The Lion of the Covenant

HIGHLANDS
DUNDEE
PERTH
LEUCHARS
ST. ANDREWS
CUPAR
FALKLAND
LOCH LOMOND
R. FORTH
LOCH LEVEN
STIRLING
FIFE
KIRKCALDY
FIRTH OF FORTH
R. CLYDE
GLASGOW
TORPHICHEN
EDINBURGH
LOTHIAN
RUTHERGLEN
BOTHWELL
HAMILTON
DARMEAD
STRATHAVEN
LANARK
KILMARNOCK
DRUMCLOG
BLUE CAIRN
FIRTH OF CLYDE
AIRDSMOSS
AUCHENGILLOCH
TINTO
AYR
DOUGLAS
MUIRKIRK
R. AYR
HARDEN
OCHILTREE
CUMNOCK
MAYBOLE
SANQUHAR
TEVIOT DALE
R. TEVIOT
HAUGH HEAD
NITHSDALE
R. NITH
CAVERS
EARLSTON
DUNSCORE
ANNANDALE
R. ANNAN
NEW GALLOWAY
IRONGRAY
GALLOWAY
DUMFRIES
WIGTOWN
KIRKCUDBRIGHT
ENGLAND

The Lion of the Covenant

The story of Richard Cameron

Maurice Grant

EVANGELICAL PRESS

EVANGELICAL PRESS
12 Wooler Street, Darlington, Co. Durham, DL1 1RQ, England

First published 1997

British Library Cataloguing in Publication Data available

ISBN 0 85234 395 7

Cover picture: Detail from *Covenanters' Communion* by George Harvey, reproduced by courtesy of the National Gallery of Scotland.

Printed and bound in Great Britain by
Creative Print and Design Wales, Ebbw Vale.

Contents

List of illustrations

Foreword

It may seem strange that an Englishman, and a Baptist at that, should be writing this foreword. The only excuse that I shall offer for my temerity is a lifelong interest in the Covenanters. Over fifty years ago on my parents' bookshelves stood the stout volumes of the *Cloud of Witnesses* and *The Scots Worthies,* both of which fascinated me as a child even though at that stage my understanding was necessarily limited. Impressions gained in this way were reinforced by quotations from the Covenanters and illustrations drawn from their lives which I heard from the pulpit of the chapel I attended. Thus it was that Samuel Rutherford, Alexander Peden and Donald Cargill, among others, became familiar names to me. Over the intervening years I have learned to value two things found in the Covenanters and in their contemporaries, the English Puritans: a warm, experiential Calvinism and a high esteem for the church of God.

Richard Cameron was a controversial figure in his own day, even among those who shared his understanding of the gospel. He remains such. However, he is a man who demands attention, even from those who have difficulty in accepting the correctness of some of his actions. What cannot be doubted is his godliness. Sermons quoted in these pages reveal an evangelist with a passion for souls seldom surpassed. He loved the church of God and had a high respect for church order. Some of us can agree to differ from his understanding of the form and government of the church and also from the methods he employed to defend his church, but no Christian can fail to be moved by his insistence that Christ alone should reign in the church. That is a lesson which we are all too prone to forget and which is challenged widely at the present time. It is good, therefore, that this intense, powerful figure should be presented to another generation.

It is not always easy to paint a clear picture of the lives of some of the great church leaders of the seventeenth century. Lengthy and painstaking research is essential. Mr Maurice Grant has put us all in his debt by this work. Richard Cameron is set against his background and not left as a figure in isolation. Although his preaching ministry was confined to a few brief years the power of that ministry comes through strongly in these pages. Mr Grant has enabled us to see why Richard Cameron was so significant a figure in his own day. More than that, he compels us to face the challenge of his life and ministry today.

Robert W. Oliver,
Bradford on Avon

Preface

Of all the names associated with the cause of the Scottish Covenanters, and their heroic resistance to arbitrary power, none is better known than that of Richard Cameron. As preacher, public figure and popular leader, he epitomized the steadfastness of a people in the face of a bitter and protracted persecution. Such was the impact of his life that, even in his own day, his name came to be synonymous with uncompromising adherence to a cause — a cause that was of the very essence of civil and religious freedom. After his death, his name was kept alive in the public memory by those who continued to witness for the values in which he believed, and it was later adopted by a distinguished military regiment which was formed to defend those very same values.

This is all the more remarkable as Cameron was on the stage of public affairs in Scotland for only two short years. For much of that time — indeed, when some of the most stirring events of the period were taking place — he was not even in the country. Yet, for most of his public life, there was no one who was so keenly hunted by the forces of authority; nor, for very different reasons, was anyone so eagerly sought after by those who valued the testimony he held and the message he proclaimed.

The main events in Cameron's life are well enough known, and have been frequently documented. Yet relatively little is known of the man himself. In his *Life* of Cameron, published in 1896, Professor Herkless expressed frustration at how little biographical detail he had been able to collect. I cannot claim to have been a great deal more successful in that respect. I have, however, been able to throw some more light on Cameron's family background, and particularly to trace his West Lothian origins, in the person of his grandfather, after whom he was named and who provided the family's first link with Fife. I have also sought to trace several of the formative influences on Cameron's later career, dwelling particularly on John Welwood, whose place in the events of the period has perhaps not always been given the attention it deserves. I have taken the liberty to refer in places to my biography of Donald Cargill, which was published in 1988 under the title *No King But Christ.*

Again I wish to thank the staffs of the National Library of Scotland, the Scottish Record Office, the Edinburgh and Glasgow University Libraries and the British Library for their ready assistance with my researches. I am also grateful to the Scottish Catholic Archive for permitting me to examine the records of Blairs College, Aberdeen. My particular thanks go to Professor H. M. Cartwright who read the manuscript and offered valuable suggestions.

Maurice Grant
Edinburgh
June 1997

1.
The Cameron family

Fife has for many years occupied a distinctive position within Scotland. The reason for this lies chiefly in the geography of the area, as a glance at the map will show. In our own day, that distinctiveness has been in a measure eroded by the greater ease of communication between the population centres to the north and south. But in earlier days, when the great estuaries of the Forth and Tay remained unbridged, the relative insularity of Fife was very real.

This comparative isolation brought its own benefits. First, it insulated Fife from the civil commotions which for so long agitated the heart of Scotland, and protected it from the worst excesses of invading armies. Second, and no less important, it encouraged a spirit of sturdy independence among the people, which earned for the area the title of 'The Kingdom of Fife'. This independent spirit was stimulated by factors inherent in the very fabric of the region. As in many other parts of Scotland, the pattern of land tenure in Fife was based on the feudal system, under which individual portions of land were 'feued', or rented out for a fixed annual payment. But what made Fife different was the fact that there the portions of land divided up in this way were smaller, and so more numerous, than in other parts of the country. This gave rise to a class of small landed proprietors, each proud of his own possession, and of the social status that went with it.

As the generations passed, these small proprietors gained considerable influence, and this in turn helped to foster still further the spirit of independence for which the region was to become noted. This was to manifest itself in various directions, not least in the spirit of enterprise and endeavour which came to be associated with the sons of Fife. The county which in the eighteenth century was to nurture Adam Smith, and in the nineteenth Andrew Carnegie, in the seventeenth bred Richard Cameron.

Richard Cameron, indeed, was a product of the class of small landed proprietors, or 'portioners', for which Fife had become noted. In his case, however, the connection with the region went back for only two generations, for his grandfather had not been a native of Fife. The course of events through which Richard Cameron came to be born and brought up in Fife is an interesting history, and one which displays clear evidence of the workings of God's providence.

Historically, the Camerons have been particularly associated with Lochaber, and it has been suggested that Richard Cameron's family may have had a connection with that part of the country in the not too distant past. That view is impossible to sustain, however. It is not to Lochaber, nor to any other part of the Highlands, that one must look for Richard Cameron's antecedents, but to West Lothian, in the farming country around Torphichen, where from the mid-1500s, and possibly earlier, there had lived a family whose name was variously spelt Campbroune, Cambron, or simply Cameron.[1]

The Camerons had a long connection with West Lothian. As early as the 1490s a certain Gilbert Cameron of Linlithgow was noted as a supplier of fine horses to King James IV.[2] Patrick Cameron,[3] who appears to have held a position of some standing in the local community, was in occupation of the small farm or estate of Birkenshaw, in Torphichen parish, as early as 1538.[4] Patrick died in or around 1563, leaving his estates to his eldest son Gilbert.

The condition of the country at that time was unsettled, and following the deposition of Mary Queen of Scots in 1567 a state of near anarchy prevailed. Perhaps keeping up a royalist tradition, Gilbert Cameron fought for Mary's cause at Langside in 1568, an action for which he, with others, was heavily fined.[5] Gilbert died in May 1571, when still a relatively young man, leaving his estates to his four children — Patrick, Richard, Gilbert and Janet — none of whom had reached the age of majority. The eldest son, Patrick, was to die young like his father, and when his widow remarried after his death the estate of Birkenshaw finally passed out of the hands of the Cameron family.[6]

Patrick's brother Richard was no more than eight years old at the time of his father's death.[7] He had been left the small farm of Woodend in his father's will, and for some years he stayed on in the family inheritance.[8] But he had his eyes set on wider horizons. When still a young man, he disposed of his share of the estate and entered the service of Alexander Lindsay, Lord Spynie, a chamberlain and favourite of James VI.[9] It is interesting to speculate how a young man from Torphichen should have come to be noticed by one of the most influential young noblemen of the time, but Spynie would no doubt have been in attendance on the king during James' frequent visits to Linlithgow and it may well have been here that the two first met. Also it is distinctly possible that, in entering the service of one so close to the king, Richard was following in the same royalist tradition which had seen his father fight at Langside — a tradition which would certainly have recommended him for his new sphere of service.

Richard's new master had been created Lord Spynie in 1590, and it is likely that Richard entered his service soon after that date.[10] The Spynie estates were in Morayshire, but the family seat was at Kinblethmont House near Arbroath, and it was here, and at the family's town house in Edinburgh, that Richard would have been based during his period of service.

There is every reason to suppose that he became a trusted servant of Lord Spynie, and that over a period of time he made the acquaintance of many of the noble families with whom his master came into contact.

However, this happy state of affairs was not to last. In June 1607 Spynie was tragically killed in Edinburgh, when attempting to intervene in a quarrel on his nephew's behalf. His son and successor to the title was still a minor, so that Richard was left without employment. However, his reputation as a trusted servant was to stand him in good stead. Perhaps benefiting from an earlier acquaintance, he then entered the service of Sir David Carnegy, later Lord Carnegy of Kinnaird, whose family seat was within a few miles of Kinblethmont and whose wife Margaret was herself a niece of Lord Spynie. Here Richard was to continue a further ten years until in 1617, when he was past fifty, he decided to marry and set up a home of his own. His master, apparently in appreciation of his services, granted him a charter for the lease of the lands of Fordell, near Leuchars in Fife, where the Carnegys possessed extensive estates.[11] Here Richard and his bride, Elizabeth Carstairs, settled and raised a family of two sons — the elder called Patrick, after Richard's elder brother and grandfather, and the younger Allan.

Richard was to remain at Fordell for the rest of his life, enjoying a position of some influence which his previous career had no doubt helped to foster. The dominant local family, the Bruces of Earlshall, held him in high regard, and there is evidence that his relations with them were both friendly and cordial.[12] Richard had long enjoyed a fairly prosperous lifestyle, and his tenure of Fordell did nothing to diminish his fortunes. The property was situated in a fertile corner of Fife, and the nature of its soil made it an ideal site for cultivation. The times were peaceful, and well suited to the pursuit of agriculture. In due time, Richard became a man of fairly substantial means. However, despite his prosperity and influence, he did not enjoy the benefit of even a basic education; the various legal instruments he was called upon to sign bear testimony to the fact that his hand had to be 'led by the notaries' because he was unable to write himself. His wife Elizabeth laboured under the same disadvantage, but the couple saw to it that their two sons received at least the rudiments of learning, no doubt at the parish school of Leuchars.[13]

Richard died in the late 1630s, when he was well over seventy, and his elder son Patrick succeeded him at Fordell. Tragically, however, Patrick enjoyed the inheritance for only some five or six years, dying unmarried around 1645. On his death the estate passed to his younger brother Allan, who with his bride Margaret Paterson, a native of Falkland, entered formally into possession of Fordell on 15 April 1646.[14] It was here that, for the next sixteen years, they were to live and bring up their family — at the same time managing the estate and the responsibilities which went with it.

Richard Cameron, the future 'Lion of the Covenant', was the eldest son of Allan and Margaret Cameron. From the available evidence, he appears to have been born in 1647, or possibly 1648. There were to be at least three other members of the family — Michael,[15] David[16] and Andrew.[17] Tradition tells of a daughter, Marion, and while there is no documentary evidence to prove her existence, this cannot necessarily be discounted.[18]

The environment in which Richard Cameron grew up was a turbulent one. Politically, the state of the country had changed radically since the more peaceful days of his grandfather. The misguided attempts of Charles I to enforce episcopacy on the Scottish church had led to a popular revolution which culminated in 1638 with the signing of the National Covenant. For the next decade and more, the country was in a ferment of agitation. By 1643 Scotland had become embroiled in the civil war which had begun in England the previous autumn, and Scottish armies were fighting side by side with the Parliamentary forces against the king. Soon, the war was to spill over into Scotland itself. The Marquis of Montrose, a former Covenanter turned royalist, placed himself at the head of a mixed band of Highland and Irish troops, and set out to reduce the country to the authority of the king. It was an ambition in which he almost succeeded, and the series of victories which he won throughout Scotland sent the cause of the Covenant into a temporary decline. Though the Covenant was strongly supported in Fife, the region was mercifully spared the excesses to which other centres of support were subjected by Montrose and his troops. None the less, Fife suffered severely through the loss of many of its men, particularly at Kilsyth in 1645, when Montrose inflicted terrible slaughter on the inexperienced and ill-equipped troops opposing him.

At its start, the Covenant was a great national movement, and many sided with it who had little interest in its great spiritual aims and who were later to throw off their allegiance to it. The most notable of these was Montrose himself. The marquis could count on relatively little support from the Scottish nobility, but there were a few ardent royalists who nevertheless sided with him. Among these was the second Lord Spynie, who was with Montrose at the sacking of Aberdeen and was captured and imprisoned for his pains. Other royalists, however, adopted a much lower profile. Andrew Bruce of Earlshall, who succeeded his father in 1642, maintained a strictly neutral position throughout. For the Camerons, with their traditionally royalist sympathies, it was no doubt a time of testing and challenge. It may well be that, if only for the sake of conformity, they threw in their lot with the Covenant, and it is even possible that Patrick Cameron's early death — apparently in 1645 — may have been directly connected with the disaster at Kilsyth.[19]

It is reasonable too to assume that the attitudes of the Cameron family would have been affected, to some degree at least, by the influence of Alexander Henderson, who was minister at Leuchars from 1620 to 1639. It was Henderson who presided over the famous Glasgow Assembly of 1638 and whose initiative formed the driving-force behind the Covenant, and it is certain that in his own parish he wielded a formidable influence. At the same time, it cannot be claimed that the Camerons' adherence to the Covenant was anything other than nominal; there is certainly nothing to suggest that they saw it in terms which went any way beyond a merely political significance.

By the late 1640s — when Richard Cameron was still in his infancy — the tide of affairs had taken a further turn. In England, both king and Parliament had come under the domination of the Independents under Cromwell, who in 1649 brought the king to the scaffold. The result was to rekindle sympathy in Scotland for the royalist cause, and to rally Scottish support solidly behind the claims of Charles II to the throne. There were many in Scotland who cherished fond hopes of seeing Charles as a king who would maintain and uphold the Covenant — hopes that he, for his own ends, did his best to encourage. These found expression in the coronation of Charles as King of Scotland in January 1651. But Scotland was to pay dearly for its support of the royalist cause. Scottish arms proved fruitless against Cromwell's military might, and by the end of 1651 the young king was in exile and Cromwell and his military government were masters of Scotland.

2.
The early years

Richard Cameron was therefore to grow up in a country under military occupation. But, in many ways, the period of the Commonwealth, as it was called, was one of the most constructive of the century. The country was weary of war, and ready for a period of stability. Business proceeded unimpaired, and apart from a ban on meetings of the General Assembly, the church was left relatively unmolested. For small landowners such as Allan Cameron, the return to a period of peace would have been welcome in many respects. It offered him the opportunity to pursue his affairs unhindered and, as a man with a young family, it allowed him to make arrangements for his children's education in an environment free of tension and turmoil. There is clear evidence that he used these opportunities to the full.

As the heir, through his brother, to his father's property, Allan Cameron inherited a well-run and prosperous estate. It continued to prosper under his management, and appears to have provided him with a comfortable income. There is evidence that he employed servants and that, like his father, he enjoyed a position of some standing in the local community. Records survive of several of his business transactions, showing that, like many of his contemporaries, he regularly lent and borrowed money on a short-term basis; in an age when there were no banking facilities, this was a common practice. Interestingly, one of these transactions was with the kirk session of Leuchars parish church, from whom, in May 1651, he borrowed the sum of 200 merks, or £133 Scots.[1] There may be a clue here as to Allan Cameron's relations with his local church, since he would scarcely have been awarded a facility of this kind if he had not been in good standing with the church.

The minister of Leuchars at this time was Patrick Scougall, who had entered on the charge in 1645 and was to remain there until 1659, and so was minister during Richard's early life. Scougall was what might best be described as a moderate Covenanter; after the Restoration in 1660 he conformed to episcopacy and was rewarded in 1664 with the bishopric of Aberdeen. It is probably characteristic of Allan Cameron and his family at this time that they should have been on terms of obvious goodwill with Patrick Scougall and his elders. However, Scougall is reckoned to have been among the better of the conforming ministers and his son Henry later achieved fame for his devotional classic *The Life of God in the Soul of Man*, which is said to have been instrumental in the conversion of George Whitefield. Henry Scougall was of the same age as Richard Cameron, and it is intriguing to think that the two boys may well have played together in those early days at Leuchars.

It is possible that Richard Cameron received his early education at the parish school at Leuchars, where his father had no doubt been educated, but it would seem more probable that he was sent to the grammar school at St Andrews, which at that time enjoyed a high reputation. This is all the more likely since the education provided by the parish schools was only of a basic nature and was not fitted to prepare pupils for a career in any of the professions. Since it is clear that Richard Cameron early showed some promise — at least enough to warrant his father taking special pains with his education —

the likelihood is that he would have been sent to St Andrews at a fairly young age. There he would not only have received a thorough grounding in the basic skills, but would also have become proficient in Latin, which was a dominant feature of the curriculum and a vital piece of equipment for any scholar wishing to pursue his studies to a more advanced stage. Thus equipped — and at no more than thirteen or fourteen years of age — he was judged ready for university, and he duly enrolled in the Arts faculty at St Salvator's College, St Andrews, on 5 March 1662.[2]

The start of Richard's university career coincided with some radical changes in his family circle. The expense of educating his sons and maintaining a growing family imposed an increasing burden on Allan Cameron, and a succession of poor harvests compounded his difficulties. Richard's needs at university no doubt imposed still further pressure. But for Allan Cameron the crowning blow appears to have come from an unfortunate business transaction in which he had involved himself several years earlier. In June 1658 he had become guarantor of a loan taken out by a friend, Arthur Forbes, from a trust fund set up for the education of Anna Napier, daughter of a former Provost of St Andrews. Forbes defaulted on the payments, and Allan Cameron was called upon to make good his guarantee. The penalty was a levy of twenty pounds a year on his property at Fordell.[3] Allan Cameron appealed against the decision, but in vain. For him, it appears to have been the final straw. On 31 May 1662, some three months after his son Richard entered university, Allan Cameron and his wife sold Fordell to Alexander Wedderburn, minister of Forgan, and his wife Helen Turnbull.[4] It was a decision no doubt taken with considerable regret, but at the same time it shows evidence of careful deliberation and forethought. For Allan Cameron now had sufficient means not only to advance his son's education, but also to attend to the needs of the other members of his

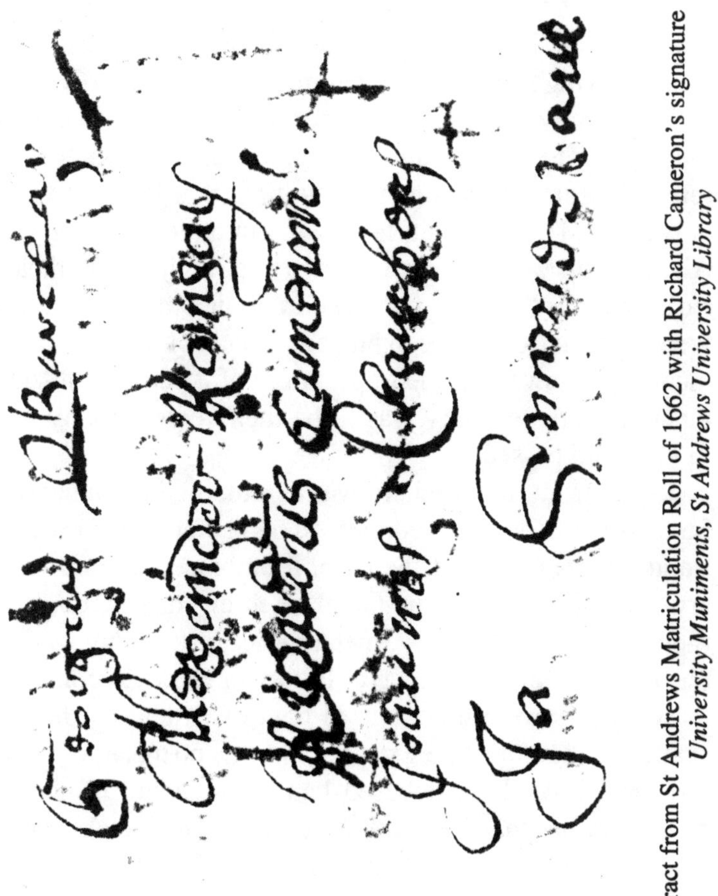

Extract from St Andrews Matriculation Roll of 1662 with Richard Cameron's signature
University Muniments, St Andrews University Library

family. Later that same year, his son David, who may well have been the second eldest, was sent to Edinburgh to serve his apprenticeship with a merchant named John McNeish.[5] Throughout his life, Allan Cameron was to manifest a solicitous concern for the welfare of his family, even when, as on this occasion, it involved considerable personal sacrifice.

On leaving Fordell in the summer of 1662, Allan Cameron and his family made the short journey to St Andrews, where they appear to have obtained temporary accommodation and remained for at least some of the time that Richard was at university. They did not, however, continue there long, for Allan and his wife are on record as being resident in Kirkcaldy early in the following year.[6] The inference may be that they were moving from place to place as Allan could find employment, while awaiting the opportunity of a permanent settlement. That opportunity was to be theirs before many more months had passed.

In the meantime, Richard was continuing his education at St Andrews. The course on which he had embarked was the standard arts course of the time. It embraced an impressive array of subjects — Latin, Greek, Hebrew, arithmetic, logic, rhetoric, ethics, geometry, metaphysics, astronomy, geography and anatomy. However, as Professor Herkless points out, these studies were more varied than exact and the level of academic attainment they required was by no means out of the ordinary.[7] Indeed, so debased had the standard of the arts course become that the Commission of the General Assembly, when they visited the university in 1642, urged the faculty to see to it that due trial was taken of students undergoing their degrees and that those who were found to be 'altogether unworthy' were excluded from graduation. By the time of Richard Cameron's stay at St Andrews, the standard of the degree had been raised and the course provided a good general test of a student's abilities. Students' behaviour, too, was kept

St Salvator's College, St Andrews

under firm control: they were allowed only limited recreation — golf or archery — and were required to converse only in Latin, whether inside or outside the college precincts. Whatever its limitations may have been, there can be no doubt that his university education played a useful part in moulding Richard Cameron's character and equipping him, both intellectually and psychologically, for his future career.

Richard graduated as Master of Arts at St Andrews on 22 July 1665. His family had in the meantime found themselves a new home. Around mid-1663 Allan and Margaret Cameron moved to Falkland, which was Margaret's home town, and where her father, George Paterson, was a local councillor and magistrate.[8] Largely, it seems, through the influence of his wife's family, Allan Cameron was able to settle fairly comfortably in Falkland, where he and his wife took possession of a substantial three-storey house on the south side of the High Street, and where in due time he set up in business as a merchant.[9] So favourable indeed were his circumstances at this time that he found himself able to assist some of his friends who applied to him for short-term financial relief. Among these, interestingly enough, were the Bruces of Earlshall, with whom Allan's father Richard had had such an intimate acquaintance in earlier days. In January 1663 Allan Cameron lent the substantial sum of 1,000 merks to Andrew Bruce the elder, and in April 1665 he advanced the sum of 200 merks to Andrew the younger, who had by this time succeeded his father.[10] It was no doubt a mark of the close ties which continued to subsist between the two families that arrangements of this kind could have been made, and it is significant that, even with a growing family to support, Allan Cameron thought sufficiently highly of his relationship with the Bruces to help them out of what was clearly a pressing financial need.

Some two years after settling in Falkland, Allan Cameron and his family were joined by his son Richard, newly graduated

Cameron House, Falkland

from St Andrews. At this time, Richard would have been seventeen or eighteen years of age. For a young graduate in his position, three main possibilities were open — the church, the law and the teaching profession. It is clear that at this stage neither of the first two appealed to him and, at a time when there was no formal education system to speak of, opportunities for the third were limited. It is likely therefore that, like many of his contemporaries, Richard was employed as a private tutor, or 'pedagogue', to the family of one of the prominent citizens of the town, or possibly one of the families of the local nobility. It seems clear at any rate that he continued to live in Falkland for some years after his graduation, which would suggest that he obtained employment in or near the town. But for Richard Cameron any such employment would essentially have been a short-term expedient and, not unnaturally, it would have been his intention to seek a more permanent position.

The schoolmaster of Falkland at this time was a man named George Kinloch, who was related to Richard by marriage.[11] Kinloch had graduated from St Andrews in 1658 and had married in 1665, so that he was relatively new to the post. In normal circumstances, therefore, Cameron could have expected that an opening for him in Falkland would not have arisen for some considerable time. However, events were to take an unexpected turn: in 1669 Kinloch suffered an accident which seriously incapacitated him and he was forced to resign.[12]

Cameron's credentials for the post were well enough known, and there is strong evidence to suggest that some influential citizens, including members of the town council, were personally acquainted with his abilities. His family connections, too, were important: his mother's family had given distinguished service to the local community and his father was by now a respected local citizen. These factors would certainly have counted in his favour and were clearly influential in determining the outcome. In late 1669 or early 1670, Richard Cameron was appointed schoolmaster of Falkland.

The development of Scottish education owed its impetus in large part to the church, and in the rural, or 'landward' parishes, the local kirk sessions continued to control appointments to the schools. While responsibility in the burghs (i.e. self-governing towns) was exercised by the town councils, the links with the parish church remained strong. Thus it was still the case in many towns that the local schoolmaster was also expected to act as clerk to the kirk session and as precentor, or leader of the praise, in the parish church. George Kinloch, Richard Cameron's predecessor, had acted as clerk to the Falkland Kirk Session from 1663 to 1669. There is no evidence, however, that Richard Cameron acted as session clerk at Falkland, and the kirk session minutes of the period, which are still extant, are certainly not in his hand. He did, however, act as precentor, though apparently only as stand-in for the regular incumbent, and then only for a relatively limited period.[13]

As schoolmaster of a burgh grammar school, appointed by authority of the town council, Cameron would have enjoyed a position of some status. The post carried with it a comfortable salary, and this was augmented by the fees paid by the pupils. For pupils living within the burgh, these fees were fixed by the town council, but for those attending from the rural areas the schoolmaster was free to prescribe what fees he chose. As in other parts of Fife, the school at Falkland would have been attended by children from the country districts whose parents could afford to give them the higher standard of education that the burgh schools could provide, in the same way that Richard himself had probably attended school at St Andrews. These pupils from rural areas may well have included the children of neighbouring landowners and even of the local nobility.

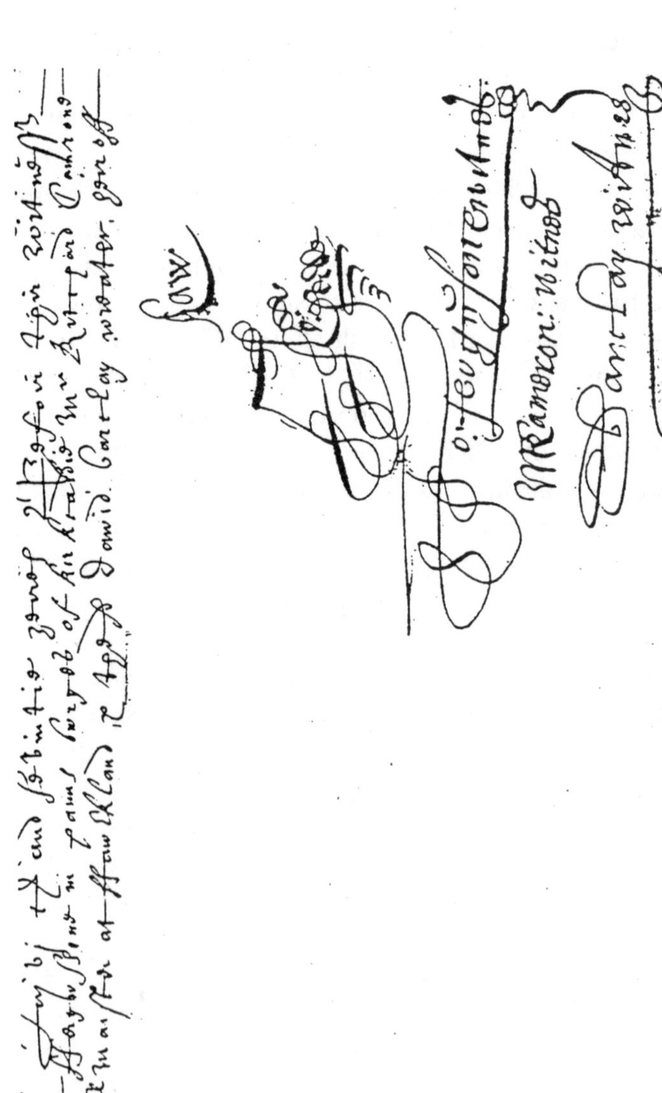

Extract from a legal bond of 1670 referring to 'Mr Ritchard Camrone scoollmaister att Faulkland' and showing his signature as witness (see note 14, page 307).

By permission of the Keeper of the Records of Scotland

While little information survives about the curriculum of the time, Cameron's duties would certainly have included giving his pupils a knowledge of the basic skills — reading, writing and arithmetic — as well as teaching Latin and the more advanced subjects to those who were planning to go on to university. The age of the pupils would have ranged from about five to ten in the case of those who were receiving only a basic education, though those destined for university would have continued longer. In some cases, however, it was not unknown for students to enter university at the age of only eleven or twelve.

What is clear is that at this point, early in 1670, Cameron's career was bright with promise. At the age of only twenty-two, or at most twenty-three, he already occupied a prestigious position in the local community.[14] He was in a secure post with a comfortable income. He was close to people of authority and influence. So long as he fulfilled his duties, there was no reason why he should not have continued in his post for the rest of his working life, or perhaps moved on to higher things in the course of an academic career. That indeed may have been the kind of future he anticipated for himself at this point. But events were destined to move differently.

3.
Church and state in Scotland

Up to this point in his career, there is nothing to suggest that Richard Cameron had been influenced in any personal way by the great spiritual and religious issues which had so dominated public life in Scotland since the Reformation 100 years earlier. His family connections and background would have been unlikely to predispose him towards considering these matters seriously. However, from this point onwards — though he was not yet aware of it — these issues were increasingly to govern the whole course of his life, and some understanding of them is essential if his later career is to be viewed in its proper context.

The Scottish Reformation of the sixteenth century had been a radical movement which had affected every area of the nation's life. Above all, it had freed the people from the bondage of a spiritually corrupt regime and laid the foundations of a new spiritual order firmly grounded upon Scripture. In abolishing the authority of the pope, the Scottish Reformers repudiated the idea that any mere man could be head of Christ's church, and in contrast to the position in England, where the authority of the pope had been transferred to the Crown, they maintained that Christ alone could be head over his church. This principle was clearly reflected in the *Scots Confession* drawn up by John Knox and his fellow-Reformers in 1560, and in succeeding years its consequences were carefully worked out in a system of church government which owed nothing to hierarchical structures, but was based on a collective jurisdiction of ministers and elders in kirk sessions, presbyteries, provincial synods and general assemblies.

This Presbyterian system, as it came to be known, was not only a logical extension of the Reformation concept of the church, but in itself provided a practical safeguard against any erosion of its spiritual independence. Thus any assault on the system came to be seen as an attack on the church itself. 'Take from us the liberty of assemblies', said Knox, 'and take from us the Evangel.' Knox was shrewd enough to know that, without the right to govern itself, the church would inevitably be exposed to influences which would mar its witness and blunt its testimony. But above all, the issue for Knox and his fellow-Reformers was one of loyalty to Christ, who, they believed, had clearly revealed in his Word that he, and he alone, had the authority to rule over his church. And, as his appointed officers on earth, they were responsible only to him.

The doctrine of the church's independence inevitably raised questions for its relationship with the state. The Scottish Reformers yielded to no one in their regard for the state as an ordinance of God, with full rights and responsibilities in its own sphere. But that sphere was strictly limited; it extended only to matters of civil government and the general good of society. It certainly did not include jurisdiction over the church. That was not, however, to say that church and state had no mutual interests. The church, as the representative of Christ, had a duty to guide the state in its responsibilities and to ensure that these were carried out in a God-honouring way; and the state, for its part, was responsible for promoting the temporal interests of the church and safeguarding its rights and liberties. This relationship has traditionally been described as 'mutual subordination and co-ordinate jurisdiction'. In its developed form, it was given fullest expression in the *Second Book of Discipline* of 1581, and it became central to the Scottish Reformed tradition.

The concept of the dual jurisdiction of church and state was to dominate political and religious life in Scotland in the years following the Reformation and beyond. It was perhaps never put more clearly or forcefully into words than in Andrew Melville's celebrated interview with King James VI at Falkland in 1596 when, taking the king by the sleeve, Melville told him: 'Sir, there are two kings and two kingdoms in Scotland: there is King James, the head of this commonwealth, and there is Christ Jesus, the king of the church, whose subject James the Sixth is, and of whose kingdom he is not a king, nor a lord, nor a head, but a member.'[1] This idea of two kingdoms was repugnant to James, who saw it as a challenge to his own authority as king, and to the divine right which he claimed, and he set himself resolutely to bring the church under his control. The instruments he chose were diocesan bishops, appointed by himself, who would exercise control over the affairs of the church and ensure that it did not operate in a way contrary to the king's interests.

So long as he remained merely King of Scots, James was careful to avoid a direct confrontation with the church; indeed in 1592 he approved an Act of Parliament which confirmed Presbyterian church government in all its essentials. However, when he succeeded to the crown of England in 1603, he felt more strongly placed to advance his plans. Bishops were formally introduced under an act of 1606, and in a series of measures over the next twenty years the Presbyterian government of the church was gradually eroded in favour of a moderate form of episcopacy. Festival days, kneeling at Communion, and other practices banished at the Reformation were re-established. The church's assemblies were deliberately packed with the king's supporters, and ministers who opposed the innovations were imprisoned or banished.

James would doubtless have proceeded still further with his plans, but his death in 1625 left affairs in the hands of his son, who succeeded to the throne as Charles I. Charles inherited all his father's antipathy to Presbyterianism, but less of his father's subtlety. Spurred on by wrong-headed advisers, he embarked on a series of measures which brought him into disastrous conflict with his subjects in Scotland. In 1637, at the instance of Archbishop Laud, he introduced a new service-book and canons to the Church of Scotland and ordered that these should be used in the church's worship. Charles' Scottish subjects had for many years tolerated the Crown's encroachments on the government of their church, but now that its worship was also under attack they could stand no more. The outcome was a popular revolution which culminated the following year in the signing of the National Covenant.

Basically, the Covenant was a restatement of an earlier document of 1580 in which king and people had pledged themselves to maintain the Reformed religion. Now it became something of a national charter. A great popular movement swept the country. Later that year, at a General Assembly in Glasgow, the episcopal innovations were abolished and the authority of Presbyterianism restored. The bishops were deposed and the exiled Presbyterian ministers reinstated. At one stroke, the church had recovered all the ground lost since the Reformation. Indeed, so radical was the change that the 1638 Assembly has been seen by historians as ushering in a second reformation period in Scotland.

The years that followed, turbulent as they were in the civil sphere, saw the church attain a dignity and stature unsurpassed in her history. Indeed, at no other time, before or since, can it be said that her institutions, worship and government conformed so closely to the Reformation ideal. Men of outstanding merit, such as Rutherford, Dickson, Durham and Gillespie, adorned her ranks. And, as happens in times of spiritual renewal, the influence of the church pervaded the whole of society. One contemporary writer even went so far as to say that 'As to the public profession of the truth, and almost as to the number of persons, the Church of Scotland was of equal extent with the nation.'[2] And another put it like this: 'Then was Scotland a heap of wheat set about with lilies, uniform, or a palace of silver beautifully proportioned; and this seems to me to have been Scotland's high noon.'[3]

This was the Scotland to which the young king Charles II was brought by commissioners from the Scottish Parliament in 1650, a year after his father's death. Opposed as they had been to the policy of Charles I, the Scots deeply resented his treatment at the hands of the English under Cromwell and, in their repugnance at what they saw as a usurpation of lawful authority, they were only too ready to see in Charles' cause the opportunity to realize their ideal of a covenanted king. It was a noble ambition, but directed at an unworthy object. Indeed, there are few more pathetic episodes in Scottish history than the blind devotion with which the Scottish church and people attached themselves to a cause which was to prove so disastrous for them.

Charles, for his part, was perfectly ready to play the role in which he was cast. Friendless and in need of support wherever he could find it, he saw the Covenants merely as a convenient foothold to regain his father's throne. On two occasions he subscribed them: first on his landing in Scotland in June 1650, and then a second time at his coronation at Scone in January 1651. And between these two occasions he put his name to a declaration at Dunfermline in August 1650 in which he faithfully pledged support for the Covenants and for the Presbyterian government of the church. His Scottish subjects were well content. To all appearances, they had a king who would uphold the cause of the Covenants and the Reformed religion they sought to defend. Events were to show how sadly misguided these hopes had been.

The immediate effect of Scottish support for Charles was to draw down the vengeance of Cromwell and his Ironsides, who in a short, sharp campaign overran the country and made themselves masters of Scotland. English support for the royalist cause was similarly ineffective, and following Cromwell's final victory at Worcester in September 1651 Charles was forced to flee to the Continent, where he remained for the next nine years in exile. Scotland, meanwhile, lay under the heel of a military dictatorship. But while the economic effects of the occupation were serious, the church continued to flourish. Cromwell, true to his policy of toleration, allowed the Scottish Presbyterians full religious freedom, the only exception being a ban on meetings of the General Assembly.

Even this restriction had its advantages, for the Assemblies of the late 1640s and early 1650s had been the scene of much internal dispute. This centred around the church's attitude to those who had sided with Montrose, or were otherwise suspected of disloyalty to the Covenants. Under Acts of Parliament passed in 1646 and 1649, such persons were disqualified from holding any positions of public trust in the kingdom. However, in the face of the increasing threat being posed by Cromwell, the view gained ground that all available resources should be recruited in the common cause. Those who favoured this policy became known as Resolutioners; the minority who opposed it were termed Protesters. Though the Resolutioners had their way, and the disqualifying acts were repealed by the Scottish Parliament, the issue remained a source of contention in the church throughout the 1650s. Thus although the spiritual life of the country may have flourished, the constitution of the church was being weakened from within. This was to have serious consequences before many years had passed.

By the late 1650s, both Scotland and England had tired of military rule. Cromwell's death in 1658 was the signal for a general outbreak of unrest, and to prevent the country from lapsing into anarchy it was agreed by all parties that the unifying influence of the monarchy should be restored. On 29 May 1660 — his thirtieth birthday — Charles II returned to take up his throne. It was an occasion for universal joy. After years of repression, a new age of liberty appeared about to dawn. Nowhere was the rejoicing greater than in Scotland, which had welcomed Charles when he was a friendless outcast and had been the first to recognize his claims as king. The church, and particularly the supporters of the Covenant, now looked to him to fulfil his promises.

The reality was to be very different. No sooner was Charles II on the throne than he commenced a systematic attack on Presbyterianism in general and the Covenanters in particular. The Marquis of Argyle, who had set the crown on Charles' head at Scone, was arrested, tried and executed. A similar fate befell James Guthrie, the Protester minister of Stirling, one of the leaders of the cause of the Covenant. A third victim was Lord Johnston of Warriston, the former Lord Clerk Register, who had been Clerk to the 1638 Glasgow Assembly and one of the main architects of the Covenant. Acts of Parliament were passed declaring the Covenants to be illegal, and forbidding the renewing of them under heavy penalties.

At the same time, a determined assault was made on the government of the church itself. In violation of the rights previously granted by Parliament, the authority of the king was declared supreme in all matters concerning the government of the church. Bishops were restored and ministers commanded to submit to their jurisdiction. In an earlier day, these innovations would no doubt have been opposed vigorously, but in its present divided and weakened state the church was powerless to resist. Not only so, but it had been betrayed from within; for one of its own ministers, James Sharp of Crail, who had been deputed to negotiate the church's interests with the king, surrendered the cause he was commissioned to defend and was himself rewarded with the chief position in the new ecclesiastical hierarchy — that of Archbishop of St Andrews. For the Reformed Church of Scotland, the reversal of its fortunes could scarcely have been more extreme. From the high point of 1638, when the church had thrown off the yoke of episcopacy, it had reverted to a subjection more profound than any it had endured since the Reformation. And it had suffered all this at the hands of a king who had sworn to uphold the Covenants and the Reformed religion they represented.

By September 1662, when the second session of Parliament ended, the dismemberment of the church was virtually complete. It remained only to put the new statutes into effect and to enforce obedience to them on the part of the ministers. This task was entrusted to the Privy Council, the executive instrument of government in Scotland, which in October 1662 issued a decree, known as the Act of Glasgow, requiring all ministers who had been ordained since 1649 to seek confirmation of their appointment from the bishops in order to continue in their charges. In the nature of things, many of the ministers in this category were in the younger to middle-aged group, representing the best of the church's strength. To many of them the temptation to conform was clearly strong, and significant numbers of them yielded. But for many others there could be no question of compromise. When the day of decision came, no fewer than 400 ministers — around a third of the church — chose to give up their charges rather than submit to the authority of the bishops. For these ministers it meant a very considerable sacrifice, but they had counted the cost and in many cases their congregations rallied to their side.

For the next twenty-six years, these ejected ministers were to suffer persecution on a scale unparalleled in the history of the Church of Scotland. The government, intent as it was on asserting the royal supremacy in all causes — ecclesiastical as well as civil — saw any disaffection in religion as a challenge to the king's authority, and tantamount to rebellion. There was no scope for liberty of conscience; there was no recognition of any church order other than that sanctioned by the state. True, the outward forms of Presbyterianism were preserved: church courts — kirk sessions, presbyteries and provincial synods — were permitted to meet, and there was no attempt to change the church's form of worship. But for loyal Presbyterians, the basic issue was the right claimed by the state to regulate the affairs of the church. The principle of Christ's headship over the church had been laid down firmly at the Reformation and had been endorsed by the Covenants. To compromise that principle would not only be to betray the church's Reformation heritage; it would be an act of disloyalty to Christ. Viewed in that light, it was a step that true-hearted Presbyterians could never contemplate. They sought no confrontation with the state. Indeed, Charles had no more loyal subjects than those whom his agents now sought to persecute so unmercifully. But when it came to a choice between the claims of Charles and the honour of Christ, they had no doubt where their duty lay.

As time passed, the gulf between the government and the non-complying Presbyterians grew steadily wider. The 'outed' ministers, as they were called, gathered round themselves a growing body of hearers and sympathizers. With the appointment by the bishops of replacement ministers, many of whom were untrained and unqualified, the exodus from the churches gathered pace. Soon the ejected ministers could number their congregations in hundreds. To satisfy the demands of their hearers, several of them began to travel around the country, preaching in houses and churches as they found opportunity and, where this was not possible, in the fields. These unauthorized meetings, or 'conventicles', as they were termed by the authorities, were seen as an increasing challenge to the government. To suppress them, rigorous measures were brought into force. Fines were levied for non-attendance at the parish churches. Attendance at conventicles was punishable by heavy fines and imprisonment. Landowners were made answerable for the conduct of their tenants. To enforce these measures, troops of soldiers were sent to the most disaffected areas. These caused great hardship and evoked much resentment from the local population.

It was just such a situation which in November 1666 led to the first serious challenge to the government, when a local revolt against the exactions of the soldiers in Galloway led to an armed rising which for a time assumed serious proportions for the authorities. The revolt was ruthlessly put down, the insurgents and their little army being scattered on the slopes of the Pentland hills, outside Edinburgh, by government forces under the redoutable General Dalyell. But the 'Pentland Rising', as it came to be called, had some salutary lessons for the authorities. For one thing, it showed the determination of the people not to be cowed by repressive measures, however severe, directed against their most cherished religious beliefs. And it demonstrated, perhaps as nothing else could, the strength of feeling among ordinary Scottish people — many of them men and women of a humble station in life — on matters of faith and conscience. It was that spirit which was to motivate them throughout the dark days ahead, and to strengthen them for the trial they were to be called on to face.

4.
The Indulgences

As time went on, and the dissenting Presbyterians showed no signs of capitulating, pressure grew on the authorities to come to some sort of accommodation with the dissenters. These calls were supported by a number of influential sources, and on 7 June 1669 the king's Secretary of State, the Duke of Lauderdale, wrote to the Privy Council intimating the king's decision to grant an Indulgence, or licence to preach, to certain of the non-complying ministers. The choice of the men to whom it would apply was left to the Council themselves. However, the condition was stipulated that the ministers in question must have lived 'peaceably and orderly' since their ejection; in other words, they must not have engaged in irregular preaching or other anti-government behaviour. Strict conditions were also laid down for their enjoyment of the favour offered: they would be required to remain within the bounds of their own parishes, they would not be allowed to baptize or marry persons from elsewhere, and would be liable to discipline, and in some cases to be deprived of their office, if they countenanced the attendance at their services of people from neighbouring parishes.

The Council's proclamation, based on the Secretary of State's letter, was issued on 27 July 1669, and between then and March 1670 over forty ministers availed themselves of the permission to preach. These were based mainly in the west and south-west, and included only four in the Lothians and none at all in Fife. In the nature of things, they were men who had not distinguished themselves by any overt act of disobedience to the episcopal order, but had been content to remain in their places of banishment and not unduly to trouble the authorities. Only for such men, indeed, had the new favour been intended.

It was thus incongruous, to say the least, that the letter should have gone on to infer that, with the granting of the Indulgence, the need for unauthorized preaching was at an end. Events soon showed the hollow nature of this claim, if indeed it had been made genuinely at all. The field-meetings, far from being abandoned, increased in both numbers and frequency, so that the authorities were obliged once more to resort to repressive measures to enforce their will. A large field-meeting at Hill of Beath, near Dunfermline, on 17 June 1670, was made the pretext for the most extreme measure yet brought in by the government — an Act of Parliament prescribing death for preachers at field-conventicles and the most draconian penalties for their hearers. Even this, however, failed to stem the tide. Baffled by a movement they could not control, the government vacillated between a policy of repression on the one hand and accommodation on the other.

On 2 September 1672 a Second Indulgence was offered, on terms broadly similar to the first. The very next day, a proclamation was issued confirming the repressive 1670 Act in all its rigour. The hope was, apparently, that by these means the government would be able to control the general body of the field-preachers, while isolating those it considered irreconcilable. If that was indeed the policy, it was doomed to failure: the response to the Second Indulgence was minimal, and the great majority of the field-preachers continued to defy the government.

By now, the field-meetings had extended over the central and eastern lowlands. While their influence was fairly general throughout those parts, there were some areas of particularly intense activity, of which Fife was one. Field-meetings had been relatively sparse in Fife before 1670, but the meeting at the Hill of Beath in that year had given the movement a substantial impetus. In the early and mid 1670s Fife was to become one of the most noted centres of field-preaching in Scotland. The first effects of this are to be seen in the Privy Council records for 1672, which list large numbers of people from Fife who were prosecuted for attending conventicles in the early part of that year. On 2 April 1673 a young field-preacher, Robert Gillespie, appeared before the Privy Council on a charge of holding a house-conventicle in Falkland, and was sentenced to imprisonment on the Bass Rock.[1]

But the greatest upsurge in field-preaching in Fife was to come in 1674. In March of that year the government granted a general indemnity rescinding all penalties imposed for past offences, including attendance at conventicles. One result of this, according to the contemporary historian James Kirkton, was that 'Scotland broke loose with conventicles of all sorts, in houses, fields and vacant churches.'[2] Nowhere was this to be seen more dramatically than in Fife. Indeed, it seemed that Fife had been prepared in a special way for the preaching of the gospel. The field-meetings began to attract all classes, from the highest to the lowest. Demands on the field-preachers grew intense. John Welsh, the most prominent of them, undertook a preaching tour in Fife between April and June in which he preached to audiences of many thousands. Other leading field-preachers followed him. The Privy Council minutes of the time record up to twenty places in Fife where Welsh and his colleagues preached regularly. Among these, significantly, were several in and around Falkland.[3]

Richard Cameron, meanwhile, continued in his post as schoolmaster. It is likely that, throughout this time, he had continued to live in the family home in Falkland with his parents and brothers. Since coming to Falkland in 1663, the family seem to have lived in relatively comfortable circumstances. However, towards the end of the 1660s, Allan Cameron's fortunes appear to have undergone a reversal. What caused this change is unknown, and it is fruitless now to speculate. The evidence does, however, suggest some financial calamity, perhaps associated with the failure of his business, which occasioned him to take some drastic steps to safeguard the future of his family.

First, in July 1669 Allan Cameron, in conjunction with his wife and his eldest son Richard, took out a bond on their house in Falkland in favour of George Bayne, a merchant in Edinburgh.[4] In the following February they went further by mortgaging the whole property to David Ferguson of Kirkcaldy.[5] At or around the same time Allan Cameron found temporary employment in the service of the second Earl of Wemyss, at his newly-built port development at Methil Harbour.[6] These steps were clearly taken in an attempt to ward off some financial crisis, or to meet some pressing need, but the nature of this cannot now be known. What is reasonably certain is that these circumstances must have cast a cloud over the start of Richard Cameron's career as schoolmaster, however satisfying he otherwise found his new position to be.

At the same time, Cameron could hardly fail to be moved by the events taking place around him. In a small close-knit community such as Falkland it was impossible for him not to have known several who attended the field-meetings, some of whom no doubt had an influence on his thinking. But there is strong evidence that, for some time before this, Cameron had been developing his own interest in spiritual matters. What led

A corner of old Falkland

to that interest is not clear; it may well have been a gradual process, extending over a period of years. It is perhaps significant that, as early as 1670, Cameron's name is found linked to that of John Geddie, a prominent local nonconformist who had already been in trouble with the authorities.[7] Geddie occupied a prominent position in the local community; he was clerk to the local stewartry court and factor to the second Earl of Atholl, the hereditary keeper of Falkland Palace.[8] From the available evidence, Geddie's friendship with Cameron was sufficiently close for him to involve Cameron in his personal affairs; on 27 July 1670, for instance, Cameron is on record as having witnessed a bond granted by Geddie at Kirkcaldy to one of his many creditors.[9] It is in fact possible that Geddie may have been influential in securing the schoolmaster's post for Cameron. The contacts between the two families also appear to have been close, since Richard's youngest brother Andrew was employed for some time as an assistant in Geddie's office in Falkland.[10] Apart from Geddie, other prominent local citizens came under the influence of the gospel about this time, and they could also have had an effect on Cameron.

It is not unlikely therefore that Cameron's interest in spiritual things had developed over some time before the field-meetings became established in Fife. This appears to be borne out by the scant biographical account in the *Cloud of Witnesses,* where it is recorded that 'He used to attend the sermons of the indulged ministers, as he had opportunity,' until 'At length it pleased the Lord to incline him to go out to the field-meetings.' To have forsaken his parish church to go to hear the preaching, first of the ministers who had been resettled in their churches by the Indulgence, and then that of the field-preachers, certainly suggests a degree of spiritual hunger on Cameron's part which he was seriously striving to satisfy. Since there were no ministers in Fife who had accepted the terms of the Indulgence, Cameron must have had to travel some distance to hear them, unless the record means that he had taken the opportunity to do so when away from home on business. At all events, the compulsion which drove him to attend the preaching of these ministers eventually led him to go and hear the gospel preached in the fields.

Cameron must have been well aware of the implications of his new interest for his career prospects in Falkland. For a man in a prominent local position such as his, it was highly improper, to say the least, to be seen to be frequenting meetings which were forbidden by law and which were presided over by declared traitors and rebels. To his conformist friends in Falkland it must have seemed inconceivable that a young man with such bright prospects ahead of him should put them all at risk in the manner he was doing. He had already made a favourable impact on the local scene. His work both as schoolmaster and church helper had given general satisfaction. His parish minister had formed a high opinion of his abilities. Not surprisingly, strenuous efforts were made to reclaim him. Foremost in the attempt to do this was his minister, John Hay,[11] who went so far as to recruit several of his fellow-ministers to join him in urging Cameron to reconsider his position. These ministers pressed upon the young schoolmaster the value of his work in the community, the regard in which he was held and the prospects which lay before him. Cameron, however, remained unmoved. At length, inevitably, flattery gave way to threats. It was made clear to him that, if he persisted in attending the field-meetings, he could expect the full consequences of the law. The objective, of course, was to render his position as schoolmaster untenable, and to force him either to conform, or to resign.

Had the pressure been directed at Cameron alone, it is quite possible that he would have stood his ground. As it was, however, it was also directed at his immediate family. Over the previous few months his father Allan, his mother Margaret and his brother Michael had all come under the influence of the gospel. It is tempting to conclude that this was a result of Richard's personal testimony. While this cannot be proved, it is by no means impossible that the conversion of his immediate family was the first work in which Cameron was engaged for his Lord. In the fulness of time, there was to be much more of such work ahead of him.

By the spring of 1675, or possibly earlier, it had become clear to Cameron and his immediate family that their continued presence in Falkland was no longer tolerable. Apart from the pressures on Cameron himself, the persistence and prevalence of the field-meetings had called forth an unprecedented surge of persecution on the part of the government. In Falkland and other parts of Fife, these measures were particularly severe. Special courts were held to try offenders, and there were frequent searches by parties of soldiers.

Jean Collace, who was visiting Falkland with her sister in the autumn of 1674, recorded in her diary: 'There was immediately before we came a great calm from trouble, and a clear blink of the gospel universally throughout Fife; yet it pleased the Lord to alter this providence on a sudden and to tryst us at our first entry with the storm in our face.'[12] She goes on to record that in January 1675 there was 'very hot persecution in the whole shire of Fife' and that in April of the same year this was particularly severe in and around Falkland.

Another source records that on 16 April a large number of the local inhabitants, including Richard Cameron, his parents and his brother Michael, were summoned to appear before the local stewartry court.[13] The specific charge against the Camerons was that of 'keeping conventicles at the house of John Geddie in Falkland, and field conventicles' and 'withdrawing from the parish church'. The outcome of the case is not recorded, but if, as seems likely, the offences were punished, probably by fines, it clearly fuelled the Camerons' determination to leave Falkland as soon as they could.

In the normal course of events, the prospect of leaving a well-established, familiar environment and setting out for the unknown would have been a daunting one, particularly since the Camerons had no assets or property to call their own. As it was, however, they were remarkably favoured by providence. On 30 October 1674 Richard Cameron's brother Michael married Rebecca Turner, whose father, Stephen Turner, had been a burgess of the Canongate of Edinburgh.[14] Michael's parents-in-law had been in comfortable circumstances, and his wife had inherited from them a property in the Canongate which formally passed into her possession on 8 January 1675.[15] Later that year Allan Cameron, his wife Margaret and their entire family moved from Falkland to Edinburgh. It is likely that on their first arrival, and for some time afterwards, they lodged with Michael and his wife in the Canongate, though at a later stage Allan Cameron and his wife took up residence in a house in the Potterrow.[16]

One advantage of being in Edinburgh was that it offered greater freedom from persecution than a small country town such as Falkland. The realities of life had, however, to be faced. In particular, a living had to be earned. Allan Cameron had, of course, previously been in business as a merchant, and it was this calling which he chose to pursue in Edinburgh. His son Michael joined him in the same trade. His third son David, who had been apprenticed to an Edinburgh merchant in 1662, had since spent some time in England but now returned to Scotland to join his father and brother.[17] Together, the three Camerons — Allan, David and Michael — set about building up their merchants' business in the city. It was no easy task, and to raise working capital they were obliged for some time to borrow heavily. The Edinburgh deed registers of the day

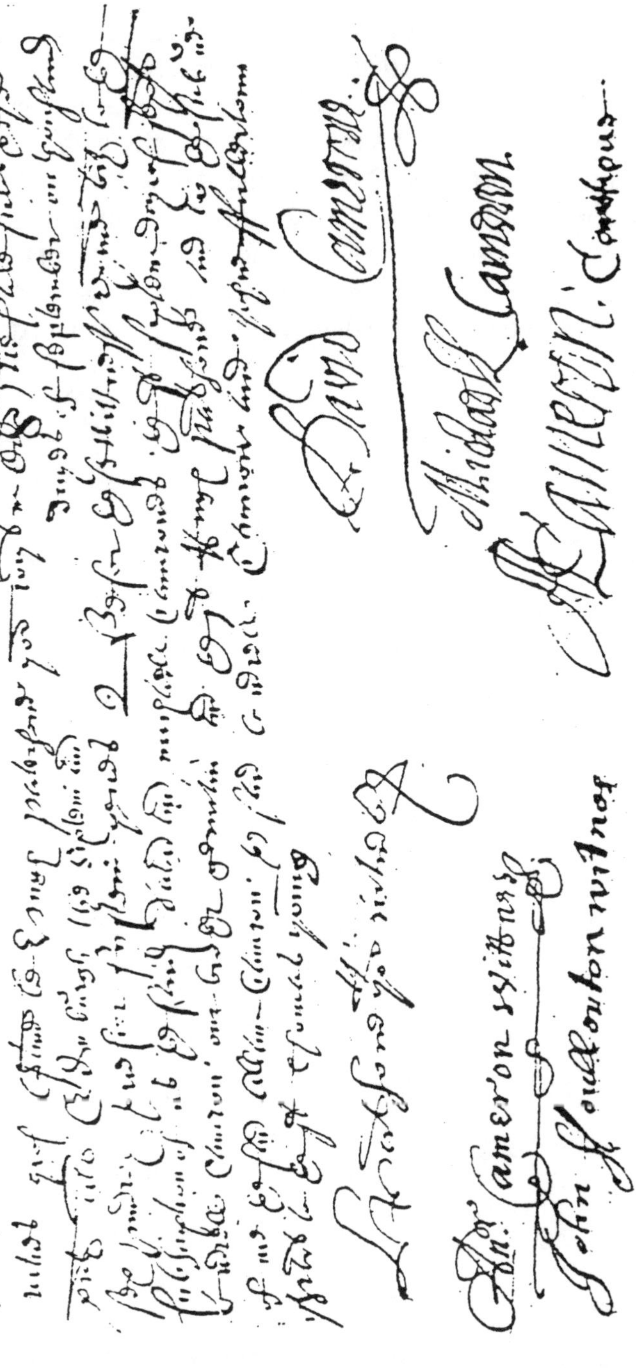

Extract from a legal bond of 1675 showing the signatures of Allan Cameron and his sons Andrew, David and Michael.
By permission of the Keeper of the Records of Scotland

bear ample testimony to the legal obligations they incurred and the extent of their indebtedness to creditors.[18]

Interestingly, many of the deeds themselves were drawn up by Allan's youngest son Andrew, who had gone into training as a 'writer', or lawyer's assistant, in the city with a view to pursuing a legal career. Over a period of time, the family were to become reasonably well established in Edinburgh, though sooner or later the causes which had motivated them to leave Falkland were, perhaps inevitably, to exert at least as great an influence on their lives in their new home as they had done in Fife.

5.
The influence of John Welwood

Either at the time of his family's move to Edinburgh, or shortly before, Richard Cameron gave up his schoolmaster's post in Falkland. For him, as for his family as a whole, this was a time of severe testing and trial. Above all, it was a challenge to his new-found faith. From a situation of relative security, he had been cast into the wilderness. The future course of his life was uncertain. Given his known sympathies, he could expect few opportunities to exercise his talents. From what is known of him at a later stage, it can be safely assumed that Cameron spent much of this time in seeking God's will in earnest prayer.

He was not, however, altogether bereft of guidance at the human level. It is uncertain who was the person instrumental in Cameron's conversion, but the evidence points strongly to John Welwood, a young preacher who had recently come to prominence, and who was destined to play a vital part in Cameron's subsequent spiritual development. John was a son of James Welwood, minister at Tindergarth in Dumfriesshire, who had been ejected from his charge in 1662 for nonconformity.

John Welwood had been licensed, and probably ordained, by a group of nonconforming ministers in the early 1670s, and had then embarked on an itinerant ministry. His preaching made a profound impact. Though dogged by persistent ill-health, which was to result in his early death, he preached extensively through southern and central Scotland, attracting a devoted following. Welwood's preaching was earnest and direct; he challenged his hearers powerfully, yet had a tenderness and a sympathy which evoked a strong popular appeal. Indeed, at a time when the ministry of the field-preachers was greatly prized, there were few who attracted so much affection and respect among all classes of the people.[1]

In the summer of 1674 Welwood went over to Fife, where he preached in a number of places in company with the other field-preachers. He seems, however, to have developed a particular affection for Falkland. The reasons for this are of some interest. They centre around the Collace sisters, one of whom, Elizabeth, was a sempstress, or sewing mistress, in Falkland. The other two, Katharine and Jean, were resident in Moray, where they frequently went to hear some of the field-preachers in the north, including the noted Thomas Hog of Kiltearn.

In the summer of 1674 Katharine and Jean visited Elizabeth at Falkland and stayed with her until the spring of 1675. Both have left accounts of their experiences.[2] Shortly after arriving at Falkland, they heard John Welwood and were immediately impressed. Welwood, for his part, recognized the worth of the sisters, and a strong bond grew between him and them. Largely through their encouragement Welwood continued to preach regularly in and around Falkland, often at great personal hazard. Jean Collace records that his preaching was with power, and that 'The Lord comforted our hearts by bringing in several by the preached gospel.'

Both Jean and her sister could well have wondered at the providence which had brought them to Falkland at this particular juncture in time. Jean had no doubt that the Lord's hand was in it. 'I was very clearly called by the Lord', she writes, 'from Moray to Fife.' Katharine, for her part, was humbly thankful that, through their influence, Welwood himself visited Moray, where he met Hog and other worthies and enjoyed much profitable fellowship. Of her visit to Falkland she records: 'It brought Mr Welwood north ... he himself professed that he was much edified by conversing with some in the north, and many times spoke of them in the south, to professors, for imitation.' However, it is not too fanciful to suggest that there may have been a yet deeper purpose in the visit of these two gracious women to Falkland at this time. They may well have been the means used by God to bring John Welwood into touch with Richard Cameron.

Whether or not Welwood was instrumental in Cameron's conversion, it is certain that he had a profound influence on Cameron's life subsequently. It is clear from later events that his influence was not limited to spiritual guidance, important though that was; it also extended to the major public issues of the time. Welwood had carefully thought through such issues as obedience to rulers, the right of popular resistance and the relative responsibilities of church and state. From a close study of Scripture and the writings of the Reformers, he had developed a high view of the spiritual independence of the church and its freedom from state domination. This, of course, was what lay at the heart of the dispute between the nonconforming Presbyterians and the government, but in Welwood's thinking it assumed a particularly highly developed form. Welwood formed the conviction that any action carried out in obedience to the state in its claims and pretensions over the church was an act of disloyalty to Christ as the church's head. While others may have been prepared to accept this as a principle, Welwood pressed it to its logical, practical conclusion. This found expression in the view, which he was the first to propagate publicly, that those ministers who had accepted the government's Indulgences had, in doing so, recognized the king's supremacy and, by virtue of that fact, they were disobedient to Christ and had forfeited the right to a hearing.[3]

The Indulgences granted in 1669 and 1672 had been accepted by around sixty ministers, who were now settled in charges while their non-complying colleagues continued to feel the full wrath of the government. The upsurge of field-preaching which followed the Second Indulgence had called forth new acts of repression: on 16 July 1674 a proclamation was issued declaring all the continuing field-preachers public traitors and rebels; and on 6 August 1675 a further proclamation declared them 'intercommuned', and so denied all sustenance and comfort, at the highest peril. John Welwood's name figured in both these proclamations, with some forty of his fellow-ministers. However, it would be a mistake to think that Welwood's opposition to the Indulgence derived from any personal resentment against those who had accepted the government's favour. On the contrary, both he and others who later adopted his position were careful to point out that they continued to respect those who had accepted the Indulgence as ministers, while deploring the defection of which they were guilty.

It was not, indeed, difficult to see the Indulgence from the point of view of those who had accepted it. It had been welcomed by them as a timely relief, enabling them once again to occupy their pulpits without openly acknowledging the episcopal order. For those with families in particular, it meant access to a means of livelihood and all the benefits of a settled ministry. While some, no doubt, had reservations, it is easy to understand the readiness with which the Indulgence was embraced by men who had spent years in the wilderness. The opportunity to exercise their chosen calling was, once again, theirs, and to many of them it must have seemed a direct intervention of God's providence in their favour.

But there were others who took a different view. The Indulgence, they pointed out, had been a direct exercise of the king's authority. It had been a reflection of the right which he claimed to regulate the affairs of the church. As such, it was inconsistent with Presbyterian principles, and with the authority of Christ as the church's head. This was the position held by the leading field-preachers, such as Welsh, Dickson, Semple and Blackader. There was, of course, common ground between this position and that taken up by Welwood and, later, by Cameron. But there was one essential difference. For the leading field-preachers, attitudes to the Indulgence were basically a matter of conscience. While they could not accept it for themselves, they were not prepared to condemn those whose consciences allowed them to do so. Objectively, they argued, acceptance of the Indulgence could not be regarded as sinful until it had been condemned as such by a free General Assembly. In furtherance of this policy they made it their practice not to touch on the Indulgence in their preaching, nor to reflect in any way on those who had accepted it. Their duty, as they saw it, was to preach the gospel, and they did not want to introduce any note which would cause controversy or mar the success of the gospel.

This was, of course, a perfectly understandable attitude. At the time that the First Indulgence was granted, and more particularly at the time of the Second Indulgence, there were tokens of increasing success for the preaching of the gospel. It seemed churlish and divisive to introduce a note of criticism of fellow-ministers, thus creating a party spirit among the people and possibly scandalizing those who had newly come to the faith. So the argument ran, and, indeed, it appeared to be justified by events.

As we have already seen, the period after the granting of the Second Indulgence in 1672 was one of unparalleled advance for the cause of the gospel. Particularly after the granting of the general indemnity in March 1674, the number of field and house-meetings grew beyond all bounds. The main focus of this activity, of course, was in the fields, where Welsh and his colleagues preached regularly to congregations of thousands. Alexander Shields, who was himself one who took part, has left a moving account of this memorable time:

> The Word of God grew exceedingly, and went through the southern borders of the kingdom like lightning, or like the sun in its meridian beauty: discovering so the wonders of God's law, the mysteries of his gospel, and the secrets of his covenant, and the sins and duties of the day, that a numerous issue was begotten to Christ, and his conquest was glorious, captivating poor slaves of Satan, and bringing them from his power unto God, and from darkness to light. Oh who can remember the glory of that day without a melting heart! A day of such power, that it made the people, even the bulk and body of the people, willing to come out and venture, upon the greatest of hardships and the greatest of hazards, in pursuing after the gospel, through mosses and moors and inaccessible mountains, summer and winter, through excess of heat and extremity of cold, many days and night-journeys; but this was a day of such power, that nothing could daunt them from their duty, that had tasted once the sweetness of the Lord's presence at these persecuted meetings. I have not language to lay out the inexpressible glory of that day; but I will make bold to say of it, I doubt if ever there were greater days of the Son of Man upon the earth since the apostolic times.[4]

These remarkable events took place against a background of at least external unity among the nonconforming ministers. True, there was little contact or association between the field-preachers and the ministers who had taken advantage of the Indulgence to be resettled in churches. But, in the main, the Indulgence was not at this time a focus of controversy. And, for their part, the generality of those who attended the preaching made little distinction between going to hear the ministers who had accepted the Indulgence in their churches and those who had rejected it in the fields.

Such was the state of affairs when Welwood started his preaching ministry. Being a young man, and respecting the views of his older brethren, he appears to have refrained at first from propounding his radical views on the Indulgence. But, as time went on, the conviction appears to have grown on him that he could not keep silent and, by the time he met Cameron, he may well have already come to notice as the first to oppose it publicly. At all events, it seems fairly certain that the Indulgence featured prominently in Welwood's early contacts with Richard Cameron. It would not, doubtless, have emerged as an issue in isolation, but as an element of the disputed supremacy claimed by the state.

There is reason to believe that Cameron had already reached his own conclusions on this score. For him, as for any true convert, the Word of God had become his only rule. It was there, and there alone, that he could find where the path of obedience and duty lay. Cameron was determined to bring all the issues that troubled him to the supreme authority of Scripture. Among these was the whole question of the rights and government of the church. This, of course, was a matter much in public agitation, as Cameron well knew, but there were also a number of personal reasons which forced it on his attention. He had himself been a participant in a system of church order and government imposed by the state. He had, to some extent, been a beneficiary of that system. Yet he had been brought to spiritual light and liberty through the ministry of men who had defied the established order and, indeed, had risked their lives in opposing it. It was natural that he should feel prompted to ask what had motivated them to do so. It is also possible that he sought the advice of some of these men themselves — notably, no doubt, John Welwood — in seeking to resolve his problems. At all events, the outcome was clear. Cameron emerged from his heart-searching with an unbreakable conviction that the state's assertion of authority over the church was a violation of the prerogatives of Christ, and that the path of obedience lay in resisting that supremacy with all the power at his command.

In reaching this position Cameron was on common ground with the majority of the non-complying Presbyterians — field-preachers and others — who continued to resist the government. But he was not yet satisfied. There was an inner com-pulsion driving him forward — a compulsion to know the will of God perfectly, to render that complete obedience which alone would satisfy his conscience. He had advanced far, but doubts continued to trouble him.

The particular object of his concern was the Indulgence. Cameron was, of course, familiar with the Indulgence as an established fact in the affairs of the church. Indeed, he had himself attended the preaching of ministers who had availed themselves of it. Now, however, he began to see it in a different light. The conviction grew on him that it could not be isolated from the supremacy claimed by the state over the church. However, at this stage in his spiritual development he appears to have found it difficult to reach a considered view. The Indulgence was, after all, a particularly intractable issue. No pronouncement had been made upon it by the general body of non-complying ministers, and it had certainly not been made a matter of public testimony. To that extent it would have been difficult for Cameron to reach a definitive view on it without advice or guidance from a source he could respect.

It was here that his contact with Welwood was crucial. The issues on which Cameron needed guidance — the Indulgence in particular — were precisely those on which Welwood had reached his own, carefully considered, views. In other ways, too, Welwood was well fitted to act as Cameron's spiritual guide. The two men were of similar age and temperament. Both were of strong character and conviction and they shared an abhorrence of evasion and compromise. In Welwood Cameron found a counsellor with whom he could identify and in whom he could confide. From this point on, the two were to develop a mutual friendship and confidence, sharing in fellowship when together and exchanging correspondence when apart.[5]

The results of that confidence were to emerge in Cameron's adopting a view of the Indulgence which owed much to Welwood's influence. That view, which Cameron would come to champion, was that the Indulgence was an integral part of the supremacy claimed by the state over the church and that those ministers who had accepted it were disloyal to Christ as the church's head, and on that account should not be countenanced nor given a hearing.

So far, indeed, did Cameron become convinced of the sinfulness of the Indulgence that, according to his own later account, he 'longed for an opportunity to witness against it'. That opportunity was to arise perhaps rather sooner than he had anticipated.

It is likely that on leaving Falkland Cameron spent some time with his family in Edinburgh, though in the event he was destined not to remain there long. Within a few weeks, through the influence of Edward Jamieson, one of the non-complying ministers, he was offered a position as private chaplain to Lady Scott, wife of Sir William Scott of Harden, in the Border country. The Scotts were well-known Presbyterian sympathizers, and Lady Scott in particular was known to favour the non-complying ministers. To Richard Cameron, in his circumstances, the offer could well have seemed providential, and he appears to have accepted it with some alacrity. He duly took up his new appointment in or around September 1675.

Cameron's duties at Harden would probably have involved conducting worship in the family, instructing the servants and generally upholding the moral order of the household. It was not, by its nature, a work which attracted much popularity, and Cameron appears to have had his share of difficulties. But his employer, at least, was on his side and, from the evidence available, he was able to enjoy fellowship with others in the neighbourhood who shared his sympathies. He wrote with his initial impressions to Welwood not long after his arrival at Harden, and in his reply, dated 5 October 1675, Welwood offered him words of encouragement. 'Brother', he wrote, 'I am glad (and you may think it strange) that Satan and his instruments love you not; for it is a token that you are none of theirs. I am glad that the Lord is encouraging you and that you have the love of his people; the Lord help you to walk humbly, watchfully and thankfully with God. As for that work, I wish that the Lord may continue it and increase it, and make you instrumental in your station therein. Be not high-minded, but fear, for there may be storms before you. The eyes of God, angels, Satan, the wicked, the godly and of your own conscience are upon you; your soul and the honour of God are at stake; therefore be watchful. But if you be diffident of yourself, and your own strength, and trust in him in whom is everlasting strength, keeping near him by faith, he will carry you through.'

Welwood went on to give Cameron some news of his family and of affairs in Fife. Richard's father, Allan Cameron, had returned on a visit to Falkland the previous week and had there been arrested and imprisoned by the authorities. In a postscript, however, which must have brought Cameron much relief, he added: 'I have heard this night that your father is let pass free, and is gone this day to Edinburgh.' He ended his letter, in typical vein, by asking Cameron to convey his regards to Lady Scott: 'Present my humble regards to your lady, and tell her from me it will be her joy and crown in the day of Christ to own him and his people and his way, and to disown Satan and this abominable and apostate generation.'[6]

Two months later, on 13 December 1675, Welwood wrote again to Cameron. It appears that, in the meantime, Cameron had reported some further problems, but had expressed some satisfaction at his success in handling them. Welwood thought it right to register a note of caution. 'Brother', he wrote, 'you have the honour to be persecuted for righteousness; have a care, be not lifted up; for there may be several trials before your hand. If you keep near him, all is well. You know, all that go heavenward are wrestlers, and through many tribulations we must enter. All things are ebbing and flowing, but God is ever the same, and he alters folk's lot, and makes them to have changes, that they may build all their hope and happiness on the Rock of Ages. Your heart will fail, and your flesh will fail, but your God will never fail you. He will be with you, as long as you are with him.' It was a word calculated to bring much comfort to Cameron in the trial which he was soon to face.

6.
Licensed to preach

There is a strong hint in Welwood's letter, quoted at the end of the previous chapter, that he expected events to turn to Cameron's disadvantage, and so it was to prove. Indeed, whether or not Cameron was aware of it, the storm clouds were already gathering. The crisis, when it came, was to hinge on his view of the Indulgence. Edward Jamieson, who had recommended him for the place at Harden, claimed afterwards that he had warned Cameron that Lady Scott attended the preaching of ministers who had taken advantage of the Indulgence, though Cameron himself denied any knowledge of this. Be that as it may, a day came when Cameron, as Lady Scott's chaplain, was called to attend her to a church where one of these ministers was to preach. To Cameron, the summons appears to have been unexpected. Here, however, was surely the opportunity he had sought — the prospect of making a public testimony against the Indulgence and all the evils it had brought on the church. But at the same time, he could not be unaware of the consequences. By making a protest, or refusing to do what was required of him, he would certainly give offence, and possibly risk losing his employment. Despite his initial difficulties, there is evidence that Cameron had settled down reasonably well at Harden and had gained the confidence and respect of his employers. As in his schoolmaster's post at Falkland, he had a comfortable situation and a regular income. And, once again, the temptation to conform, and to stifle his beliefs, must have been a very real one.

When the critical day came, Cameron duly accompanied Lady Scott and her husband to the church. He had given them no hint of his intentions, nor, it appears, had discussed with them his opposition to the Indulgence. It therefore came as a total surprise to them when, at the door of the church, Cameron excused himself, left them and returned home. He spent the remainder of the day in his room, where, as he later recorded, he 'met with much of the Lord's presence, and very evident discoveries of the true nature of these temptations and suggestions of Satan, which had like to have prevailed with him before'.

The next day, inevitably, Cameron was called to account for his conduct. He had, of course, expected this, and was well prepared. Characteristically, he made no attempt at mitigation or excuse. On the contrary, he saw it as an occasion for plain speaking. Tracing the Indulgence back to its origin, he testified fearlessly against it as an endorsement of the state's supremacy and a betrayal of the interest of Christ. And, he argued, the ministers who had accepted the Indulgence had compromised their calling and on that account should not be given a hearing.

Lady Scott and her husband listened patiently to what he had to say, but were not impressed. On the contrary, they seem to have been taken aback that a young man in Cameron's position should express himself so dogmatically, and by implication condemn their own conduct. The result of the interview was that Cameron was told that his services were no longer required. There is no reason to conclude that Cameron's parting with the Scotts was marked by any bitterness; their reaction appears to have been one more of sorrow than of anger. But, for Cameron, it meant the loss of his employment and, for a time at least, the disappointment of his hopes. This clearly mattered less to him than maintaining a clear conscience, but Cameron would have been less than human had he not felt the loss keenly.

One of his first reactions was to write to Welwood, telling him of the turn of events and asking what he should do — in particular, whether he should stay on in the Borders or return to Edinburgh. Welwood's reply, written on 12 January 1676, was full of the consolation Cameron needed. 'Brother', he wrote, 'I am glad that the Lord helped you to be faithful to him in that family you were in, and that the enemy hath no evil to say of you; and that it is given to you not only to believe, but also to suffer for his name's sake. The Lord hath been training you in the high court gate to heaven, which is through many tribulations. I know a little of it in my own experience, that the Christian's life is a warfare, and he that standeth hath need to take heed lest he fall. We have need often to sit down and to count the cost; and heaven will cost us no small toil, and no few crosses, and many ups and downs will we meet with ere we come there. Oh but it takes much to humble us, and it is not done all at once, but piece by piece. For though the Lord should keep us humble many a day, yet the very second that he lifts us up, we are ready to miscarry. Oh but it takes a long time and much pains to teach us wisdom, for we are at first as a wild ass's colt. But in this we may comfort ourselves; all our springs are in him. The fountain is full.'

Welwood went on to answer Cameron's request for guidance: 'Now for what you speak about advice anent your tarrying or returning, I hope the Lord will guide you by his counsel. Acknowledge him in all your ways, and he will direct your steps. But I will tell you in brief what I think; except you have hope of some convenient place in that country, I know of no advantage you can have in tarrying in it.' 'And', he added pointedly, 'note this, all is not gold that glitters.'

It is difficult not to see in Welwood's remarks a hint of his feeling that Cameron had acted too hastily in accepting the post at Harden, and his fear that he might meet a similar disappointment again. Welwood had sensed a tendency to impetuousness in Cameron's character, and he was doing what he could to curb it. While he may not have been altogether successful, his wise counsel certainly had a beneficial effect on Cameron, both at this time and afterwards.

Welwood ended his letter with a profoundly interesting comment. Reminding Cameron that his father was now living in Edinburgh — and hinting that it was his duty to be there also — he went on: 'Possibly you may get yourself licensed there; I am not sure of it, but the Lord may bring such a thing to pass.' This is the first known reference to Cameron's future career as a preacher of the gospel. Clearly this had already been discussed between the two, and Welwood, no mean judge of men, had become convinced that this was where Cameron's duty lay. In suggesting that he might be licensed in Edinburgh, Welwood may well have had in mind that the non-complying ministers, in their determination to continue the witness of the church, had appointed some of their number as tutors, or instructors, of young men aspiring to the ministry. Some of these tutors were, no doubt, to be found in Edinburgh, and Welwood may have been suggesting that Cameron should place himself under their instruction for a time.

It is not known for certain whether Cameron acted on this advice, though his apparent presence in Edinburgh for at least a good part of the following year does suggest that he may very well have done so. It is otherwise difficult to account for his movements during the period immediately following his departure from Harden. Indeed, the only clues are some fleeting references to him in Welwood's letters to other correspondents, which suggest that the two men were in frequent contact at this time. The absence of any recorded correspondence between Welwood and Cameron over this period would seem to support that view. Welwood himself was a regular visitor to Edinburgh, where his kinsman James Welwood was a prominent local notary and friend of the Cameron family. The evidence, therefore, seems to point to a fairly extended stay by Cameron in Edinburgh at this time, during which he may have availed himself of the instruction which Welwood recommended to him.

It is also possible that Cameron may have joined Welwood on some of his preaching tours, which during this period extended not only to Fife, but also to the Lothians, the eastern Borders and Northumberland. Cameron had proven skills as a precentor, and could well have used these to support Welwood. He would also, of course, have had the opportunity to hear Welwood preach, and to learn from him some of the skills which he would later use to such telling effect. If this was indeed how Cameron was engaged at this time — and the presumption in its favour is fairly strong — it clearly marked a major stage in the preparation for what was to become his life's work.

By the end of 1676, Cameron could well have been in a favourable position to apply for licence to the ministry. That he did not choose to do so remains something of a mystery. Instead, he once again left Edinburgh, this time to take up an appointment at some considerable distance, but of which very little is known. Again the only clues come in a letter from Welwood, who wrote to him on 26 January 1677 offering him advice and counsel. It is difficult to avoid the impression that Welwood regarded Cameron as having once more acted hastily and against his better judgement, and there are hints that there may have been factors in Cameron's domestic circumstances which impelled him to make the move. Welwood, however, as was his wont, saw the hand of the Lord in the whole situation. 'Brother,' he wrote, 'I do not love the place to which you are gone; I suppose there is nothing of religion there. But I trust the Lord has sent you thither for your good, and it may be for some others' good. You are far from the vexation of your family, and it may be he has taken you to the wilderness that he may speak kindly unto you. And, for ought I can conjecture, there are and are like to be more troublesome days with us, and who knows, but this may be a hiding-place to you for a while? Wherefore I would not have you to weary, though you have not the converse you would desire, for it is the day of Jacob's trouble (though he shall be delivered out of it) and everyone must look to have their share in it.'

Welwood went on, in terms which were to prove prophetic: 'Truly, I think you are at no disadvantage to be in a retired condition as at this day; neither be troubled for want of work; for if you be spared to see the good that he shall do for his people, you shall have work enough.' He ended by saying, 'He, it may be, is preparing you for it; you know in your experience that it hath been good for you that you have been afflicted, and if things had gone as you and I would have had them going, we would never have done well. It is hard indeed to submit to his disposal, and to judge it fitter that he carve out our lot than that we ourselves do it; but he will order it, whether we choose or refuse. Now the Lord be with you, and work all his good pleasure in you.'

It would certainly have been interesting to know Cameron's circumstances at the time of Welwood's letter, but nothing of this has been recorded. The inference, however, would appear to be that he had accepted a post — possibly that of a tutor/chaplain — which had once again proved a disappointment to him. Where that employment was, and with whom, it is impossible now to speculate. To judge from Welwood's letter, it was in an area remote from the main centres of population and relatively untouched by the gospel, though there is no need to conclude — as some have done — that it was outside Scotland altogether. The probability is that Cameron had moved to a part of Scotland where field-preaching had not yet penetrated, and which was therefore in Welwood's terms a 'wilderness'. He may have thought that by going to such an area to work he would be able to exert some influence for good, but, to judge from Welwood's letter at least, the outcome did not match his expectations. At the same time, it is difficult not to see in it, as Welwood did, the providential ordering of Cameron's life in a way that would fit him for the work that lay before him. In writing to Cameron, Welwood appears to have had before his mind the analogy of the apostle Paul in Arabia, and he was convinced that, in a similar way, Cameron's wilderness experience was being used to prepare him for the life of public witness which lay ahead.

By the beginning of June 1677 Cameron had found a new situation, as chaplain to Lady Douglas of Cavers, near Hawick.[1] Lady Douglas, who had been recently widowed, was a noted sympathizer with the non-complying Presbyterians and a staunch friend and supporter of the field-preachers. Not content with going to hear them, she was in the habit of giving them shelter and hospitality, and her house became a well-known place of sanctuary. For this she was kept under close surveillance by the government, and she was later to suffer much for her self-sacrificing loyalty.[2] Around this time, however, she was left relatively unmolested, and she used the respite to render what service she could.

Cameron was at last in a situation he could find congenial. His new employer was sympathetic to his views, and he had ample scope to exercise his talents. But the main significance of Cameron's stay at Cavers was the opportunity it brought him for contact with the field-preachers. For several years, the eastern Borders had been one of the main centres of field-preaching activity. The leading field-preachers visited it regularly. John Welsh, John Blackader, Gabriel Semple and many others are all known to have been in the area around this time. While there, they were given sanctuary at Cavers, where they would certainly have come into contact with Cameron. There is good reason to believe that the contacts which Cameron forged at Cavers were decisive in shaping his future career and giving him the impetus he needed to take up the work to which God was calling him.

On no one, it seems, did Cameron make such a strong impression as on John Welsh. Welsh was beyond doubt the leading field-preacher of his day, and the one most keenly sought by the authorities. A grandson of the noted John Welsh of Ayr — himself a son-in-law of John Knox — he had been active in field-preaching since the earliest days and travelled extensively throughout central and southern Scotland, gaining an immense popular following. In the Lothians, Borders and Fife his meetings were attended by many thousands. Among the field-preachers, and the people generally, there was none who exercised a greater influence. Such a man it was who had now been brought into close contact with Richard Cameron.

It is possible that Welsh and Cameron may have met before, in Fife, but any acquaintance at that time would have at best been slight. Now, however, Welsh's interest was thoroughly awakened. Cameron had, of course, matured substantially in the interim, and he made a strong impression on Welsh. Over the next few months, Welsh had ample opportunities to assess Cameron's character. It seems that Cameron, while still based at Cavers, joined Welsh, and possibly others of the field-preachers, on preaching tours, as he had earlier accompanied Welwood. The more Welsh saw of Cameron, the more he was impressed with his fitness for the work of the ministry. To achieve that end, Welsh now applied all his efforts. He represented to Cameron the undoubted natural gifts he possessed. He pointed out to him the need there was for a man of his abilities. And, it appears, he recruited the support of other field-preachers, and of influential local sympathizers, to reinforce his case.

Cameron was not easily persuaded. His reluctance did not stem from any doubt about his own personal qualifications; indeed, he did not attempt to plead inability or lack of confidence. He did, however, make clear to Welsh the main objection he saw to his acceptance. It concerned the Indulgence. He had, he said, been led into such a view of the evil of the Indulgence, and the disloyalty of those ministers who had accepted it, that he could not in conscience keep silent about it in his preaching. At the same time, he was anxious to preserve the peace of the church and not to cause disunity among brethren. He well knew that the Indulgence was a matter of particular sensitivity, and that it was agreed policy among the field-preachers not to deal with it in their preaching. He made it plain that, before committing himself, he wanted the likely consequences of his acceptance to be fully recognized.

Welsh heard him patiently, but was not prepared to be diverted from his purpose. To judge by later events, he may not have fully appreciated the strength of Cameron's views on the Indulgence, and his determination to witness against it when he had the opportunity. At all events, his only response was to redouble his efforts to win Cameron over. It is by no means certain that Cameron would have capitulated, even to the entreaties of such an influential pleader as Welsh, had not a circumstance intervened which he may well have seen as providential.

His old friend Welwood, with whom he had shared so many confidences, and whom he regarded as his father in the faith, now lay dying. Welwood's health, never robust, had finally given way, and early in 1678 he withdrew to Perth, where he was faithfully tended by loyal friends until his death the following April.[3] In the pressure put on him by Welsh, Cameron may have heard an echo of the words of Welwood, who two years earlier had suggested that he seek licence for the ministry. It is not, indeed, beyond belief that in the closing days of his life Welwood may have contrived to send a message to Cameron, reminding him of their earlier talks, and once again pressing the claims of the ministry on his attention. Be that as it may, Cameron finally gave way to the pressure, and early in 1678 he submitted himself to the required procedures for licence.

Under legislation of the General Assembly, candidates for the ministry were required to give evidence of their preaching gifts, their ability in theological disputation and their proficiency in the original languages of the Scriptures. These 'trials for licence', as they were called, continued to be conducted by the groups of non-complying ministers who formed themselves into 'field presbyteries' during the persecution. While, no doubt, the strictness of the requirements was somewhat modified in these extraordinary times, the ministers still required a high standard of attainment from those who presented themselves for licence. It can certainly be assumed that they would not have been prepared to license Cameron had they not been satisfied that in both gifts and abilities he met the general standards laid down by the church. By the same token, Cameron would not have presented himself for licence had he not been confident of his own ability to meet these standards. His university training was, of course, a strong factor in his favour, as was his teaching experience at Falkland. At the same time, his ability to satisfy the ministers, which he clearly proved, was a tribute to his diligence and application, particularly during his time of study in Edinburgh.

Cameron was duly licensed to preach the gospel in or around March 1678.[4] The licensing, according to Patrick Walker,[5] took place in the house of Henry Hall, a Border landowner and staunch friend of the non-complying ministers, at Haughhead near Kelso. The ministers present, apart from Welsh himself, were Gabriel Semple, Welsh's close friend and colleague, David Williamson, later of the West Kirk of Edinburgh, and Thomas Douglas, a field-preacher with whom Cameron was to be closely associated in later days. Henry Hall also attended as an elder of the church, and the licensing was carried out according to the due form. The ministers, doubtless, were well satisfied with their day's work, and with the addition of such a recruit as Cameron to their ranks. They could scarcely have known that one of the most remarkable ministries in the history of the Church of Scotland had finally been launched on its way.

7.
Troubled times

Cameron began his preaching ministry at a time of fast-moving change in events in Scotland. Throughout the mid-1670s—indeed, ever since the Indemnity of 1674—the field-meetings had continued to flourish. By the middle of the decade they had overspread much of the central lowlands and the south. The field-preachers had regular congregations of many thousands. Areas not previously penetrated were being reached with the gospel.

By 1677 the field-meetings began to take on a new dimension. Field-communions began to be celebrated, where multitudes assembled from far and near, remaining together for up to three days. These became particularly memorable occasions, and several who attended them have left moving accounts of their experiences.[1]

The government, inevitably, viewed these events rather differently. Irritated as they were by their failure to curb the field-meetings, they saw these new developments as a further affront to their authority. The impression grew on them that the non-complying Presbyterians were planning some sort of direct challenge to them. Various events around this time gave a show of credence to this view. In late October 1677 a well-attended field-communion was held at Girvan, in south Ayrshire, at which it was reported that arms and weapons were openly paraded.[2] In early November Robert Ker of Kersland, whom the government saw as a leading troublemaker, made his escape from prison in Glasgow.[3] And later in the same month a violent incident took place at the home of John Balfour of Kinloch, in Fife, in which a party of government troops was repulsed by force of arms, and one of their number was seriously wounded.[4]

Much was made of these incidents in an attempt to justify the need for still more repressive measures by the authorities. On the part of the people generally, of course, there was no intention of seeking an armed confrontation with the government. The only aim of the majority who attended the field-meetings was to worship God according to their consciences — and to resort to justified self-defence if pushed to extremity. But with the continued harassment and provocation by the authorities, which was daily reaching new levels of intensity, it was perhaps inevitable that some should have begun to take a stronger line. By 1677 — or at least by the end of that year — a movement had become established which sought to stiffen the pattern of resistance, and in various ways to carry the battle to the authorities.

The acknowledged leader of this movement was Robert Hamilton, the second son of Sir Thomas Hamilton of Preston, in East Lothian.[5] Hamilton, who had earlier had a reputation as a profligate, had apparently undergone a radical spiritual experience, and had set himself up as a champion of orthodoxy and of opposition to compromise. His natural zeal, his dominant personality and, perhaps not least, his aristocratic background, soon secured for him a position of influence.

Hamilton's movement was not, however, an isolated phenomenon. It grew out of a perceptible change of mood among the people, particularly in their attitude towards ministers. The field-preachers still continued to be held in the highest regard, but towards others there was a basic shift of ground. The very endurance of the field-preachers, and the evident tokens of blessing which attended their ministry, tended to reflect adversely on those ministers who did not share the same principles, or suffer the same privations. Ministers who preached privately, or otherwise avoided the wrath of the government, were increasingly held in low esteem. And to none did this feeling extend more than to the ministers who had taken advantage of the Indulgence and been reinstated in their parishes. More and more, these men became associated in the popular mind with compromise and a readiness to purchase liberty at the expense of truth. While this may not have been a totally fair conclusion, it gained much popular currency, and Hamilton and his associates exploited it to the full. With their support, and primarily at their instigation, some of the younger preachers began to hold meetings on the boundaries of, and even within, the parishes of such ministers, with the object of drawing away their people from attending their services. This unmistakably aggressive stance was fully in line with Hamilton's view of how to proceed. And his management of affairs was to become more influential as time went on.

Hamilton's closest coadjutors — at least in the early stages — were in Fife, and he himself had been involved in the incident at John Balfour's house in November 1677 which so inflamed the government. The escape from prison of Robert Ker of Kersland was an undoubted encouragement to Hamilton. Kersland, as he was usually called, was a veteran of the Pentland Rising who had been kept in various prisons since his arrest in 1669, and had endured numerous privations. He enjoyed a reputation as a folk hero, and to Hamilton and his supporters he became something of a father figure. There is no doubt that Kersland strongly supported Hamilton's aim of taking a more forceful stance against the government, and that the two men collaborated closely in the months following his escape from prison. Nor can there be any doubt that Kersland's influence gave Hamilton's movement a respectability which it might not otherwise have had.

The overall position, then, by the latter part of 1677, was one of gathering tension, with the prospect of open conflict a very real possibility. This state of affairs was viewed by the moderate Presbyterians with great alarm. It seemed to them that the government was seeking an excuse for, or could be provoked into, a new wave of persecution, and that the Presbyterian testimony of the church as a whole was under threat. Their response, perhaps predictably, was to close ranks in the common cause. Differences of policy were seen as subservient to the overriding need for unity. In this critical state of affairs, what mattered most of all was that the church should show a united front. In no other way, it was argued, could it now hope to survive.

There was, of course, nothing new in all this. The same pragmatic spirit had been in evidence some thirty years before when the country as a whole had been under threat from Cromwell. Then, the prevailing party, the Resolutioners, had counselled the policy of united action against the common enemy, irrespective of party. So it was now. Cast in the role of the Resolutioners were the majority of the non-complying ministers, including some of the leading field-preachers. And as the aim of the Resolutioners had been to enlist the aid of those disaffected from the Covenant, so these ministers now sought to court those who had accepted the Indulgence. Once again, the need for external unity was to take priority, and expediency was to triumph over principle.

The new policy duly manifested itself in practice. A meeting was held at which it was agreed that the ministers who had accepted the Indulgence should be invited to preach alongside their non-complying brethren, while the latter would be given access to their pulpits. At the same time steps were to be taken to silence any opposition to the Indulgence on the part of the younger preachers. Up till now, Welwood had been virtually a lone voice, but there were already signs that others were ready to follow in his footsteps. To forestall this, it was agreed that those presenting themselves for licence should in future be required to give a promise not to preach on any matters which might create division — by which, of course, the Indulgence was primarily intended. All the non-complying ministers were strictly enjoined to enforce these requirements when licensing young men to preach.

These instructions were in force by the beginning of 1678, and the requirement not to preach on matters that might cause division was no doubt a major factor in Richard Cameron's hesitation in applying for licence. This also, no doubt, explains his anxiety to ensure that his implacable opposition to the Indulgence was fully understood by those who licensed him. If he did not succeed in this, it was scarcely his fault and, having made his position clear, as his conscience required, he could scarcely be blamed for accepting what the ministers were more than eager to bestow on him.

He was later to maintain that no promise had been required of him to refrain in his preaching from matters which were the subject of controversy, though he admitted that he had been instructed not to touch on matters which might provoke division or cause offence. The Indulgence, he claimed, had not figured in the proceedings at all, though when one of the ministers had raised it with him privately he had categorically refused to refrain from preaching against 'that very great and public sin'. The ministers, it seemed, had been so persuaded of Cameron's abilities that they had stretched to the very limits the discretion allowed to them in licensing him.

It was a condition of Cameron's licence that, as an unordained preacher, he should preach only under the 'advice and direction' of ordained ministers. In his case this responsibility fell to the ministers who had licensed him, particularly

John Welsh. It was Welsh who, according to Patrick Walker's account, sent Cameron on his first preaching mission.

The place chosen for him was Annandale, in the western Borders, an area then noted for its lawlessness. Cameron was apprehensive, knowing the area's reputation. Welsh, however, persisted. 'Go your way, Ritchie,' he is said to have told Cameron. 'Set the fire of hell to their tail.' It is clear from these words that Welsh regarded Cameron as the ideal instrument for bringing the gospel to the unevangelized, and so indeed it was to prove. Annandale had only recently been reached by the field-preachers, and in a letter to Katharine Collace on 4 August 1677 John Welwood had claimed that a field-meeting he had led there the previous day had been the first ever held in the district. The people, according to Welwood at that time, were 'exceeding ignorant and rude'.

It was scarcely surprising, then, that Cameron should have been apprehensive at the thought of going to Annandale. His fears, however, were misplaced. The people flocked to hear him, and, though many came out of curiosity, there were evident tokens of blessing. He preached from Jeremiah 3:19, 'How shall I put thee among the children?', suiting the words to the condition of his audience. 'Some of them', records Patrick Walker, 'who got a merciful cast that day, told it afterwards that it was the first field-preaching that ever they heard; and that they went out of curiosity, to see how a minister would preach in a tent, and people sit on the ground; but if many of them went without an errand, they got one that day.'

Cameron's reception in Annandale was typical of that which he was to meet with elsewhere. It soon became evident to the people that there had come among them a preacher of no ordinary power. The account of his preaching in the *Cloud of Witnesses,* published in 1714, notes that from the very outset the people were 'warmed and affected with his doctrine'. The choice of words is significant. It shows that Cameron was able, even in his early days as a preacher, to move his audiences and to relate to them in a way that few of his contemporaries could. This was not merely a matter of personality, important as that was; it drew on all the experience of his past life. His academic training, his years as a schoolmaster and chaplain, his fellowship with men such as Welwood, his months of contemplation and solitude — all had fused together to produce a mature and well-balanced Christian character. And when these were allied to a strong and vigorous temperament, the effect was to produce a personality whose influence on the contemporary scene was to be both enduring and memorable.

8.
Cameron speaks out

As we saw in the previous chapter, the start of Cameron's preaching career coincided with a time of remarkable prosperity for the persecuted church in Scotland. Despite tensions within and without, the year 1678 marked the high point of gospel preaching in the fields. Huge meetings were held, attracting thousands from far and near. The preaching of the Word on the Lord's Day was supplemented by public fasts on weekdays and, increasingly, by field-communions in various places. One of the most memorable of the latter was at East Nisbet, in the eastern Borders, over the three days from Saturday, 20 to Monday, 22 April. Five ministers took part, and the sacrament was administered to 3,200 people. The occasion has been immortalized in a graphic description by John Blackader, which has often been quoted.[1]

Cameron was almost certainly present at the East Nisbet communion, though he took no part in the preaching. However, on the following Lord's Day, 28 April, he preached with Welsh at Blue Cairn, a favourite preaching-spot between Lauder and Earlston, where some 3,000 people had assembled. It was the first time he had preached to an audience of those who regularly attended field-preaching, as distinct from the unevangelized in Annandale, and the occasion would have provided a stern test of a young preacher's abilities. While no record of his sermon remains, there can be no doubt that he acquitted himself very much to Welsh's satisfaction, and to that of his hearers. The occasion was distinguished by the baptism by Welsh of a man of twenty-seven years of age — a highly unusual event which attracted much notice, and which added greatly to the solemnity of the meeting. In the words of a contemporary, 'The man's confession of sins and renouncing them, and engagement to duties, was an edifying and wakening sight; he gave a great testimony to these meetings and made 3,000 people at least weep to hear him.'[2]

Moving west again, Cameron accompanied Welsh towards Dumfries, where he preached the following Lord's Day, before moving on into Galloway. Over the succeeding weeks he preached regularly under Welsh's supervision, mainly in Galloway, Dumfries and the western Borders, and probably made several return visits to Annandale. It is likely too that he was present at the field-communion held at Irongray — Welsh's old parish — from 1 to 3 June, of which Blackader has again left a vivid description.[3]

Throughout this time Cameron kept himself strictly to preaching the Word, and studiously refrained from touching on controversial matters such as the Indulgence. However, it was inevitable that this state of affairs could not continue for long. By the time that he had been preaching for some weeks, Cameron felt sufficiently attuned to the prevailing climate of opinion among his hearers to know that there was a deep-seated discontent with the state of affairs in the church. He saw it as his duty to give expression to that discontent. At the same time, of course, he was anxious to keep his own conscience clear and, irrespective of the state of feeling among his hearers, it is certain that he would have felt constrained to declare himself before long. An opportunity duly presented itself.

The occasion was the holding of a public fast in Galloway. As was usual on such occasions, the sins of the land and the church were confessed, and God's forgiveness earnestly sought. Cameron was one of several who were called on to take part. He duly enumerated the various sins it was customary to mention — breach of the Covenant, failure to perform duties, forgetfulness of obligations towards God — and then, contrary to all expectation, he included among them the Indulgence. Nor did he stop there; he then proceeded to denounce the Indulgence as a particularly grievous evil, and the ministers who had accepted it as guilty of compromise and disobedience to Christ.

Not surprisingly, Cameron's words were greeted with dismay by the older ministers. They had licensed him in the full knowledge of his views on the Indulgence, but had clearly been prepared to stifle any misgivings on the grounds of his outstanding abilities for the work of the ministry. Now, it seemed, their worst fears had been confirmed. Cameron's action had not only broken the convention that nothing should be said about the Indulgence in public; it was also in defiance of the requirement placed on him at his licensing that he avoid dealing with matters which could cause division. Cameron, of course, did not see it in that light. From his point of view, the Indulgence was in its essence contrary to the established principles of the church, to which all church members were required to conform, and on that ground it could not properly be a cause of division. He did not therefore regard his action as in any way violating what had been required of him at his licensing. And he was to confirm that view, in the face of increasing pressure, as his ministry continued.

Whatever dismay Cameron's action may have caused the ministers, it did nothing to diminish his popularity among the people. He had clearly caught the prevailing mood and among his hearers there appears to have been general satisfaction that one of their preachers had finally dared to express what many of them thought. The opportunity soon presented itself for him to do so again.

Over the three days 3 to 5 August there took place near Maybole in Carrick what was reputed to be the largest field-meeting ever held in Scotland. Some 14,000 people attended, and the communion was observed. Welsh, as usual, took the leading role, accompanied by several of the older ministers. So vast was the crowd, however, that the sacrament could be administered only to sections of them at a time and, after the first group had been served, it was decided to hold preaching services while the sacrament was dispensed to the remainder. Cameron, though present, had not been engaged to preach, but at the instance of one of the ministers, Samuel Arnot, he was pressed into service. Though unprepared, he seized the opportunity readily.

Accompanied by another young preacher, John Kid, he withdrew some distance from the main meeting, and soon attracted a large crowd. His text, significantly, was Psalm 85:8: 'The Lord ... will speak peace unto his people, and to his saints: but let them not turn again to folly.' Taking the latter part of the verse as his theme, he spoke forcefully of the dangers of compromise, applying his words particularly to ministers, and going on to denounce vigorously those who had accepted the Indulgence. In an unprecedented way, he directly challenged his hearers to examine their consciences, and to declare openly if they had ever received any good from the ministry of these men. Not surprisingly, no one spoke — and of course this was precisely the response Cameron had anticipated by his novel way of pressing home his point. But his sermon and his unconventional style were scarcely designed to improve his standing among the older ministers, some of whom now started to agitate against him. However, Cameron still had his supporters among the ministers, and encouraged by one of them, John Dickson — one of the most respected of the field-preachers — he preached again the following day.

If Cameron's behaviour at Maybole had caused controversy, his actions later that week at Kilmarnock were to precipitate a crisis. There the local elders were out of sympathy with the minister of the parish, who had accepted the Indulgence. Supported by the local people, they arranged a public fast and preaching day for Wednesday, 7 August, to which Welsh and the other preachers at Maybole, including Cameron, were invited. There was much debate over the location of the meeting, and some of the visitors suggested that out of deference to the local parish minister the meeting should be held in the neighbouring vacant parish of Fenwick. The elders, however, resisted this and, in an attempt at compromise, a place was chosen which was just marginally within the Kilmarnock parish boundary.[4] This was not enough to satisfy Welsh, who forthwith declared that he would take no part in the meeting.

Cameron, however, felt no such inhibitions. Suiting his preaching to the occasion, he summed up the various sins of which the church was guilty, singling out the Indulgence as 'one of the woefullest pieces of our defection'. And, once again, he roundly denounced the ministers who had accepted it, urging that, so long as they remained unrepentant, people should not go to hear them.

Relations between Cameron and the older ministers had now come to an open breach. In preaching at all at Kilmarnock he had plainly disregarded Welsh's feelings, and made clear that in the matter of his preaching he saw himself as responsible not to the dictates of any man, but to his own conscience and the call of the people. Both these conditions had been met, to his satisfaction, at Kilmarnock. He saw no reason to regret what he had done; indeed, as the sequel showed, he was ready to repeat it when opportunity offered.

The ministers, not surprisingly, took a different view. As they saw it, Cameron's actions were fraught with the gravest consequences. The carefully constructed consensus over the Indulgence was in danger of being breached irreparably. Once released, the tide of popular feeling against the ministers who had accepted it could prove too strong to stem. It could sweep away the long-preserved unity of the church, and perhaps do lasting damage to the Presbyterian cause. Such was the reasoning of the ministers and, as reports of Cameron's preaching spread, the conviction grew on them that the time for decisive action had come.

On leaving Kilmarnock, Cameron preached the following Lord's Day at Fenwick, and then turned his steps towards Edinburgh. It is possible that reports had reached him of his mother's recent ill-health, but in any event it was now several months since he had parted from his family and he had a natural desire to see them again. It is likely that while in Edinburgh he stayed at his parents' house in the Potterrow, where he may well have presided at some of the house-meetings which his father used to hold in defiance of the authorities.

It was there, late in the evening of Wednesday, 21 August, that Cameron received a visit from Robert Ross, one of the non-complying ministers, who had been active for some time in the fields.[5] With him Ross brought a summons, in the name of a meeting of ministers in Edinburgh, citing Cameron to appear before them the following evening. No reasons were stated, and there was no attempt to specify charges. Cameron, of course, could have been in no doubt as to what these were, and he was equally clear as to his defence. Though taken aback by the peremptory nature of the summons, he determined at once to comply. He had nothing of which to be ashamed, and he may well have welcomed the opportunity to state his position openly, as his conscience required. He was prepared for whatever the ministers had in store for him.

The ministers, for their part, were at somewhat of a disadvantage. Those who had issued the summons were part of a group — around twenty in all — who met occasionally in

Edinburgh for mutual conference and discussion, and for general oversight of the affairs of the church in their area. Their meeting on this occasion had been arranged some time in advance, and Cameron's conduct had certainly not been on the agenda then. Indeed, it appears that few of them knew Cameron personally, or had heard him preach. They had, not surprisingly, heard reports of the controversy his preaching had caused, but this in itself was unlikely to have prompted them to act.

What appears to have forced their hand was a formal complaint made by John Welsh, in which Cameron's name was bracketed with those of two other young preachers, Thomas Hog and John Kid. Welsh had been deeply offended by Cameron's conduct at Kilmarnock, and he no doubt hoped that by bringing him to the notice of the Edinburgh ministers he could bring pressure to bear on the younger man from an influential source. The Edinburgh meeting was only one of several such groups which met around the country, but because of its influence and location it appears to have carried particular weight. Indeed, to judge from some contemporary attitudes, it seems to have had an almost unquestioned authority vested in it. Since Cameron was, at least occasionally, resident in Edinburgh, he could in any event have been regarded as subject to the jurisdiction of the Edinburgh ministers, but Welsh probably also thought that an appearance before this respected body of men would be sufficient to bring him into line.

Welsh's complaint duly came before the Edinburgh meeting on 21 August. It was supported by several of those present, who claimed to have heard, in their visits around the country, of the outcry Cameron's preaching had caused. Faced with these claims, the ministers felt compelled to act. Cameron's presence in Edinburgh was known, and it was decided that he should be sent for; hence the summons he received later that day. However, what the ministers hoped to achieve was by no means clear, and it is doubtful if they themselves knew. Their rights of jurisdiction were uncertain, and in the disorganized state of the church at the time it was doubtful what form of discipline they could claim to exercise. Furthermore, the business had been gone about hastily, and with little preparation. These factors were to become all too evident as the proceedings unfolded.

9.
The Edinburgh meeting

The next evening, Thursday, 22 August, saw some sixteen ministers convened in the house of John Mossman, one of their number.[1] For the most part they were men who had held charges in and around Edinburgh and who had continued to preach in the city and its vicinity, mainly in houses, but occasionally in the fields. Some of them had already suffered persecution. They included Robert Gillespie, who several years earlier had been arrested for holding a field-meeting at Falkland and had spent some time as a prisoner on the Bass.[2] Edward Jamieson, former minister of Swinton in Berwickshire, presided as moderator.[3] The group included one minister who had himself accepted the Indulgence — Ralph Rodger of Kilinning — his presence perhaps giving a fair indication of the prevailing mood among the ministers.

At the appointed hour Cameron appeared, and after the meeting was opened in prayer by the moderator he was asked to withdraw for some time while the ministers deliberated. He was then brought in to face his questioners.

For a young man, who had been licensed to preach for only five months, the prospect of being interrogated by sixteen older ministers was a daunting one. Despite his confidence in the rightness of his own case, Cameron could well have been excused for feeling apprehensive. In the circumstances, it might have been expected that the ministers would have sought — at least in some measure — to put him at his ease. This was not, however, what happened; on the contrary, the meeting adopted a confrontational tone from the outset.

Jamieson, as moderator, started by challenging Cameron as to whether at his licensing he had given a commitment not to meddle in matters of controversy. Cameron denied it, but said that he had been enjoined not to foment division, nor to speak or do anything that might give offence. 'Nor', he added, 'do I intend to speak or do anything which may foment division or give just cause of offence to any person.'

'Was there no other engagement required?' asked the moderator.

'Yes', replied Cameron, 'by one of the ministers in private, anent [i.e. concerning] the Indulgence. And', he added, 'I altogether refused to conceal that so very great and public sin.'

Jamieson then made a digression, apparently with the aim of discrediting Cameron in the eyes of the other ministers. He revealed that, before Cameron had gone to take up his post at Harden, he had himself told Cameron that Lady Scott frequented the meetings of ministers who had been resettled in churches following the Indulgence, and claimed that Cameron had raised no objection at the time.

Cameron acknowledged that Jamieson had written to him, and to Lady Scott, alleging that Cameron had said, supposedly in the presence of one James Douglas in Edinburgh, that he had no scruples about hearing ministers who had accepted the Indulgence. However, he went on, he had replied to Jamieson refuting the allegation, and on the first opportunity of seeing James Douglas, had obtained from him an assurance that he had never heard him say any such words.

Jamieson then tried a new tack. He alleged that, on his return to Edinburgh from Harden, Cameron had asked him to intercede on his behalf with the Scotts and to write to Lady

Scott asking her to reinstate him in his post. Cameron merely smiled, by way of response, and said he remembered no such thing, repeating his denial for further emphasis.

Jamieson was allowed to proceed no further in this strain, for the other ministers, feeling that time was being wasted, urged him to get back to the issue which lay at the heart of the complaint against Cameron. He then proceeded to challenge Cameron directly with having preached separation from the ministers who had accepted the Indulgence. Cameron at first declined to answer, claiming that, if the ministers had an accusation to make against him, this should be set out as a formal charge, and that he should not be expected to act as his own accuser.

Jamieson reminded him that the ministers had already concluded that nothing should be spoken in public against the Indulgence, and told him that 'It became not any, far less a young man, a probationer, to meddle with these things.' Cameron replied, with some spirit, that he had spoken nothing but what was warranted by Scripture, the Covenants and the Acts of General Assembly.

Some of the ministers then demanded to know what precisely he had said and, when he continued to demur, charged him with prevarication. Cameron, however, stood firm, and for a time the meeting threatened to degenerate into confusion.

At length Gillespie, who apparently felt able to exert some influence over Cameron, urged him at least to tell them what had first prompted him to speak out against the Indulgence. Cameron answered that, after being licensed to preach, he had for some time forborne to speak on the subject, but when he was called on to speak at public fast-days he had 'found himself necessitate' to witness against it. Pressed particularly about his right to preach at Kilmarnock, since the meeting was held within the parish of one of the ministers who had been settled in a charge after accepting the Indulgence, he claimed that the elders of the Kilmarnock and Newmilns parishes had expressly invited him to do so. His call to preach there had been 'as valid as the call of those who preached in those churches, save that we wanted the order of the king and council, which in public that day I preached and now this day own'.

It was now growing late, and the ministers were anxious to come to a decision. Cameron was asked to withdraw for a further half-hour while they reflected on what he had said. There was general agreement that he deserved a rebuke, and that he should be required to give an undertaking not to preach against going to hear the ministers who had accepted the Indulgence, and not to preach in any of their parishes. However, if this was to be effective, the meeting had to be clear that he would submit himself to its jurisdiction and so, when he was called in again, they first sought from him an assurance on this point. Cameron, somewhat taken aback, asked for an explanation.

'It need not be explained,' answered Jamieson.

'There is need', urged Cameron, for I do look upon you as a judicatory, yet you may act that anent me which I neither can, nor in conscience dare, submit unto.'

Some of the ministers took this as a direct affront to their authority and charged Cameron with violation of Presbyterian principles. Jamieson, growing increasingly exasperated, remarked that it would be very hard even for a General Assembly to find that the ministers who had taken advantage of the Indulgence to return to their parishes had in so doing acknowledged the king's supremacy over the church: 'Far less should a probationer take upon him to meddle with it, whose reading and learning scarcely comes the length of knowing what Presbyterian government is.'

Cameron, to his credit, refused to be provoked by this calculated insult. The fact that he had been brought before the ministers was, he said, sufficient proof that he was a Presbyterian and, if the meeting wished it, he could prove the point further as occasion required.

There followed a further quarter of an hour's deliberation, during which Cameron was once more asked to withdraw. When he returned, he was again asked if he would submit himself to the meeting. 'I will submit', he replied, 'in the Lord.'

Jamieson then read out the judgement: 'It is decided by the brethren that both by preaching and practice you have fomented division, and that you should humble yourself before God for what you have done; and that you have not been ingenuous and plain in telling the ministers what you have spoken in public, and that you engage in time coming not to preach in indulged ministers' parishes, nor against hearing the indulged.'

Cameron listened in silence, then spoke his mind. He was not convinced, he said, that he had fomented division either by his preaching or practice. Nor had he been less frank before ministers than others about his principles; there had, after all, been five or six ministers who heard him preach at Kilmarnock, when he had been 'most free' in speaking about the Indulgence. And, as for giving promises for the future, he could not in conscience do any such thing.

Matters had now reached an impasse. Once again Cameron was asked to withdraw while the ministers deliberated. Their confrontational tactics had clearly failed and, now that Cameron was openly defying them, their credibility as a court was at stake. Faced with this dilemma, they tried conciliation. Predictably perhaps, they chose as their spokesman Gillespie and sent him out to negotiate with Cameron. Gillespie told him that the meeting would be satisfied with a general assurance from him that he would not attempt in future to stop the people from going to hear the ministers who had accepted the Indulgence.

Far from being appeased, Cameron was horrified. 'Oh, dreadful!', he exclaimed. 'I would not do it for the world.'

Gillespie tried to reason with him. 'You mistake things', he said. 'They intend, if you be contumacious, to send to the brethren in the south and through other parts of Scotland, and they will recall your licence; and is it not better for you to forbear preaching against that sin than be deprived of your liberty of preaching all other things?' Cameron was unmoved. 'I will take my hazard', he replied.

Gillespie then asked what answer he should carry back to the meeting. By this time Cameron was becoming thoroughly weary of the whole business. 'I value not what you say', he told Gillespie dismissively.

Gillespie's report of the interview threw the meeting into even greater confusion. With a hint of desperation, the ministers decided to suggest that some of their number should meet with Cameron the following evening to discuss matters at fuller length.

When Cameron was brought before the meeting and told of this, he said that he could see no need for any such discussion, since his position was well enough known, and in any case he had arranged to be out of Edinburgh over the next few days and could not conveniently attend.

This went down very badly with the meeting, and several of the ministers accused him of contumacy, or stubbornness. Cameron denied the charge, maintaining that he was perfectly willing to give an account of himself 'in time and place convenient', but he was not prepared to break off a commitment he had already given to others. He did hint, however, that he would be available the following week and, after asking him once again to withdraw, the ministers were left with no option but to accept his terms.

When he was called back to the meeting yet again, Cameron was merely asked if he would meet the ministers again the following Wednesday, 28 August, and to this he assented.

As he left the ministers that evening, Cameron had reason to be satisfied with the outcome so far. He had not compromised his principles, and he had certainly not let the ministers intimidate him. Indeed, in the view of some, he had treated the meeting with scant respect. One of those present, John Scott of Hawick, was later to write of Cameron's 'insolence' towards the ministers.[4] But while he respected them as ministers, Cameron was far from accepting them as his judges. It is clear that, from the outset, he seriously doubted their competence to try him, and this had coloured his conduct throughout. In the interval between the meetings his misgivings grew, and by the time the meeting reconvened on the 28th his views on this point had become even more firmly entrenched.

The proceedings on 28 August took place in the house of John Lidderdale, former minister of Tynron in Galloway, who was now resident in Edinburgh.[5] Eleven ministers attended in all, with John Scott of Hawick acting as moderator. As usual, following the opening prayer, Cameron was asked to withdraw while the meeting deliberated. This time, however, he stood his ground and requested permission to speak.

When this was granted, he reviewed briefly the proceedings of the previous meeting, saying that he had since made them the subject of earnest reflection and prayer. To the embarrassment of the ministers, he then posed a question: 'I humbly desire to know what sort of a judicatory you are. I know you will not call yourselves a session; I humbly desire to know then whether you are to be looked on as a presbytery, synod or general assembly.'

Cameron then proceeded to say that since they appeared to be acting as a general assembly — which he did not accept they were — they ought to have given notice of their meeting to all other ministers of the church, including those who had licensed him and those who had attended his preaching at Kilmarnock. Also if they regarded themselves as a church court, they ought by the basic laws of Presbyterianism to have ruling elders with them as well as ministers. These, he submitted, were sufficient grounds for him to decline their authority. But most serious of all, in his view, was their disloyalty to Presbyterian principles through their connivance at the Indulgence. 'I am made to think it strange', he went on, 'that Presbyterian ministers, whom God had once honoured with suffering, should have vented themselves — and that publicly — so very far contrary to the principles of the Church of Scotland, the Covenants, and the faithful and honest Acts of the General Assembly.'

Having stated his position clearly, Cameron was about to leave the meeting, but was prevailed on by the ministers to wait in another room while they reflected on what he had said. There was, of course, little that they could do, and such had been the impact of Cameron's words that they appear to have been thrown into some confusion. Their only response when he was brought back before them was to ask him once again not to 'meddle' with the Indulgence, to agree to meet two of their number for discussion and to promise to attend a further meeting at which the ministers who had licensed him would be present.

Cameron refused to accept any of these terms. The Indulgence, he declared, was a public sin, and he could not refrain from speaking against it 'when called to it by God and it comes in my way, for to this I am obliged by the Scriptures, Covenants, and Acts of the General Assembly'. As to the proposed discussion with two of their number, he would agree to it only if he were allowed to have supporters of his choice to accompany him. And as to attending a further meeting, he had already made clear his view that he had committed no fault and so was not liable to a judicial process.

The ministers were having no more. They rejected Cameron's request for supporters at the discussion, and told him that, in view of his attitude, they would now report the proceedings to those who had licensed him, asking them for their concurrence and support. With this, he and the ministers parted.

So ended the first attempt to bring Cameron to account. For the ministers it had been an abject failure. The seeds of that failure were inherent in the meeting itself. As Cameron had pointed out, it had been merely a gathering of ministers, with no constitutional status. It had sought to exercise a judicial function which it did not possess. When its authority was challenged it could give no answer. Its supposed jurisdiction had no basis in orthodox Presbyterianism. From that viewpoint, of course, there was a supreme irony in the fact that the ministers had charged Cameron with ignorance of Presbyterian principles. He had shown that, when it came to disputations on church government, he was more than a match for them. He had seen through their pretensions very well; and while he may have appeared to show them scant respect, he felt justifiably resentful of the violence they were doing to the Presbyterian principles which he cherished. It was that regard for the principles and traditions of the church which alone had motivated his conduct. His critics — and they were now more numerous than before — did not see it in that light, however.

10.
A mounting chorus of criticism

Had Cameron had the time to reflect on it, he could well have felt satisfied with the outcome of the meeting. As it was, however, his attention was claimed by a distressing turn of events within his own family circle, which must have grieved him deeply. After an absence of a few days on his preaching duties, he had returned to Edinburgh to find that his father had been taken into custody by the authorities on 25 August.

Since moving to Edinburgh, Allan Cameron had been accustomed to hold illegal preaching meetings in his house. These had previously remained unmolested, and there must therefore be at least some grounds for suspicion that the authorities' action on this occasion was connected with Richard Cameron's known presence in Edinburgh. If this was so, it failed of its main purpose, and the authorities had to be content with imprisoning his father in the Tolbooth. A fine of 100 merks was demanded of him to secure his liberty and, since he refused to pay, he was held in prison. Allan Cameron was not to be liberated again in his son's lifetime.[1]

Grieved as he must have been by his father's arrest and imprisonment, Cameron did not allow it to divert him from his supreme task of preaching the gospel. He had promised to preach the following Lord's Day, 1 September, at Monkland, to the east of Glasgow, and he was determined not to disappoint those who had invited him. Among that number, significantly, was Robert Hamilton of Preston.

Over the spring and summer of 1678 Hamilton and his friend Robert Ker of Kersland had been developing their plans to stiffen the forces of resistance against the government. Two important factors had combined to give further impetus to their campaign: the depredations of the Highland soldiery in the western shires in the spring of the year, and the decision of a Convention of Estates, or Parliament, in June to levy a 'cess', or tax, for the express purpose of raising additional troops to suppress the field-meetings. To Hamilton in particular, opposition to this tax became a test of orthodoxy, on a par with opposition to the Indulgence. There is considerable evidence that in the summer and autumn of 1678 both he and Kersland sought to influence the younger field-preachers to adopt an increasingly militant tone in their preaching, and to condemn both those who payed the 'cess' and the ministers who had accepted the Indulgence.

It is also clear that during this period both Hamilton and Kersland became increasingly associated with Richard Cameron. One of the bishops, writing in September 1678, referred contemptuously to 'Kersland's curates', among whom he included Cameron, Hog, Kid and Dickson. What is less clear is how far Cameron identified himself with the policies of Hamilton and Kersland. There is evidence that it was they, rather than he, who formed the attachment, hoping no doubt to benefit from his popularity among the people. At the same time Cameron — for the present at least — did nothing to discourage these attentions, and inevitably as time went on he was to become increasingly identified with the policies they represented.

In the late summer of 1678 Kersland went over to Holland, from where, despite Hamilton's repeated entreaties, he was never to return.[2] It is not clear whether this move was dictated by fear for his own safety, or by increasing suspicions about

Hamilton's motives, and it is futile now to speculate. His departure, however, deprived Hamilton of his counsel and experience, and left Hamilton very much to his own devices. The results were to become only too apparent as time went on.

Throughout the 1670s it had been customary for the leading field-preachers, such as John Welsh, to be accompanied by armed bodyguards as they moved around the country. This was seen as a necessary precaution for their own safety, in circumstances where they could be at risk from sudden attack. Having attached himself to Cameron, Hamilton concluded that Cameron too should enjoy the same protection. He therefore gathered a body of men — several of them from Fife — whom he engaged to accompany Cameron around the country, and to attend on him while preaching. Hamilton himself assumed the command of this group. A show of military order was observed, though neither Hamilton himself, nor, it appears, any of those whom he led, had any military experience. However, it satisfied Hamilton's fondness for demonstration and for display, and it was, of course, fully consistent with the militant approach which he advocated.

What Cameron thought of it is not on record, though the evidence suggests that, as time went on, he found Hamilton's activities an undoubted embarrassment. They certainly did nothing to improve his standing among the ministers, and he came increasingly to be seen by them and the moderate Presbyterians as the representative of a faction. On the other hand, there can be no grounds for concluding, as some have done, that Cameron was beholden to Hamilton for the views he put forward. Cameron's opinions were his own and, however much Hamilton may have felt able to influence him, he never countenanced the brand of militancy which Hamilton advocated.

A day or two after his second interview with the ministers Cameron kept his appointment with Hamilton, with a view to his day's preaching at Monkland on 1 September. However, when they arrived there late on the Saturday evening, it was to find that the ministers in Glasgow had sent a probationer of their own, Matthew Selkirk, and the stage was set for a confrontation.[3] Cameron and, even more so, Hamilton were determined not to give way and, predictably enough, Selkirk was forced to retire without opening his mouth.

Writing many years later to Robert Wodrow, Selkirk gave his own version of the events of the day. He had, he said, been told on his arrival at Monkland that Cameron and Hamilton were already there, and that he need not expect to be allowed to preach. He had tried to speak to Cameron before the morning's preaching began, but Cameron had evaded him. Denied the opportunity to preach, Selkirk busied himself in taking notes of the sermon, with the intention of reporting them to the ministers who had sent him. When Cameron preached again in the afternoon, he showed that he had noticed what Selkirk had been doing. Looking him full in the face, he 'took sun, moon and stars to witness' that he had been saying nothing but what was right and, addressing Selkirk directly said, 'Betwixt God and you be it, if you write anything but what I have said.'

Selkirk also recalled that while Cameron was preaching, Robert Hamilton had come up to him with a company of musketeers and, surrounding him 'on the one side and the other', had challenged him with the words: 'Is this all that you are come here for, to write?' Hamilton had then added, with a sneer: 'Write this also,' and had proceeded to parade his armed followers up a hillside overlooking the meeting.

When the day's preaching was over, Selkirk waited for Cameron and complained to him about the proceedings. Cameron replied, rather wearily, that he wished Selkirk had been somewhere else, where he might have been useful. Selkirk protested that he had been called by the people. Cameron questioned whether those who had invited him had any power to do so. Selkirk countered that all the call he sought was 'people's necessity'. There the confrontation ended, and Selkirk was left to report the day's events to those who had sent him.

In his preaching that day Cameron had certainly given ample opportunity to his critics. Taking as his text Isaiah chapter 7:14, which is in the context of the attack by the kings of Syria and Israel upon Jerusalem, he declared, 'There were two kings, of Syria and Israel, going up to Jerusalem to war against it: the one an enemy, though not professed; the other a professed enemy. The occasion of that preaching is the occasion of ours. There are two parties raised against us, the one malignant and prelatical, the other an Erastian party — a party that has revolted from the house of David, a party that has received an Indulgence from the prelatic party, but it is our comfort they shall not prevail, as these did not.'

He continued: 'There are some who get their mission from men. These may be sent forth, but not from God.' And, clearly referring to himself: 'There are some who have a mission first from God, and then seek it from men. Those who have their mission thus, though men should take it from them without a ground, they are not called to obey them. We are necessitate to speak these things, having a commission from God for it.' All this was faithfully taken down by Selkirk and, as Cameron no doubt expected, it was to be used in evidence against him at no very distant date.

By preaching in this manner, so soon after he had met the Edinburgh ministers, Cameron had served them with clear notice that he was not to be deflected from his chosen path. The ministers had, of course, been left in no doubt on this point and soon after his departure they wrote to Welsh and the others who had licensed Cameron, reporting their own lack of success in influencing him and urging Welsh and his associates to take him in hand. Welsh, by way of response, wrote to

Cameron, asking him to come to Galloway to meet him and the rest.

Cameron, who still cherished a regard for Welsh, replied that he would come, 'even from the ends of the earth', to meet his request. At the same time, since Welsh had apparently not set a date for the meeting, Cameron was in no hurry to comply. Accompanied by Robert Hamilton and some others, including on this occasion his brother Michael, he made a leisurely progress through Clydesdale and Ayrshire, turning his journey into an extended preaching tour.

Over the days that followed, Cameron had ample opportunity to return to the theme he had taken up at Monkland, and he used that opportunity to the full. Preaching shortly afterwards at Hamilton he said, 'How sad is the condition of our church, that all have made defection; for even they who were instruments before against backsliding have themselves now made so far defection that they have turned to be persecutors of faithful witnesses.'

On 27 September an incident took place which gave added point and poignancy to Cameron's words. James Learmonth, a young man from East Lothian, was executed in Edinburgh for having resisted a party of soldiers who attempted to break up a field-meeting at Whitekirk, opposite the Bass Rock, in May of the same year. Preaching the following week at Strathaven, as he continued on his way south, Cameron went probably as far as he was ever to go in his denunciation of the ministers who had accepted the Indulgence. According to an account later quoted in evidence against him, he compared these ministers and their followers to Cain, and their worship to Cain's sacrifice, calling them idolaters and persecutors, and declaring them 'guilty of the blood of the young man who suffered last week'. According to the same account, he went on to say that 'The indulged ministers had never profited a soul, and never should,' and had appealed to the consciences of his hearers to endorse his words. He warned that neither these ministers nor their hearers would find mercy without public repentance.

Reports of this and similar utterances were carried far and wide. Not surprisingly, they were often embellished in the telling, and lurid indeed were the terms in which some of them were retailed. Ralph Rodger, the minister of Kilwinning, who had himself been reinstated through accepting the Indulgence, wrote to Robert M'Ward in Holland complaining that in a sermon preached at Galston, as he made his way south from Strathaven, Cameron had charged his hearers on pain of damnation not to go to hear the ministers who had accepted the Indulgence. 'And shall Mr Cameron', asked Rodger, 'not be brought to account?'

However exaggerated some of these reports may have been — and Cameron was later to refute several of them — they certainly served to fuel the resentment which his treatment of the ministers had caused. According to Hamilton, whom there is no reason to doubt, the non-complying ministers in Glasgow, hearing of his journey, sent one of their number ahead of him, to warn the people of his principles, stigmatizing him and his party as Jesuits, or, at best, independents and separatists.

Meanwhile the shock waves from the Edinburgh meeting continued to reverberate. The ministers there deeply resented their defeat at Cameron's hands, and made it their business to discredit him by what means they could. John Scott, who had presided on the second day of that meeting, wrote scathingly of 'worthy Mr Cameron's humility', and of his 'forehead that cannot blush' adding, 'If you add not "worthy" to Mr Cameron you shall be none of his disciples.'

But amid the chorus of hostile criticism there were some who took a different view. The most notable of these was John Brown of Wamphray in Annandale, who had been exiled to Holland in 1662 for his opposition to the new episcopal order in Scotland. Brown, a man of massive intellect and learning, had spent his exile in writing works on theology and on church and constitutional government, and had earned for himself an international reputation. With his fellow-exile Robert M'Ward, formerly minister in Glasgow, Brown had conceived a strong antipathy to the Indulgence, believing that it had brought the displeasure of God upon the church.

Brown had been impressed by what he had heard of the success of Cameron's preaching in Annandale, where he had himself ministered, and the news of the treatment the young preacher had suffered at the hands of the Edinburgh ministers stirred him to resolute action. On 7 October 1678 he penned a letter of warm support to Cameron, thanking him for his uncompromising stand and encouraging him to stand firm in the face of all opposition.

'Dear brother', Brown wrote, 'though I have no acquaintance, yet the report I have heard of your appearing for Christ and his cause, now when so many are not so zealous as sometimes they were thought to have been, and particularly the report I have heard of the Lord employing of you to hold up his banner in dead and desolate Annandale, and blessing your labours there, as elsewhere, so that a great change is wrought, and among the rest in and among the people of Wamphray parish, where, alas, I did little or no good (blessed be he, who honoureth himself and carrieth on his work by what instruments he will) hath excited me to write this line of hearty thanks for my part. But you know whom you serve, and you know what a rich and great recompense of reward is awaiting, out of pure grace, such as are honoured to carry on his work, as co-workers with him: besides the inconceivably great honour that is in the service itself, and the rich incomes and supplies of new strength, furniture, peace and joy in the Holy Ghost that attend the faithful endeavour to lay out ourselves to the uttermost in singleness of heart for him and his service.'

Brown went on: 'I have likewise heard of the trouble you have met with at the hands of some, of whom sometime other things were expected, because of your faithful and zealous, yea and seasonable appearing against that woeful Indulgence, the evil that God's soul hateth. I bless the Lord that helped you to stand in that day of trial. Stand fast, my dear brother, and speak freely and boldly; fear not.'

Brown did not content himself with writing only to Cameron. He also wrote to Welsh and Dickson, expressing his concern about developments among the non-complying ministers, and particularly their vacillating stance on the Indulgence. His letter to Dickson is typical of his forthright style. 'I have been much surprised', he wrote, 'to hear that almost all the suffering ministers of Scotland are of late (for formerly I never heard nor dreamed of such a thing) begun to speak in favour of the Indulgence; yea some, yea the generality for anything I know, are come that length as to be ready to question and censure such as preach against it or preach but upon the ground where any such indulged minister is.'

He wrote to Welsh even more strongly, reminding him of the honourable example of his grandfather (the son-in-law of Knox) and going on to refer specifically to the affair at Kilmarnock: 'My dear brother, I was surprised to hear that you were among those who would not speak against that piece of defection, nor preach if the tent were but set one length of your staff within their bounds, and that even upon a weekday when called to countenance a fast. This looked so unlike you, and your usual way of following the call of God, that I could not but impute it more to some others influencing you, than to your own genius and inclination. I am loth to tell you my fears that, if you go on in this course, your testimony is near an end.'

Brown's intervention, not surprisingly, caused great offence. It was one thing for such opinions to be propagated by a young probationer such as Cameron, but if they were to be supported by men of Brown's standing and authority, the ministers' policy of moderation was in danger of losing all credibility among the people. A campaign was set afoot to contradict Brown's views, and to discredit them so far as possible.

John Carstairs, one of the senior ministers who had not submitted to the Indulgence, wrote bitterly to Brown's fellow-exile M'Ward, complaining of Brown's 'magnifying Mr Cameron as if he were one of the greatest, most countenanced and most successful preachers of the Church in Scotland', and alleging that, as a result, Brown had lost all his standing among the ministers.

John Blackader, trying to exercise moderation, took on himself to write to Brown suggesting that he had been misinformed of the proceedings about Cameron. Brown was not impressed. 'You suggest', he replied, 'that we were misinformed about the resolution of that meeting against Mr Cameron; and this medium is ordinarily made use of to make anything we say of no effect.' 'But', he continued drily, 'if we have been misinformed, it is our mishap that we cannot get right information.'

For good measure, Brown went on to make crystal clear his objections to the Edinburgh meeting and to what it had attempted to do. 'If', he maintained, 'a company of presbyters meet occasionally, or of their own head, and think that because they are presbyters they may assume the power of a General Assembly, or of a Grand Commission, and so call before them any man of the Church of Scotland, for a crime, real or supposed, committed within Scotland — I know of no Presbyterian principles of order that will allow this, nor know I what sort of government (that presupposes order) can give countenance to it.'

Brown elaborated in a further letter to Dickson: 'This to me is a very unusual and untrodden path, yea I may say is a way not only not agreeing to Presbyterian principles, but even repugnant to the principles of all government whatsoever; for all government, as such, is orderly, and knoweth nothing of anarchy or confusion, nor yet of tyranny.'

He was no less critical of the decision of the Edinburgh meeting to refer Cameron's case to those who had licensed him: 'As for that course which is now fallen upon of rolling him over on the individual persons that opened his mouth, I do not understand it; nor do I know what principles of Presbyterian government will allow it; it looketh to me rather like a piece of prelatical inspection, in one respect, and to draw nigher to independency in another respect; but because of the persons interested, whom I desire to reverence in the Lord, I forbear to enlarge.'

In a day when communications were slow and correspondence between Scotland and Holland was closely watched, it was some time before news of Brown's intervention reached Cameron. When it did, it came as a real encouragement to him and it appears to have prompted in him a desire to cultivate a closer acquaintance with Brown and his fellow-exile M'Ward. He was not at that time in a position to take any immediate steps towards the fulfilment of that desire, but he cherished the prospect of doing so when the opportunity arose.

11.
A formal indictment

While there were, as we have seen, some encouragements for Cameron in the midst of all his difficulties, the consequences of the Edinburgh meeting still had to be faced. In a curious way the efforts to discredit him had actually proved beneficial to Cameron, since they helped to stimulate interest in, and concern for, him among the people. As he and Hamilton made their way south, they found considerable evidence of popular support, although attitudes varied from place to place.

Arriving at Ayr on 18 October 1678, they were informed that such was the animosity against them on the part of some moderate Presbyterians that they were in danger of being handed over to the authorities, and they were forced to leave the town for their own safety. At Dalrymple, on the road south from Ayr, they met with a very different reception. There, Cameron was invited to preach by some local sympathizers, and ventured to do so on the following Lord's Day. Such was the impact of his preaching that the elders of the local parish, which was without a minister at the time, pressed him to give another sermon during the following week, and this he agreed to do. By this time, reports of his presence had spread widely through the surrounding country. Many flocked to hear him, not only from Dalrymple itself, but from neighbouring parishes where ministers had been resettled after accepting the

Indulgence. Cameron saw this as evidence, not only of a popular hunger for the Word, but of growing disillusionment with the ministers who had accepted the Indulgence, and it strengthened still further his resolve to witness against it.

By 26 October 1678 — a Saturday — Cameron and Hamilton had reached Irongray, Welsh's old parish, where they heard that Welsh himself was to preach the following day. After some hesitation, for they were unsure how Welsh would react, they decided to go to hear him, but not to make themselves known. Welsh, however, was told of their presence after the morning's preaching and immediately sought them out. He welcomed them warmly, saying to Cameron, 'Mr Richard, I hope there is no difference betwixt you and me, for all that is come and gone.' He then went on to invite Cameron to preach in the afternoon. Though somewhat surprised and unprepared, Cameron gave a fervent evangelical sermon, avoiding all mention of the Indulgence or other public matters, and at the end of the day he and Welsh parted on the best of terms.

Cameron and Hamilton pressed on to Dumfries, where they decided to remain for some days. While there, Cameron received an invitation to share a day's preaching with Welsh at Irongray on Friday, 1 November. Thinking it right to consult Welsh beforehand, Cameron, accompanied by Hamilton, visited Welsh on the night before the meeting to discuss the arrangements for the day. Welsh, as Hamilton later recalled, was 'very kind' and, addressing Cameron as 'Richard', asked him what part of the preaching he wished to take. Cameron, deferring to the older man, left him to make the choice, and Welsh then suggested that Cameron might preach first. He accompanied Cameron and Hamilton back to their lodgings, and once again they parted amicably.

As he reflected on the events of these days, Cameron could well have felt he had cause for satisfaction. The prospects for the future now looked brighter. Despite the opposition he had met with, and the attempts of some of the ministers to silence him, it seemed that he had found his way back into Welsh's favour. The influence of Welsh continued to matter a great deal, and Cameron knew that in defending himself against any further charges it would clearly be highly valuable to have Welsh on his side. By the same token he also knew that, if he were to alienate Welsh, his own position would be made very much more difficult. Much depended, therefore, on how he conducted himself in the meantime, particularly when Welsh was present.

The issue was not left long in doubt. Preaching the next day as arranged, Cameron took as his theme the defections of the land and church. Quoting extensively from Reformation standards and from the Covenants and the Acts of the General Assembly, he enumerated at length what he saw as the main sins of the time, dwelling upon each in turn. Among those catalogued was the Indulgence. Hamilton, who was watching Welsh closely as Cameron preached, saw the former become increasingly agitated, and then leave the meeting.

When his own turn came to preach, Welsh could scarcely contain his anger. He launched into a vehement denunciation of Cameron, berating him for his 'impertinence', and going on to inveigh bitterly against his preaching and character. Hamilton, true to form, walked out halfway through the tirade, but Cameron stayed on. When he had finished preaching, Welsh went over to Cameron and in the presence of the people said to him, 'Sir, since I was instrumental in licensing you, I will now exert myself in retracting your licence,' and forthwith summoned him to a meeting of ministers to be held near Dumfries the following week.

Cameron protested that he had not said anything that had not already been said by Welsh himself, and in this he was supported by some of Welsh's own elders and others present. Indeed, such was the resentment against Welsh on the part of some that they challenged him with contradicting not only Cameron, but the whole work of reformation. Welsh, however, was not to be moved, and from that moment he appears to have viewed Cameron as unreclaimable. Cameron, for his part, clearly regretted the breach with Welsh, though Hamilton, with his more argumentative nature, was more inclined to glory in it than otherwise. But for Cameron, as always, the issue was one of conscience. He could not be silent when conscience urged him to speak. And if that meant breaking friendships, even influential ones, it was a price he was prepared to pay.

The rupture with Welsh also inevitably widened the breach between Cameron and the other ministers. On the following Lord's Day, 3 November, Cameron was due to preach at Locharbriggs, some four miles west of Dumfries. According to Hamilton, Welsh and his colleagues went to considerable trouble to stop this meeting, or to dissuade the people in neighbouring parishes from attending it. However, these efforts were of little avail. Huge crowds gathered — estimated by Hamilton at up to 5,000 — and, as he records, 'We had a great day of the gospel.' Even allowing for some exaggeration in this account, it is clear that Cameron had achieved wide popular appeal and, for a man licensed to preach only a few months earlier, it was a considerable tribute to his powers as a preacher. Its effect on himself, not unnaturally, was to encourage him still further in his preaching career and to strengthen his resolve to resist any dilution of his testimony.

The following Tuesday, 5 November, four ministers — Welsh, Douglas, Semple and Williamson — met at an agreed spot near Dumfries. Cameron duly attended, in obedience to Welsh's summons the previous week. Hamilton, however, had been busy in the meantime, and on his prompting the meeting was made the occasion of an elaborate demonstration in support of Cameron from the surrounding parishes. This secured the desired result: the ministers felt sufficiently intimidated to break off the meeting, and nothing was done. But they remained firm in their resolve to bring Cameron to account. This time, they set about preparing a 'libel', or indictment, setting out a series of specific charges that he would be called upon to answer. The meeting to hear his replies was arranged for the following week at Dumfries, and again he was served with a summons to attend.

After preaching the next Lord's Day at Lochmaben, Cameron received the indictment the following day. It was a lengthy document containing no fewer than fifteen charges. It started off by reminding him of the engagements he had entered into at his licensing, and went on to rehearse a series of allegations which had been made against him.

> It is informed [it ran] that you preach ordinarily and most frequently without the advice or direction of a minister; that when you preach, you frequently call yourself an ambassador of Christ, and speak in the name of the Lord, with all the authority of a minister, without putting any difference betwixt you and them…
>
> You said rarely or never the Lord had punished a people for their own faults, but for the faults of their magistrates, of the kings and princes…
>
> You said in discourse in a certain place, speaking about your licensing, that if the ministers had not licensed you, you would have taken instruments and have preached at your own hand without licence…
>
> At the communion of Maybole, where there were so many grave and able ministers, you preached several times upon slender or no invitation, which seems not to

> savour of that sobriety and modesty which becomes any minister, much less a young preacher...
>
> The scope of your doctrine on the Sabbath day [i.e. at Maybole] drove much to reflect on ministers, particularly the indulged ministers, and with much boldness you charged all your hearers as an ambassador of Christ to declare their consciences presently if any of them had got any good of those ministers...

So the indictment went on, dwelling mainly on Cameron's preaching against the ministers who had accepted the Indulgence, and quoting extensively from his preaching at Monkland, Hamilton, Strathaven and other places.

The document also charged him with insubordination before the meeting of ministers at Edinburgh:

> You did not carry with that reverence and respect as became a meeting of so many reverend and worthy ministers, rather challenging the meeting than giving due regard to it, as though a company of ministers might not take an account of any young man, though a preacher or other, for any offence or scandal.

Another of the charges against Cameron, obviously included on the instigation of Welsh, concerned his conduct at Irongray:

> You preached upon the very same strain to the great offence of your hearers, particularly Mr John Welsh, whom you provoked, contrary to his inclination, to bear witness against you before all the people ... so that it would appear your coming into this country has been to prosecute your old design and not to give satisfaction for what you have done or said.

This was a formidable indictment, and Cameron could well have been excused had he felt daunted by it. Quite the reverse was the case, however. Borne up by the support he had received, and supremely confident in his own cause, Cameron awaited the meeting of the ministers in a composed frame of mind. He was particularly encouraged at this point by the arrival of Henry Hall, who had been present at his licensing, and who made plain his support for Cameron's stand.

On Tuesday, 12 November, Cameron and his party took up their quarters in Dumfries. Meanwhile Hamilton had spread the news of the meeting widely, in the hope of another popular demonstration in Cameron's support. This time, however, the ministers had the advantage of him. At short notice they changed the place where the meeting was to be held to a remote spot known as Sundewal, or Sundaywell, in the parish of Dunscore, some fifteen miles north-west of Dumfries, and in the brief time available Hamilton was able to muster a retinue of only thirteen men. These duly accompanied Cameron when he presented himself at the meeting of ministers on 14 November.

In contrast to the meeting in Edinburgh, the one at Dunscore bore all the appearance of a properly constituted church court. Presbyterian forms were observed, with four ruling elders complementing the four ministers — Welsh, Semple, Douglas and Williamson. Welsh presided as moderator, and John McGoune, a probationer, was appointed clerk.[1] However, before the meeting could get under way it was confronted with a point of procedure. Henry Hall, who, like the four ministers, had been present at Cameron's licensing, had arrived at the meeting with Cameron's party and claimed the right to sit in the court. The problem was eventually resolved, in the meantime at least, by allowing Hall to sit as a non-voting member, and Cameron was then called in.

When he appeared, the moderator reminded him of the purpose of the meeting, and the indictment was read in full by the clerk. Cameron was then asked to state his reply. Instead of doing so, however, he raised three queries: whether the meeting was a judicatory; who were its members; and whether they judged the charges in the indictment worthy of censure.

Cameron was asked to withdraw while these points were considered. On his first two queries, the ministers satisfied themselves that they were a judicatory, and that if Cameron had an objection to any of them he should be allowed to declare it; and on his third they concluded that the charges were indeed worthy of censure, but that it would not be proper to state this until Cameron had answered the libel.

This was too much for Hall, who felt moved to denounce the meeting and claimed the right to protest against anything it might do in violation of the laws of the church. Hall's intervention met with a very hostile reception, and on the votes of all present, except that of Douglas, who abstained, he was forthwith ejected from the meeting.

Cameron was then recalled — knowing nothing of what had happened — and had the answers to his queries read out to him. He acknowledged the meeting's authority and did not press his queries further, though continuing to express reservations on the third of the points.

Cameron then turned his attention to the charges which had been made against him. He categorically denied having given any promise not to preach against the Indulgence, though he admitted, when pressed, that he had undertaken not to preach anything which might provoke division. He could not see, however, how anything he had spoken could be so construed.

On some of the other counts in the indictment he claimed to have been misrepresented, though freely admitting his preaching against the Indulgence, and indeed claiming it as his duty to urge that the ministers who had accepted it should not be given a hearing.

He defended his conduct before the Edinburgh meeting,

again maintaining that this body of ministers had possessed no judicial status.

He strongly denied being associated with any movement to cause schism and division in the church. The only movement he acknowledged, he said, was what was 'incumbent for carrying on the Reformation as it had been established in 1648 and 1649'.

And as to the meeting at Monkland and the alleged offence against Matthew Selkirk, he offered to produce a testimony from the local people affirming that they had indeed called him to preach on that occasion, and that he had not intruded on Selkirk's preserve.

There the proceedings for the day ended, and the meeting adjourned until the next morning at eight o'clock.

Hamilton, meanwhile, had been anxiously awaiting the outcome. He learned, to his satisfaction, that he was to become involved in the proceedings himself; for when Cameron offered to produce the testimony of the people of Monkland, he had informed the meeting that Hamilton was the source from whom this evidence could be obtained. With his fondness for demonstration, Hamilton judged the opportunity too good to miss. He canvassed his band of followers, and together they drew up a statement in the following terms:

> We undersubscribers, being together providentially at your calling for the Monkland testimony, judge it duty and our concernment to adhere thereto, it being a fair opportunity for contending against the present and most controverted defection of our time, and your procedure against Mr Cameron, his or any other faithful testimony upon this occasion. In witness whereof we have subscribed these presents with our hands the 14th of November 1678, in the parish of Dunscore.

There followed, in order, the signatures of Robert Hamilton, Henry Hall, Michael Cameron, Alexander Ross, Samuel Grier, Robert Gordon, John Martin, John Latimer, John Bell, Robert Gray, William McNeillie, Robert Nelson and John Fowler. Some of the signatories — notably Cameron's brother Michael, Robert Gray and John Fowler — were to be with him to the end.[2]

With this document Hamilton lodged the Monkland testimony requested by the meeting. This was in the following terms:

> We under-subscribers, elders and others in the Monklands, hearing of the great though groundless offence that is taken by many from Mr Richard Cameron's preaching amongst us on the 1st of September 1678, being Sabbath, judge it duty and our concernment for his and our vindication by these presents to testify that the said Mr Cameron was duly called to preach in our bounds the said day by certain of our number appointed by us, unto whose call we unanimously adhere, and albeit Mr Selkirk was likeways by one of our number under-subscribing to preach the same day, yet having due information afterwards of his being licensed by the indulged men, and of his being a promoter and upholder of that Indulgence to his power, we judged it our duty, without consulting Mr Cameron, upon the reasons foresaid, to oppose and hinder Mr Selkirk's preaching amongst us, and to lay the whole work of the day upon Mr Cameron, it being a fair opportunity for our giving a testimony against the present defection. In witness of the premises, we have subscribed the same with our hands at the parish of Monkland, the 16th day of September 1678 years, by all the elders and others.

When the meeting reconvened the next morning, with Gabriel Semple as moderator, the two documents were tabled. Hamilton's intervention produced the desired result — at least as far as he was concerned. He was summoned before the meeting to give an account of the statements, and he used the opportunity to the full. Quoting liberally from the indictment against Cameron, he challenged those present for their apparent support for the Indulgence and their implicit condemnation of Cameron.

The ministers protested that they had, as yet, passed no censure on Cameron. Hamilton replied that their intention was sufficiently plain from the terms of the libel, and he went on explicitly to condemn those ministers who failed to preach against the Indulgence, arguing that they should not be given a hearing. For good measure, having Welsh clearly in view, he added: 'He that in the face of a congregation or elsewhere upbraids any for his preaching against that sin, should not be heard.'

After some further robust exchanges, Hamilton was asked to withdraw, so that the ministers could interview others of his adherents. Cameron was then recalled. The ministers, according to a prearranged plan, started to question him on his attitude to those ministers who did not preach against the Indulgence but, to their consternation, Cameron refused to answer their questions and instead raised a series of complaints about the conduct of the meeting.

First, he claimed that one of the elders present the previous day — Bailie Corbet of Dumfries — had signed a bond for the peace after the Pentland Rising, and so was guilty of compromise. When the ministers protested their ignorance of this — and pointed out that the person complained of was not now present in any case — Cameron asked for an assurance that none of the other elders present had been guilty of similar defection, adding: 'You that are elders, take heed to yourselves.'

Not receiving an answer, he went on to complain about the treatment meted out the previous day to Henry Hall. To this, the ministers replied that he had been justly dealt with, having been found guilty of serious misconduct.

Cameron, however, had not yet finished. To the ministers' astonishment, he protested that Welsh, being a party to the indictment against him, had no right to sit in the court, and that his presence there was prejudicial to the outcome of the case. The ministers took time to consider this complaint while Cameron withdrew from the meeting. When he returned, the ministers told him that, though Welsh had admittedly provided information which had been used in the libel, that did not make him a party to it, and he therefore had every right to sit in the court.

Cameron did not agree, and again asked that Welsh be removed. After some further deliberation the ministers told him a second time that they regarded his objection to Welsh as irrelevant.

Cameron, however, stood his ground, and went on to complain that the ministers, having formerly found his principles to be sound, were now questioning these same principles rather than his alleged guilt as set out in the libel. The ministers countered that, from the reports reaching them, they had good reason to question his principles. After some further exchanges of this nature the ministers again asked him to withdraw while they considered their decision.

The eventual conclusion of the meeting, reached after some further heart-searching, was that any sentence should be delayed for some five or six weeks; that in the meantime Cameron must be 'circumspect and inoffensive' in his preaching; that he must not preach without the advice of one or two ministers, as he should be answerable; that he should attend the ministers further as advised; that he prepare answers to certain questions before the next meeting; and that he be ready to appear before the meeting of ministers at Edinburgh if so required.

When this formidable list was read out to him, Cameron took particular exception to the requirement not to preach without the advice of ministers, and yet again pressed for the removal of Welsh from the court. When the ministers insisted that this could not be done, he told them that he considered he had sufficiently discharged his responsibility towards them, and that he saw himself as under no obligation to submit to any censure. The moderator, seeing that further remonstrance was unavailing, said to him resignedly, 'You may go your way,' and Cameron promptly left them.

12.
The work goes on

Clearly, the second attempt to bring Cameron to account had proved no more successful than the first. Indeed, the sequel to the Dunscore meeting was remarkably similar to that of the one in Edinburgh. The Lord's Day following the meeting, 17 November, Cameron went to Annandale, where he had received an invitation to preach. The ministers at Dumfries — like their counterparts in Glasgow on an earlier occasion — sent along a probationer of their own, John Forrester, and, inevitably, there was once again a confrontation. At a meeting of the ministers and elders later that week Forrester complained bitterly that he had been prevented from preaching by 'menaces and threatenings' on the part of Cameron and his associates, and that Cameron had preached for the most part against the Indulgence.

It is not clear whether at this point the ministers had already decided to pursue further the case against Cameron, but news of this latest episode stirred them into action. The options left open to them were by now were very limited and, probably for want of any other recourse, they decided to refer the whole matter back to Edinburgh, where it had come from. They accordingly wrote to six of the Edinburgh ministers, in the name of the rest, giving them a full account of the proceedings at Dunscore and, in effect, putting the matter back in their hands.

The terms of the ministers' letter sufficiently reflected their feeling of helplessness over the whole affair. 'He so far gave up with us', they wrote, 'and declined us, as we can expect him no more to regard us in anything done and to be done by us ... we ordered him not to preach without the direction and advice of a minister or two, and as he did not engage it, so he did not perform it; for he went into Annandale, and has been looked upon to commit a greater insolency there than in Clydesdale ... therefore, reverend and dear brethren, we most earnestly desire your judgement and advice in this matter, for we find the case to be singular, and of such consequence, and we being so few in number, and none of the greatest consideration to determine a case that does so generally concern the church of Christ in this land.'

The letter went on to suggest that the Edinburgh ministers might convene a general meeting: 'We intreat that you may invite and call all the nonconformist ministers out of charge to give judgement with you in this matter, particularly the field-preachers to whom the young man's behaviour is best known in the country, and what is his influence among the people, and what may be most expedient at this juncture of time to do in the case ... that whatever be concluded in your counsels may be with the most common consent that can be had.'

Even so, the ministers cherished little prospect of success. 'We have no expectation', they wrote despondently, 'that he, nor many of the people also, will regard us or any else, as matters stand.'

They closed with some sober reflections: 'Reverend brethren, the matter upon every hand is of weight, and deserves serious seeking of God, and grave consultation amongst yourselves ... what Israel should do were a great and rich mercy to know in this case, and in many other cases, and what the watchmen should do that go about the city for its preservation from destruction by inward division and outward persecution.

Oh for wisdom to take up this matter, that the inheritance of the Lord be not swallowed up! For this end we make our application unto our reverend brethren whose piety, parts and experience is far above ours, that you may consider what is fittest to be done for the glory of God, the edification of the saints, and the perfecting of Christ's body.' The letter was signed by Gabriel Semple, as moderator, in the name of the rest, and dated 25 November 1678.

A copy of the letter found its way to Cameron himself, and his comments on it, written in his own distinctive handwriting, still survive. He had not, he said, declined the authority of the ministers, nor their jurisdiction as a court; he had simply refused to accept any censure, or to subject his preaching to their control. And he had been clearly called to preach in Annandale by the local people and had not gone there on his own initiative.

In the meantime reports of the Dunscore meeting had travelled far and wide, and the whole countryside was in a ferment. A graphic, though perhaps overdrawn, picture of things was painted by Hamilton: 'The divisions grow hotter and hotter ... the father against the son and the son against the father, the wife against the husband and the husband against the wife, everyone appearing in their true colours; the moderate and wise "fanatic" clasps hands with the malignant, all to extol their Presbytery; there is nothing now but extolling Mr Welsh for his wisdom and prudence, who by the same persons formerly was called mad, rash and desperate; yea, all oars laid in the water to break, oppress and scandalize Mr Cameron, and to withdraw all from hearing him.'

Cameron, however, was by no means without his supporters. While the older people, in the main, remained largely influenced by the ministers, the sympathies of the young were undoubtedly with Cameron. His stand at Dunscore had earned their admiration, and in his uncompromising opposition to the

Indulgence he had caught much of the prevailing mood. Among the young at this time — many of them recent converts — there was a growing disillusionment with the policies of the older ministers, and with their desire for an accommodation with those who had accepted the Indulgence.

It was increasingly felt that the church had not proved true to the testimony of the Reformers, or even to that of the earlier victims of the persecution. This extended not only to the martyrs such as James Guthrie, but to the exiles such as M'Ward and Brown. Cameron was wont to justify his stand in terms of the Reformation standards and the Covenants, and this carried a strong appeal for many who looked back nostalgically to the testimony of the church in her best days. For them, Cameron became the focus of a new radicalism, offering the prospect of returning the church to her Reformation purity.

Cameron, for his part, was quite willing to be cast in this role. From his point of view it was highly opportune that the long-delayed letter from Brown praising his conduct at the Edinburgh meeting, and commending his stand against the Indulgence, should have come into his hands just at this time. This letter was widely circulated and greatly enhanced Cameron's standing as a champion of the old values. The disaffected among the people, particularly the young, were increasingly drawn to his side. 'Everywhere now', noted Hamilton with satisfaction, 'it is the young ones that are carrying on the work.'

To the older ministers, however, these events were a cause for dismay. It appeared not only that the carefully built concordat over the Indulgence was being broken, but that the rising generation as a whole was becoming disaffected. Strenuous efforts were made to repair the damage. The leading ministers, Welsh, Semple and Williamson, set about trying to counteract Cameron's influence among the people, and to oppose his preaching as best they could. Warnings were issued about his teaching, and counter-meetings were held in places where he was to preach.

Particular indignation was directed against Hamilton, who was widely regarded as an interloper and troublemaker. Typical was an outburst by Williamson, who inveighed against 'laymen, ignorant, idle men', who had 'taken upon them to meddle in the matter of church government without a call'. The clerk to the Dunscore meeting happened to meet Hamilton in the street and told him that he 'had been a black sight to that country' and that he 'had set all on a fire'. Hamilton, true to character, rejoined that he was 'satisfied to hear of any such effect, for they stood much in need of fire to thaw their frozen spirits'.

Cameron, in the meantime, as the controversy raged around him, continued his itinerant ministry. The events at Dunscore had brought him well and truly into the public eye, and he was not left short of invitations to preach. After spending some time in Annandale, where he revisited John Brown's old parish of Wamphray, he came to the parish of Kirkmahoe, in Nithsdale, where he preached at the invitation of the local elders and their former minister, Francis Irvine.[1] His reception there was one of the most enthusiastic he had yet met. Hamilton, who accompanied him, recorded triumphantly: 'There resorted great confluences of people, yea many families new begun to seek the Lord, with many young; a very heartsome work seemed to be begun there, all training themselves in the fundamentals of religion and in the government of the house of God. The work was wonderfully carried on…'

Cameron's preaching was certainly valued highly by his hearers. Many of them, desiring that others should benefit from it as well, took copious notes of his sermons, which from this time came to be distributed from hand to hand. One of the addresses he gave at Kirkmahoe — on Matthew 18:1-17 — is the earliest example of his preaching to survive. Up till now, it had figured only in the reports of his opponents, anxious to ensnare him for his opposition to the Indulgence. From now on, however, the circulation of Cameron's sermons helped to put his preaching in its proper perspective.

The record of Cameron's address at Kirkmahoe is valuable as an early example of his preaching style. There is, indeed, much in it which was to become characteristic of his preaching at a later date. There is the initial, direct challenge to his hearers, designed perhaps to shock, but certainly to command attention: 'Unto whom are ye come here today? Are ye come to a man only? Are ye come to see a reed shaken with the wind? Those who came out to see a man only, or to be seen of men here today, will probably go away as filthy as they came.' As he often did, Cameron had hard words for the hypocrite, the formalist, the man who made a mere profession of religion, but at the same time he had words of comfort and reassurance for the true follower of Christ. Indeed, much of his address was devoted to setting out the 'marks', or characteristics, of the true Christian.

There must be humility, and a spirit of repentance — and here Cameron referred, with striking tenderness, to the example of the little child brought before the disciples:

> Our Lord takes much notice of little children. He reproves them that would have hindered little children from coming unto him, for they were all very welcome. Children, you know, are very humble creatures. The child of a nobleman will be as familiar with the child of his tenant or cotter, yea with the child of a beggar or any other poor man, as with the child of one who is of equal degree. Now this is one mark whereby folk may know whether they are in a state of grace or not, that is if they become as little children.

And with this humility, Cameron went on, must go a regard and respect for the people of God. 'Such as are humble and holy will love the image of God in their brethren. They will be very loth to offend any of those who belong to Christ. They will rather suffer the worst punishment that enemies can inflict, than offend one of their brethren in the least.'

This honouring of fellow-Christians was itself a reflection of the honour which Christ had placed on his people, and which would yet be seen in its full glory:

> However much they are despised now, the day is coming when they shall not be despised; and though all the world should despise them, yet our Lord takes a great care of them. They have each of them angels waiting upon them, that guard them while walking through the weary wilderness of this world. Will no less serve the saints upon earth, but to have angels to serve them? What is the reason? Just because it is the Lord's will and pleasure. And if he came himself to seek, save and suffer for them, well may they come, attend and guard them home to heaven, whither the forerunner is now entered to prepare mansions for them. The master Christ will not lose any of those little ones for whom he died, and whom he effectually calls; he will carry on that good work once begun by the Spirit, unto perfection; he will carry it on unto the day of the Lord.

It was this thought of the angels waiting upon God's people that led him into one of those fervent appeals which were to become his hallmark, and which when spoken would have come home to his audience with remarkable power:

> There is no doubt that the angels are looking down upon this meeting here today. They will not take a look

> only, and then go off, but they will take special notice of all that are here this day. They will carry the tidings to heaven, of what they have heard or seen. Oh if there were any soul converted, how would they fly joyfully through the first and second heaven, until they entered in among the rest, before our Lord Jesus Christ the Angel of the Covenant! 'What tidings,' will Christ say, 'have ye concerning my people today, and of that meeting at Kirkmahoe?' Who can tell how joyful the news would be, that some souls that before were strangers to Christ were converted and brought in to Christ this day? Oh but it would be joyful tidings unto the angels if some poor young man or woman, some of this or that rank, some gentleman or lady, were here brought in to Christ this day!

But his address was largely concerned with the life of the believer, with the ongoing struggle against sin, and the responsibility to deny self. And so, taking up the words of his text, he went on:

> There are many that have many things that they count as dear to them as a right hand, foot or eye. But here we see, be they what they will, be they never so near and dear unto us, when they come in competition with Christ's cause or interest and glory, they must be cut off or plucked out and cast away. Indeed there are some things very near and dear to a Christian. 'Oh,' says the Christian, 'I cannot want [i.e. be without] such a friend; I cannot be without the company of such and such a godly man; he is as dear to me as my right hand or my right eye.' Well, admit he is of singular use to you, 'Still,' says Christ, 'if it were your right eye that offends you, you must pluck it out and part with it.' 'But,' you

> say, 'I cannot give up such a friend, or such a minister; he is a worthy man; I cannot want him.' 'Well,' says Christ, 'if he be your right hand, and offend you, you must cut him off, and cast him from you.'

It was only a step from this to speak of the offence given to the godly by those ministers who had accepted the Indulgence. Cameron broached the subject fearlessly, without deviating in the least from the stance he had taken. His aim on this occasion was to refute the claims of those who saw acceptance of the Indulgence as a personal matter, amenable to private admonition rather than public rebuke. Cameron would tolerate no such idea. The Indulgence, though accepted by individuals, was a public sin of the church. It therefore had to be publicly exposed. The sin of it, in his view, was like the sin of Achan, who, though he sinned privately, brought judgement upon the whole congregation of Israel. As Achan's sin had been publicly exposed, so should this be. And as the scribes and Pharisees in the time of Christ had been publicly rebuked, so should those who had accepted the Indulgence. Cameron was uncompromising as ever on this score: 'Oh but ministers and professors have this day turned aside; they have committed abominations, and taken the accursed thing. Now, if there be no other way got, let us pray and cry unto the Lord that these may be taken away from being an offence to his church. I say, they ought themselves to be taken away.' He added: 'Now if we were rightly searching into and trying the sins of our church in Scotland, we would find that we have great reason to turn our laughter into mourning, and our joy into heaviness.'

Cameron stayed on in Nithsdale for three weeks, preaching regularly both on the Lord's Day and on weekdays. It was a time that, probably more than any other, firmly established his reputation as a preacher. Great crowds flocked to hear him, and reports of his preaching spread far and wide. To the people in the local parishes, these proved to be weeks of remarkable blessing. A strong and enduring bond of affection was forged between them and Cameron. When the time finally came for him to leave, the scene was one of unrestrained grief. 'When we parted from Nithsdale', wrote Hamilton, 'young and old hung about Cameron and all of us, begging and crying with tears that we might stay; or, if he should go, that he might not tarry from them.' Cameron was indeed later to return to Nithsdale, though in rather different circumstances, but for the moment he felt that his duty lay elsewhere.

On his way south through Ayrshire he had promised to return there to preach, and he now turned his steps northwards once again. On the Lord's Day, 22 December, he preached at Dalrymple, where, Hamilton records, there was 'a great confluence from the indulged parishes'. From there he went to Coylton — one of these parishes where the local minister had accepted the Indulgence — and then on to Cumnock, where he received, and accepted, a pressing invitation from the local people to preach to them on the following Thursday, 26 December.

While making their way through Ayrshire, Cameron and Hamilton heard some news which disturbed them deeply. This concerned an arrangement between the ministers who had accepted the Indulgence and the leading field-preachers, including Welsh and Semple, to allow young men acceptable to both sides to be settled in vacant parishes, or to respond to calls for field-preaching. This step was, of course, very much in line with the accommodating spirit of the time, but to Cameron and Hamilton it savoured of a plot to deceive the more loyal among the people into accepting preachers contrary to their principles.

Hearing of a meeting of ministers at Bridge of Ken, in Galloway, on 26 December, at which these plans were to be taken a step further, Hamilton decided to attend the meeting and to confront the ministers personally. Cameron, who was already committed to preach at Cumnock the same day, could not accompany him, but Hamilton duly set out on his mission, taking with him Henry Hall. The ministers heard that the two men were on their way and resorted to their old ruse of changing the place where the meeting was to be held, and convened instead at Dundeugh, a desolate spot between Dalry and Carsphairn. Hamilton, nothing daunted, followed them there, and demanded a hearing.

When this was granted, Hamilton vehemently denounced the ministers for their complicity with those who had accepted the Indulgence, and charged them with unfaithfulness to the cause and interest of Christ. The ministers, understandably, were deeply offended, and unanimously censured him for his conduct. The only effect of this rebuke was to impel him to an even more vehement denunciation of their proceedings, and the confrontation was only ended when Hamilton, feeling that he had said enough to satisfy his conscience, eventually walked out of the meeting.

Meanwhile, at Cumnock, Cameron was engaged in a confrontation of his own. The night Hamilton left him, he received a visit from several influential men in the parish, who urged him to leave the district and not to be a source of dissension among the people. His main critics were two local landowners, the lairds of Logan and Horsecleugh, who had represented him as a Jesuit, and sought to dissuade the people from hearing him. Cameron replied to them, quite forcefully, that he had been called by the people to preach, and he would deliver what he had to say 'if they should bury him at the tent side'. Hearing this, his visitors went to the Earl of Dumfries, the local magistrate, to ask him to apprehend Cameron. The earl, to his credit, refused, saying he had no warrant for such an act.

Cameron, having seen his opponents thwarted, preached as planned on the 26th, and for good measure went on to preach at New Cumnock the following Lord's Day, 29 December, by which time Hamilton had rejoined him. The end of the year found him at Galston, in the north of Ayrshire, as he made his way back once more towards Edinburgh.

13.
Cameron leaves for Holland

As the year 1679 opened, Cameron could take some satisfaction from the events of the previous months. He had embarked on the career to which he felt God had called him, he had seen signs of blessing as a result of his labours and he had resisted efforts to divert him from his chosen course. At the same time, he had been involved in bitter controversy, he had alienated himself irreversibly from the leading field-preachers and he was already seen as a dangerous fanatic by the more moderate Presbyterians. There can be no doubt that, for a variety of reasons, within a very short space of time Cameron had become the best-known of all of the younger generation of field-preachers. It did not in the least trouble him that this fame should be seen by some as notoriety; his own conscience was clear, and he had given ample proof, through all the turmoil of the preceding months, of his determination to maintain a faithful witness and a clear conscience.

The most serious cause of concern for Cameron at the start of 1679 was clearly the threat of further disciplinary action against him by the older ministers. The meeting at Dunscore had referred his case back to the ministers at Edinburgh, and there was a strong possibility that the latter group would summon him to appear before them again. So far as can be known, this threat never materialized, but it is impossible to be certain. One of the frustrations faced by the chronicler of Cameron's life is the complete lack of any information about his relationships with the older ministers in the months after the Dunscore meeting. This is particularly unfortunate since the events of this period were obviously critical in relation to Cameron's subsequent actions, and indeed to much of his later life.

The crucial point, and the one around which much argument has centred, is whether Cameron was prevailed upon during this time to promise to forbear, for a period, from preaching against the Indulgence. As we have already seen, at both the Edinburgh and Dunscore meetings he resolutely refused to give any such assurance. It has been asserted, however, that, at some point after the Dunscore meeting, he was finally persuaded to do so, and that the recollection of having given this promise was to prey upon his mind for the rest of his life.

There is no documentary evidence by which this claim can be tested. No record survives of any meeting between Cameron and the ministers, subsequent to that at Dunscore. The assertion that Cameron gave such a promise is, however, made quite unambiguously by Patrick Walker, Cameron's first biographer, in his short *Life* of Cameron published in 1727. Walker's account is not to be disregarded lightly. Though he himself never actually met Cameron or heard him preach, he was personally acquainted with several of his closest friends and adherents, who were in a position to give him accurate information. Some of them were still alive when Walker wrote, and could have contradicted his account if they had chosen to do so, but they did not. Walker's subsequent *Life* of Donald Cargill, published in 1732, contains some additions to his earlier *Life* of Cameron, but his record of Cameron's promise over the Indulgence remains unchanged.

Walker's account has been discounted by later biographers, who have pointed to the fact that the record of the Dunscore meeting shows plainly Cameron's determination to give no such promise.[1] Walker, however, is careful in the way he has recorded the facts. According to his account, Cameron was persuaded to give way, not by those who attended the meeting, but by 'others who would not sit with them on the same design'. The minutes of the Dunscore meeting do indeed record that other ministers had been invited to act with the presbytery, but had declined to do so. Among these could well have been men such as John Dickson and George Barclay, both of whom had countenanced Cameron at the meeting at Kilmarnock when Welsh and the other field-preachers had refused to do so.

It is certainly difficult to account for some of Cameron's actions, and words, in later life if he did not give such an undertaking. If this is indeed the case, the way in which it was achieved must remain a matter for speculation. It is not, of course, beyond the bounds of possibility that some of the ministers in Edinburgh — notably some who were basically sympathetic to Cameron, such as John Blackader — together with Dickson and Barclay, may have succeeded in persuading him that the peace of the church depended on his forbearance at this particular time. Whatever the circumstances, the evidence of the rest of Cameron's life does point to the conclusion that, possibly in the early part of 1679, he gave an undertaking of some sort, to ministers whom he trusted, that he would forbear for a specific period from preaching against the Indulgence. And the evidence seems equally clear that, for Cameron, what he did at that time was later to become a matter of bitter heart-searching and regret.

It is likely that Cameron spent the first weeks of 1679 in Edinburgh after his extended visit to the south-west. On his way homewards he had preached in West Lothian, but had met considerable opposition from the moderate Presbyterians. He later preached in and around Edinburgh where he was more favourably received. On one particular Lord's Day, Hamilton records, his preaching, in the city itself and within five miles of it, drew such acclaim from his hearers that the older ministers refused to preach to them any more. But his movements for most of this period are very uncertain, and there is no record of his having preached with any frequency. This tends to bear out Walker's assertion that, after giving the promise to the ministers, he 'turned melancholy, finding himself bound up by reason thereof from declaring the whole counsel of God'. There is no further record of his preaching until 24 April, when he took part with Donald Cargill and John King in a fast-day's preaching near Glasgow, and again on 27 April and 4 May, when he preached in the parish of Crawford in Clydesdale — on the latter occasion within only three miles of a troop of soldiers led by Graham of Claverhouse.[2]

By this time, Cameron seems to have been labouring under an oppressive burden on account of the promise he had given. He appears to have felt that, apart from compromising his own conscience, he had betrayed the trust of those who had been looking to him to give a lead in opposing the Indulgence, and he evidently concluded that he could not continue his preaching ministry in Scotland so long as the promise remained in effect.

Other events, too, pressed in upon him. The government, incensed by the continued prevalence of the field-meetings, brought in at the beginning of the year a series of draconian measures, including the stationing of troops in the main centres of resistance, and the appointment of special magistrates throughout the country. Increased rewards were offered for capture of the field-preachers, and the penalties for attendance at field-meetings were made even more severe.

These measures were rigorously enforced, in a determined attempt to subdue the people into submission. But the spirit of the people was different now from what it had been at an earlier stage of the persecution. Largely as a result of the influence of Robert Hamilton, there was less of a spirit of passive resistance and a greater determination to carry the battle to the authorities. The result was a series of confrontations of increasing violence. These started on 11 March, when Robert Johnstone, the Town Major of Edinburgh, who was noted for his persecution of those who attended unauthorized services, was lured to a house in the city under pretext of dispersing an illegal meeting, and was there set upon by a body of men, of whom Cameron's brother Michael was one. On 30 March, when a field-meeting at Cummerhead, near Lesmahagow, was challenged by a party of soldiers, the response from those present was so robust that some of the soldiers were wounded and made prisoner, and the lieutenant in charge barely escaped with his life.[3] Three weeks later a government trooper was shot dead, and another seriously wounded, in an attack by a body of armed men on their sleeping-quarters at Newmilns, in Ayrshire.

The blame for these and other incidents was, of course, attributed to Hamilton and his supporters, though there are good grounds to believe that some of them, particularly the last, were caused by rogue elements which had infiltrated his following and which he could not properly control. Be that as it may, Cameron, for his part, was clearly associated in the popular mind with the increasing aggressiveness which characterized Hamilton's dealings with the authorities, and there is good reason to believe that he found this particularly distasteful. While there is no evidence of a breach, as such, between Cameron and Hamilton, there are strong grounds for concluding that Cameron saw a break in his association with Hamilton as a necessary step at this stage of his career, and that this strengthened the resolve he had already formed to distance himself, for a time, from events in Scotland.

The outcome was that, probably in early May 1679, Cameron left the shores of Scotland and sailed to join Robert M'Ward and John Brown in Rotterdam. Cameron had several reasons for wanting to meet the exiles, quite apart from the considerations which had led him to leave Scotland. At a time when he faced almost unanimous opposition from the leaders of the church in Scotland, they had shown themselves to be his firm friends. Brown, in particular, had been a source of continuing strength and encouragement, and despite attracting criticism to himself by his support of Cameron, had stood unflinchingly by his side.

It is not clear whether Cameron went to Holland seeking some seal of approval from the exiles, though he could well have been excused if such was his intent. Both M'Ward and Brown were held in the highest regard by the most discriminating Christians in Scotland, and Brown was respected as one of the outstanding theologians of his day, even by those who opposed his views on the Indulgence. An endorsement of his ministry by such men would certainly enhance Cameron's standing at home. However, he may have had no such prospect in view, and may simply have gone to Holland to savour the spiritual refreshment and fellowship which such a visit promised. If that were so, the event was greatly to exceed his expectations.

Cameron probably arrived in Holland in mid-May. Rotterdam was already a haven of refuge for many from Scotland, and Cameron was readily accepted into the refugee community. His reception by M'Ward and Brown was all that he could have desired, and more. M'Ward, who had perhaps tended to reserve judgement about Cameron, in view of the adverse reports which had reached him, soon perceived that he had been sadly misinformed. 'The common report of poor Mr Cameron', he wrote later, 'was that not only he did preach nothing but babble against the Indulgence, but that he *could* do no other thing. And this was so confidently and commonly talked, that I was not in case to contradict it upon knowledge.' M'Ward's meeting with Cameron effectively dispelled such prejudices. 'But', he went on, 'by his coming hither, the reporters have lost their credit; and many who heard him were convinced that prejudice, heightened to malice, had given men liberty to talk so; for here he was found a man of a savoury gospel spirit, the bias of his heart lying towards the proposing of Christ, and persuading to a closing with him.'[4]

Here indeed was a true estimate of Cameron's character, given by one of unimpeachable integrity. That Cameron should have so impressed a man such as M'Ward was in itself highly significant. M'Ward stood in the very forefront of the Scottish Reformed tradition. He had studied under Rutherford at St Andrews, and had acted as his secretary at the Westminster Assembly. He had known intimately such giants of the Second Reformation period as Durham and Gillespie. In Holland he had laboured for well-nigh twenty years ministering to his fellow-exiles, sending messages of encouragement to those at home, and working on a range of literary enterprises including the editing of Rutherford's *Letters,* which he had already seen through three editions. With his fellow-exile John Brown — who had himself attracted Rutherford's notice as a young man — M'Ward lived on terms of close and happy fellowship. In some ways, indeed, the exiles formed an interesting contrast — Brown with his bias towards the theological and doctrinal, and M'Ward with his emphasis on the experimental and practical. But in their zeal for the cause and testimony of the church they were fully and completely at one; and it was on that basis, of course, that they had identified so closely with Cameron.

The support of such men was a great encouragement to Cameron. At a time of almost universal opposition at home, it was a convincing vindication of his witness and testimony.

But its implications went well beyond that. In Scotland, Cameron was increasingly portrayed as the representative of a faction, diverse from the mainstream of Scottish Presbyterianism. But here was an endorsement of his ministry from men whose credentials as representatives of the Reformed Church of Scotland could not be questioned. They themselves were products of the golden age of Scottish Presbyterianism. They were in the direct line of the Scottish Reformers. Here was convincing proof that Cameron had not strayed onto a path of his own, but was in fact upholding the Scottish Reformed tradition at a time when others were forsaking it. That alone, no doubt, would have been sufficient reward for Cameron for his visit to Holland, but God, in his providence, had still more in store for him before he again turned his face towards Scotland.

14.
Rutherglen and Drumclog

Meanwhile, back in Scotland tumultuous events were taking place. The series of confrontations since the beginning of the year had created conditions which made a crisis inevitable. On Saturday, 3 May, came the spark which lit the great conflagration. Significantly, the scene of the denouement was in Fife. A local deputy sheriff, William Carmichael — one of those appointed at the beginning of the year — had achieved notoriety through his repressive acts and his harassment of the local population. Several men of influence — among them John Balfour of Kinloch and his brother-in-law David Hackston of Rathillet, both close associates of Robert Hamilton — decided to teach Carmichael a salutary lesson. On the morning of 3 May they lay in wait for him as he prepared to go hunting, but Carmichael received warning of their presence and succeeded in eluding them.

They were about to disperse, their purpose frustrated, when word reached them that James Sharp, the Archbishop of St Andrews and Primate of Scotland, was shortly to pass by in his carriage. Their first reaction was one of incredulity, but this was soon replaced by a stern sense of purpose. Sharp, in the view of many, had been the principal betrayer of the church and one of the chief instruments in the persecution. He was also the man charged with the blood of those put to death after

Pentland, and of others who had suffered since. And Sharp, Balfour and his friends decided, had now been delivered by the Lord into their hands.

Their purpose was no sooner decided than acted upon. Sharp was pursued, dragged out of his carriage and summarily killed. The act was carried out ruthlessly, yet with a deliberation which reflected the participants' view of themselves as the instruments of divine vengeance. Sharp's daughter, who was travelling with him, and the coachman and servants were left unharmed.

The killing of Sharp provoked a predictable cry of outrage from the authorities. Not surprisingly, an effort was made to relate it to the confrontations of the previous weeks, and to portray it as the natural consequence of the illegal gatherings which the government had been doing its best to suppress. Stringent new laws were enacted against field-meetings, and extended powers given to the standing forces. Especially severe measures were introduced in Fife, where owners of land were required to produce their servants and tenants for examination by the local magistrates, under penalty of being deemed accessories to the crime if they refused. Sharp's death may have removed one of the persecutors, but it in no way lessened the virulence of the persecution.

Those responsible for the archbishop's death were of course keenly sought for, and large rewards were offered for their capture. After living for some time as fugitives, they decided that their safety lay in greater numbers, and so, making their way through the country, they sought to ally themselves with those who might give them support. Their main hope, not surprisingly, was in Robert Hamilton, whom some of them already knew, and who was known to be somewhere in the western shires. They met some of Hamilton's adherents at a field-meeting at Campsie on 22 May, and on the following Lord's Day, at Strathaven, they joined Hamilton himself.

Hamilton had not been idle in the meantime. The increased tension with the authorities had caused him to adopt a higher profile, and the series of confrontations in the spring had brought him additional support. While Cameron's absence was a drawback, he had striven in various ways to turn it to good account. Hamilton was shrewd enough to know that he could not further his objectives without the active support of one or more of the ministers, and following Cameron's departure he had sought to influence others of them on his behalf.

His main success was with Thomas Douglas, an ordained minister who had been active in the fields for some time but who had not, before now, come to particular notice.[1] Douglas had been present at Cameron's licensing and had been formerly numbered by Hamilton among those sympathetic to their position. He had, however, been reluctant to break with the older ministers and had sat with them as a member at both the Dunscore and Dundeugh meetings, but now he had apparently been won over conclusively to Hamilton's side. Douglas had preached at Strathaven on the Lord's Day when Hamilton had been joined by the party from Fife, and he was to figure prominently with Hamilton in some of the events which followed.

The arrival of the party from Fife gave an important boost to Hamilton's morale. It lent additional weight to his movement and greater credibility to his cause. Above all, it gave him the confidence to take a step he had long been contemplating — a public display of defiance against the government. He lost no time in putting his purpose into effect.

Just before nightfall on Thursday, 29 May — the day appointed as a 'solemn anniversary thanksgiving' for the king's restoration — Hamilton and a large party of horsemen rode into the town of Rutherglen, two miles from Glasgow. They extinguished the bonfires blazing in the king's honour, summoned the local magistrates to attend them and rode in procession to the market cross. Douglas prayed and gave an address, and a psalm was sung. Hamilton publicly read the Acts of Parliament and Council asserting the king's supremacy, and ceremonially set fire to them. He then read and affixed to the cross a declaration in the following terms:

> As the Lord had been pleased still to keep and preserve his interest in the land by the testimony of some faithful witnesses from the beginning, so in our days some have not been wanting, who through the greatest of hazards, had added their testimonies to those who have gone before them, by suffering death, banishment, torturings, finings, forfeitures, imprisonments etc. flowing from cruel and perfidious adversaries to the church and kingdom of our Lord Jesus Christ in the land. Therefore we owning the interest of Christ according to the Word of the Lord, and the National and Solemn League and Covenant, desire to add our testimony to the testimonies of the worthies that have gone before (though unworthy, yet hoping as true members of the church of Christ in Scotland) and that against all things that have been done prejudicial to his interest from the beginning of the work of Reformation in Scotland; especially from the year 1648 to the year 1660, against these following Acts, as,
>
> I. The Act of Supremacy.
>
> II. The Declaration whereby the Covenants are condemned.
>
> III. The Act for eversion of the established government of the church, and for establishing of Prelacy, and for outing of Christ's ministers, who could not conform thereto by an Act Recissory of all Acts of Parliament and Assemblies for the establishment of the government of the Church of Scotland according to the Word.

> As likewise that Act of Council at Glasgow, putting that Act Recissory in execution, where, at one time, were violently cast out above 300 ministers, without all legal procedures.
>
> Likewise the Act appointing a holy anniversary day to be kept upon the 29th day of May for giving thanks for the upsetting of an usurping power, destroying the interest of the church in the land, which is to set up the creature to be worshipped in the room of our great Redeemer, and to consent to the assuming of the power that is proper to the Lord alone, for the appointing of ordinances in his church; as particularly the government thereof, and the keeping of holy days, and all other sinful and unlawful acts emitted and executed by them.
>
> And for confirmation of this our testimony, we do hereby this day, being the 29th day of May 1679, publicly burn them at the cross of Glasgow most justly, as they perfidiously and blasphemously had burnt our holy Covenants through several cities of the Covenanted kingdoms; we judge none will take exception at our not subscribing this our testimony, being so solemnly gone about, for we are ready always to do it, if judged necessary, with all the faithful suffering brethren in the land. [2]

As the document itself showed, the original intention had been to publish it at the cross of Glasgow, which would have suited Hamilton's purpose even better by conferring greater prestige on the proceedings, but the presence of government troops there in some strength had made this impossible, and had forced the choice of Rutherglen as a second-best. As it was, however, his action made sufficient impact. The government, already frustrated by their lack of success in tracking down the assassins of Sharp, were roused to vigorous action. A wide-ranging commission was given to John Graham of Claverhouse, who had already carried out acts of repression in the south-west and who, the government believed, was well fitted to bring the rebels to account.

Claverhouse entered on his task with enthusiasm. Coming suddenly to the town of Hamilton on 31 May, he apprehended several people who were preparing to attend a field-meeting at Loudon Hill, near Strathaven, the following day. The next morning, driving his prisoners before him, he set out to attack the meeting itself. Douglas, who was again the preacher, had scarcely opened the meeting when the alarm was given, but his hearers were in a high state of readiness. By a prearranged plan, those who carried arms — some armed with guns, but most with only pikes and pitchforks — withdrew from the meeting and stationed themselves in a position of strength at Drumclog, in the direct line of Claverhouse's advance. A strict military order was observed, and officers were appointed to their various duties. Hamilton was, of course, prominent, and claimed later to have been appointed chief commander, but the real heroes were the party from Fife. The ill-equipped little force took up their positions and calmly awaited the arrival of Claverhouse. They weathered his initial assault bravely, then advanced on him with their full strength.

Other things being equal, the military discipline of the soldiers would have carried the day, but such was the vigour of the assault made on them that they were completely routed. Claverhouse wrote later, 'They pursued us so hotly that we had no time to rally. I saved the standards, but lost on the place about eight or ten men, besides wounded; but the dragoons lost many more. I made the best retreat the confusion of our people would suffer. What these rogues will do next I know not, but the country was flocking to them from all hands. This may be counted the beginning of the rebellion, in my opinion.' In all,

The battle of Drumclog (as depicted by George Harvey)
Reproduced by courtesy of the National Gallery of Scotland

some thirty-six of Claverhouse's men were killed, and he himself narrowly escaped with his life. No victory, indeed, could have been more complete. The prisoners were rescued, and the pursuit kept up for several miles, until Claverhouse finally found refuge in the government garrison at Glasgow.

The victory of Drumclog was an undoubted triumph for Hamilton, and those with him. Flushed with their success, the next day they attacked the government troops within Glasgow itself, but the garrison was heavily defended, and they were eventually obliged to retire with some losses. They then withdrew to Hamilton, on the south side of the Clyde, where they resolved to continue in arms in their own defence.

The government were by now thoroughly alarmed. As Claverhouse rightly divined, the movement against them was assuming the proportions of a full-scale rebellion. Urgent preparations were made to meet the challenge. Troops were assembled from far and near, and summonses issued to the principal landowners to mobilize their tenants and servants. The Duke of Monmouth, a natural son of the king, was sent north to assume overall command. By mid-June, a formidable army had been assembled and was on its way westwards from Edinburgh. A final confrontation loomed imminent.

Meanwhile, at Hamilton the victors of Drumclog were regrouping. Since the memorable events of 1st June there had been substantial additions to their numbers. Success had given Hamilton's movement a degree of credibility, and many who had previously been hesitant now saw their opportunity to strike a blow for liberty. There was still resentment over the depredations caused by the Highland troops brought in by the government, and this prompted a large influx of support from the western shires. Others joined out of a general feeling of solidarity with Hamilton and his supporters. While the new-comers did not share all their principles, they nevertheless did not wish to see them exposed to the wrath of the government, and they saw it as their duty to come to their aid. Yet others joined from a sense of self-preservation. It seemed to them that, if Hamilton and his party were overcome, the outcome would be even more stringent repression for the nonconforming Presbyterians as a whole and, by presenting a united front, they hoped to convince the government of the strength of popular feeling and deter them from any precipitate action. They may well have hoped, too, to be a moderating influence on Hamilton and his colleagues, and possibly even to persuade the authorities to avoid a final confrontation.

These varying motives brought large additions to the 'Covenanted army'—as Hamilton was now calling it—in the days following Drumclog. By the second week of June a substantial force had been gathered, numbering some 5,000 or 6,000 men in arms. By all appearances, they constituted a formidable challenge to the government army, now on its way from Edinburgh. And, given their success at Drumclog, Hamilton and his friends had good reason to believe that they could make that challenge an effective one.

But it was not to be. The very diversity of the 'Covenanted army' contained the seeds of its own confusion. The animosities created over the previous months, particularly over the question of the Indulgence, ensured that, when such diverse elements were brought together, the result was merely to accentuate the tensions and bring them into higher profile.

This was particularly demonstrated when John Welsh, and with him some of the older ministers, joined the camp on 7 June. Welsh, as the sequel showed, hoped to exercise a moderating influence on affairs and perhaps even to avoid a final conflict, but, predictably enough, his presence only served to exacerbate the differences between the parties. There can be no doubt that, whatever Welsh's own feelings may have been, many of his supporters came with a strong personal prejudice against Hamilton and his party.

Strikingly enough, these prejudices were directed not so much against Hamilton himself, initially at least, as against Richard Cameron. One of Welsh's strongest supporters, James Ure of Shargarton, later recorded that he would have taken with him a larger body of men, but, he said, 'Cameron was the stay', and on being told by Hamilton that Cameron was in Holland, he had 'prayed that all his faction were with him'. There can be little doubt that Ure's view of Cameron was shared by many who joined the camp on Welsh's side, and that it strongly coloured their attitudes towards Hamilton and to the rest. That Cameron should have become the focus of such strong feelings was, no doubt, a measure of the resentment felt against him for his treatment of Welsh, but it was also a tribute to the power of a personality which, in only a few short months, had stamped its imprint so firmly on the course of events in Scotland.

The days that followed saw a lamentable succession of disputes over the management of the army and the general conduct of affairs. Like the Protesters of an earlier day, Hamilton and his colleagues urged that only those who had not been guilty of compromise or compliance with the government should be appointed as officers. They particularly objected to the appointment of Thomas Weir of Greenridge, who had brought a party of men to the camp, but thirteen years earlier had been a government trooper at Pentland. Hamilton and his supporters pressed that, before being admitted as an officer, Weir should be forced to make a public retraction of his past conduct. Weir refused to do so, and enlisted the aid of Welsh, who supported him. He was duly appointed, though remaining an object of distrust and misgiving to Hamilton and his party, who saw his presence among their ranks as a harbinger of judgement on the army as a whole.

This was an inauspicious enough beginning, but worse was to follow. A bitter dispute developed as to what should be said by way of a public declaration concerning the aims of the army, and their justification for rising in arms.

Welsh favoured a moderate approach, which only sought redress of grievances and disclaimed any intention of revolt against authority. He and his party drew up a declaration on these lines, in which they included among their aims 'the preserving and defending the king's majesty's person and authority in the preservation and defence of the true religion and liberties of the kingdom, that the world may bear witness, with our consciences, of our loyalty, and that we have no thoughts nor intentions to diminish his just power and greatness'. This in fact restated the third article of the Solemn League and Covenant of 1643, and on that ground Welsh and his colleagues urged that no reasonable exception could be taken to it.

Hamilton and his party, however, disagreed strongly. The Solemn League, they pointed out, had been framed in entirely different circumstances from the present, and any acknowledgement of the king's interest would now be entirely out of place, in the light of the evils he had inflicted on the church. An impasse resulted, which was at last broken when Welsh and his supporters unilaterally published the declaration at the cross of Hamilton on 13 June, adding for good measure, 'God Save the King,' at the end of it. Hamilton's party bitterly protested that they had been betrayed, and the Hamilton Declaration, as it came to be known, was to be a focus of contention for many a day in the future.

The government army was now only a few miles off, and it was becoming obvious that a confrontation could not be long delayed. Hamilton and his supporters pressed for a day of fasting and humiliation, to confess the sins of which the land was guilty, and to invoke the blessing of God. As a prelude to this, they commissioned four ministers and four elders to prepare a statement of the public sins of the time, to be used in the public preaching planned for the fast-day. As drafted by the ministers and elders, this included as one of the sins to be confessed, 'ministers appearing at the courts of usurping rulers, and their acceptance from them of warrants and instructions to admit them to, and regulate them in the exercise of their ministry; their indulgence becoming a public sin and snare, both to themselves and others'.

When Welsh heard of this, he opposed it vehemently. The Indulgence, he argued, had not been condemned by any free General Assembly, and who were they to count it as a public sin of the time? He went further: if a statement of public sins was to be called for, then let it include the fact that ministers were preaching against the Indulgence and calling upon their hearers to forsake the ministers who had accepted it. And, as an example of the prime offenders in this, he singled out Richard Cameron.

Welsh's status and influence were sufficient to ensure that the statement drafted by Hamilton's party did not see the light of day, and the proposal for a fast-day which depended upon it was consequently abandoned. The result was, not surprisingly, to exacerbate feeling between the two sides still further. In fact, relations in the camp were approaching open warfare. Ministers preached in contradiction of one another, and there were even cases of physical harassment of one side by the other. The divisions among the leaders were also reflected in the army itself. Hamilton, though in nominal command, was unable to exercise any effective control, and those officers who were sympathetic to Welsh were able to do very much as they pleased. In such a situation the army was rendered virtually powerless as a fighting force. Skilled fighters there were, indeed, on both sides, and men who had years of military service to their credit, but as an effective fighting unit the army was now utterly unprepared for the challenge that it was about to face.

15.
Bothwell Bridge and its aftermath

By Saturday, 21 June, a government army of some 10,000 under the Duke of Monmouth had taken up position at Bothwell, on the north bank of the Clyde opposite Hamilton. John Welsh, in a last bid to avoid disaster, urged that a supplication should be addressed to the duke, seeking a redress of grievances and disclaiming any intentions of rebellion. Hamilton objected, and maintained that he would agree to no address to the duke except one which confronted him with his own and his family's public sins. The issue generated a great deal of heat, and Hamilton and his party twice walked out of the discussions. At length, they were persuaded to agree that a supplication be drawn up by representatives of either side, to be signed by Hamilton as overall commander, and with this uneasy compromise the issue was temporarily settled.

The next morning, 22 June, it became obvious that Monmouth was preparing to attack. Hamilton busied himself in organizing the army and preparing the best means of defence. While he was thus engaged, the supplication to Monmouth was brought to him for signature. He signed it, as he afterwards recorded, without reading it, and in the belief that it had been prepared by Donald Cargill, who had been chosen to represent Hamilton's party on the drafting committee. It was not, however, Cargill's work, but that of John Welsh and others of his party. Framed in similar terms to the Hamilton Declaration, it recounted briefly the wrongs the petitioners had suffered, their urgent need for a redress of grievances, and their expectation that Monmouth, 'of whose princely clemency, and natural goodness, and aversion from shedding of Christian blood, we have had so savoury a report', would respond sympathetically. It was scarcely in line with the respectful, and almost subservient, tone of the supplication that Hamilton should have subscribed it: 'R. Hamiltoune in naim of the Covenanted army now in armes'.

Their object secured, Welsh's party entrusted the supplication to two of their number, who, under safe conduct, crossed to the government side and presented it to Monmouth. The duke was unimpressed. While, he said, he was not unwilling to listen to grievances, he was not prepared to negotiate with men who had risen in revolt against the king, and he refused to countenance any discussions until they had first laid down their arms. Hamilton's response was equally uncompromising when the emissaries returned. 'And hang next,' he is reported to have said, dismissively.

After a brief token delay to allow for an answer, Monmouth gave the order to advance. His prime objective was control of the bridge separating the two sides, which had been stoutly fortified and defended. His initial onslaught was weathered gallantly for some three hours by a force of 300 men under the command of David Hackston and John Balfour — both from Fife — and John Paton of Meadowhead, a veteran of the wars of the Commonwealth period and earlier. When their ammunition gave out, they sent for fresh supplies, but Hamilton, instead of sending them the help they requested, ordered them back to the main body of the army. Whether this was because no supplies were available, or for some other reason, has never been satisfactorily explained, and even the most sympathetic commentators have found it difficult to justify Hamilton's action.

Monmouth immediately saw his opportunity and, seizing control of the bridge, he found strategic sites for his cannon and directed his fire against the mounted troops opposite him. In their anxiety to reach higher ground out of the range of his guns, these cavalry broke the ranks of the foot-soldiers in their rear, and a general state of confusion followed. Attempts at regrouping proved futile, and under the pressure of the continuing cannonade, the foot-soldiers broke ranks and fled.

Monmouth's troops, with Claverhouse well to the fore, pressed home the attack mercilessly. While relatively few were slain on the field, some 400 were shot down in the pursuit and a further 1,200 taken prisoner. The 'Covenanted army' was scattered to the four winds. Had it not been for the restraints imposed by Monmouth, the slaughter would certainly have been greater; as it was, the rout was comprehensive and complete. The fatal divisions of the previous three weeks had led to their tragic, and inevitable, conclusion.

In the weeks that followed, the government busied themselves with taking reprisals. Despite their most strenuous efforts, however, they failed to capture any of the army leaders. Most of these eventually fled to Holland. Some, including Robert Hamilton, were to remain there until the persecution was over, while others, such as Hall and Hackston, returned after a few months.

Foiled of their main prey, the government took vengeance on any who fell into their hands. Two ministers, John Kid and John King, were condemned and executed. The 1,200 prisoners taken after the battle were kept for several months in inhuman conditions in the Greyfriars Churchyard in Edinburgh. Over 250 of them were eventually put on board ship for the Plantations, most of whom later perished in a shipwreck off the Orkneys. A further five prisoners were later selected for execution on the spot where Sharp had met his death.

But the government, for their own ends, were anxious to avoid creating an impression of undue vindictiveness. Events were skilfully managed to produce a show of justice tempered with mercy. A general indemnity was proclaimed on the very day that King and Kid were executed. The remaining prisoners were promised their liberty on taking a bond for the peace. And a new, third, Indulgence was granted to ministers, offering them the free exercise of their functions in return for a bond for their good behaviour being given by their parishioners.

Like the earlier Indulgences, this last measure generated its share of controversy. But the situation in 1679 was radically different from what it had been in earlier days. The church was now in a seriously weakened condition. In the aftermath of Bothwell, the leading field-preachers had fallen silent, or had left the country. John Welsh had retired to London, where he was to remain until his death in 1681. Donald Cargill and Thomas Douglas had gone to Holland. The others judged it prudent, in the situation prevailing after Bothwell, not to provoke the authorities into further acts of repression. They also, quite understandably, feared for their own safety. The act proclaiming the Third Indulgence had reaffirmed the previous severe laws against field-meetings, including the death penalty for preachers, and the condemnation as traitors of all who attended such meetings carrying arms. In such an atmosphere it was scarcely surprising that a mood of compromise prevailed. Some of the ministers in Edinburgh made it their business to visit the Greyfriars Churchyard and persuade the remaining prisoners to take the bond for the peace. At a general meeting of ministers on 16 September it was agreed that the Third Indulgence could be accepted without compromise of principle, and a number of ministers — some of them former field-preachers — were settled in parishes on bonds of 6,000 merks each.[1]

By the autumn of 1679, resistance to the government had been well-nigh overcome. The confrontational tactics of Robert Hamilton had ended in disaster. Through persecution and compromise, the church had been virtually brought into submission. Everywhere the forces of repression appeared to be triumphant. That their triumph did not become complete was to be largely due to the efforts of one man, who had been remote from the scene of action, but who was now preparing once again to return to his native land.

It is one of the supreme ironies of Cameron's life that he should have been absent from Scotland when the tumultuous events of 1679 were taking place. His influence, however, was by no means unfelt. Ure of Shargarton's comment that 'Cameron was the stay' to his bringing more men with him to Bothwell has already been noted. Ure also recalled with evident distaste that Robert Hamilton and his friends had told him, after his arrival at Bothwell, that 'They owned Cameron, and were of his judgement plainly.' And in his account of Bothwell, published in 1751, William Wilson of Douglas recorded that 'Such as contended for the truth, and witnessed against Mr Welsh's corrupt courses, were by the Erastian party called by the name of the Cameronian faction.' It was a title which, though given in contempt, was to achieve an honour which those who coined it never contemplated.[2]

Cameron therefore, though absent, had an undoubted influence on the events of the time. The government, indeed, appear to have been so convinced that he had taken part in the battle at Bothwell that they included his name in a proclamation they issued on 26 June, condemning the leaders of the movement as 'the worst of traitors' and marshalling all the forces of the law to bring them to justice. It is interesting to speculate on what difference, if any, it might have made to the course of events if Cameron had been present. Doubtless Robert Hamilton and those with him would have found his presence a powerful support in their contendings with Welsh and his party. It may well be, too, that he could have rallied and inspired the mass of the army in a way that Hamilton and the other leaders found themselves unable to do. But the events of the previous months, and particularly the antagonisms between him and Welsh, leave no room to believe that even if he had been there this would have been enough to avoid the divisions between the two sides which in the end were to prove so disastrous. Indeed, if Ure's comments are to be taken as typical, there is little doubt that Welsh and his party would have reacted even more strongly against Cameron's views had he been there to propagate them himself.

In Holland, Cameron had ample opportunity to reflect on the strange providence which had taken him out of Scotland — probably for the first time in his life — at a period when events of such great moment were taking place. Not surprisingly, the news of these events featured prominently in the press of the time. The *London Gazette,* for example, which circulated on the Continent, reported in some detail the events at Rutherglen and Drumclog and carried a report of the battle of Bothwell Bridge as early as 26 June. These public reports were soon to be corroborated by correspondence from eyewitnesses and others directly involved. Cameron, M'Ward and Brown were thus fully aware of events in Scotland shortly after they took place, and were able to form their own judgements.

In the case of M'Ward, this was crucial for Cameron's future career. As he reflected on the situation, M'Ward seems to have become convinced that the witness to the truth in Scotland was in danger of becoming completely extinct unless, in the providence of God, an instrument was raised up who would carry forward the testimony, no matter what opposition there might be. To M'Ward's mind it must have seemed providential that such an instrument was ready to his hand. The conviction grew on him that Cameron, whatever his original motives in coming to Holland, must be sent back to Scotland invested with the authority to undertake the task to which, M'Ward was persuaded, God had called him.

So it was that, when the full scale of events in Scotland had become evident, M'Ward said to Cameron, 'Richard, the public standard of the gospel is fallen in Scotland; and if I know anything of the mind of the Lord, you are called to undergo your trials before us, and go home and lift the fallen standard, and display it publicly before the world.' He added: 'But before you put your hand to it, you shall go to as many of the field-ministers as you can find, and give them your hearty invitation to go with you; and if they will not go, go you alone, and the Lord will go with you.'

The 'trials' to which M'Ward referred were those to test his suitability for ordination and, as M'Ward well knew, it was only as an ordained minister that Cameron could carry the authority needed for the task before him. M'Ward was fully aware too — as was John Brown, with whom he had shared his thoughts — that what he had in mind for Cameron ran counter to the traditional practice of the church. In the *Form of Church Government* adopted by the Westminster Assembly in 1645, it was clearly laid down that 'It is agreeable to the Word, and very expedient, that such as are to be ordained ministers be designed to some particular church, or other ministerial charge.' By contrast, M'Ward and Brown were proposing to ordain Cameron to a ministry wherever his lot might be cast. This practice of indefinite ordination, as it was known, had been frowned on in the church, and M'Ward and Brown knew that their action would attract strong criticism. But they were aware too that the *Form of Church Government* had laid down that 'In extraordinary cases, something extraordinary may be done.' This, then, was the warrant on which M'Ward and Brown proceeded.

The 'trials', preliminary to ordination, were largely similar to those that Cameron had undergone for his licensing to preach. Though, as before, the requirements would no doubt have been modified to suit the nature of the case, Cameron would certainly have had to satisfy the ministers on his qualifications for the very special mission on which he was being sent. That done, the way was clear for his ordination.

It has generally been assumed that Cameron was ordained on his own, but this may not have been the case. Thomas Hog, a young probationer who, like Cameron, had got into trouble with the older ministers, had gone over to Holland around March 1679 with a strong recommendation from John Dickson in favour of his ordination.[3] 'If', Dickson wrote to M'Ward, 'you and your other brother would fall upon a way of ordaining him, it is much desired by friends here. He is a young man of no small worth for principles, piety, parts and prudence.' M'Ward and Brown appear to have satisfied themselves as to Hog's credentials for the ministry, and they prepared to ordain both him and Cameron. It is possible that the ordinations took place separately, but it is impossible to be certain of this.[4]

Cameron's ordination duly took place in the Scottish Church in Rotterdam, probably in late July or early August 1679. It was a memorable and moving occasion. M'Ward and Brown were joined for the ordination service by a Dutch minister, Jacob Koelman, of Sluiss in Flanders, so making up the quorum of three required by the law of the church. The procedure followed the traditional practice of imposition of hands, with the officiating ministers laying their hands on the head of the candidate for ordination in token of his investment in the office of the ministry.

It was precisely at this point in the service that a most striking event took place. As he and the others laid their hands on Cameron's head, M'Ward had a sudden vision of the future. So intense and vivid was it that he lost all sense of time and place. No longer was he in the Scottish Church in Rotterdam on that summer day in 1679, but on an Ayrshire moorland on a day in July 1680. Just as suddenly, the scene shifted to the

High Street of Edinburgh, a few days later, where one sight above all others fixed itself on his attention. As the vision faded, and consciousness of his surroundings returned, M'Ward, alone of the three, kept his hands firmly placed on Cameron's head. Then, turning to those assembled, he called out: 'Behold, all ye beholders, here is the head of a faithful minister and servant of Jesus Christ, who shall lose the same for his master's interest, and it shall be set up before sun and moon, in the public view of the world.' M'Ward then prayed with more than usual emotion and fervency, and so ended one of the most remarkable ordination services in the history of the Church of Scotland.

News of the ordination of Cameron and Hog was swiftly carried back to Scotland, where it caused a predictable outburst of indignation among the older nonconforming ministers. John Carstairs, one of the most senior among them, wrote bitterly to M'Ward on 20 August: 'I somewhat wonder you have there ordained those two young men — not so very acceptable, to say no more, to the Church of Scotland. I fear it offends many; nor do I see, especially at this time, how it can be so well justified. Do you think that there is no ministerial church amongst the nonconforming ministers in Scotland to ordain whom they think fit to be ordained? And is it suitable to that Christian correspondence and deference that the churches of Christ ought to have with and to one another that a few ministers of the church in Holland should ordain ministers for the Church of Scotland without their desire, consent, allowance or knowledge?'

Carstairs' view was certainly typical of many of the older and more influential of the ministers, and his letter clearly reflected their resentment at what they saw as a usurpation of their ministerial functions by M'Ward and Brown. It also gave an indication of the sort of reception Cameron could expect on his return to Scotland. A further hint of the welcome that awaited him was given in a letter from John Dickson to M'Ward on 16 July: 'As for Mr Cameron, the prejudice against him is screwed up so high that no vindication will allay the feverish spirits of some persons who are maddened against him.'

16.
Return to Scotland

There can be no doubt that Cameron faced his return to Scotland with a very keen sense of a divinely appointed mission. It would indeed be surprising had he not done so, given the particularly solemn circumstances in which he had been ordained. It would, however, be a mistake to think that Cameron entered on the work in Scotland with little regard for the consequences, either for himself or others. The evidence shows clearly that he was fully conscious of the dangers of resuming field-preaching at a time of intense and bitter persecution. Not only so, but he was also keenly aware of the new responsibilities which devolved on him as an ordained minister of the Church of Scotland. That meant, among other things, maintaining the unity of the church against schism and division. As a true son of the Scottish Reformation, Cameron had an instinctive horror of separatism. That may seem paradoxical in view of his subsequent actions, but the evidence clearly suggests that Cameron was keenly aware of the duty of maintaining communion with his fellow-ministers and not disrupting the visible unity of the church.

But there were other factors too. Like his older contemporary, Donald Cargill, with whom he was to become closely associated, Cameron cherished the highest regard for the work and office of the ministry. The minister was the instrument through whom God was pleased to declare his mind and purpose to men. He was to be a leader of the people in the ways of God, and a watchman for their souls. He was to speak with God's authority. It was through his conduct, as he moved among them, that unbelievers gained an impression of the ways of God, and were either solemnized or hardened as a result. And it was equally through the minister's example that the people of God were edified and built up in the faith, or else weakened and caused to stumble.

The basic difficulty facing Cameron was how to reconcile the claims of ministerial fellowship with his responsibilities to the people. In an ideal situation, of course, this would not have been a difficulty. But the situation to which Cameron was returning was far from ideal. The tensions of that situation are well brought out in a list of queries he addressed to M'Ward before leaving Holland. Should he, he enquired, agree to any private dialogue with the compromising ministers? What was he to do if he was invited to preach with them, or to join with them in any of their meetings? 'For', he noted, 'these two would be guarded against … giving any seeming ground of being called separatist, and giving offence, on the other hand, to any of our few most strict and zealous friends who have, alas, got great ground of offence from them.' 'As also', he went on, 'these two would be looked unto … the giving of any advantage to our contrary party of ministers on the one hand, and, on the other hand, stumbling these that are halting betwixt two.' Cameron also sought guidance on the all-important subject of field-preaching. In particular, he wondered 'if I may appear active for a field-meeting where there is the least willingness remaining amongst the people, or if I should put it wholly in the people's will, now when their hazard will be greater than before'.

While M'Ward's answer to these queries is not on record, they at least show that Cameron did not enter on the work in

Scotland without calculation of the cost, and in his readiness to submit to guidance we see clear evidence that he was acutely conscious of the weighty responsibilities which lay before him.

Cameron appears to have stayed on in Holland for some weeks after his ordination, perhaps because of difficulty in finding a suitable ship bound for home, but he eventually left Rotterdam in late August or early September.[1] It is likely that he was accompanied by Hog, who is known to have returned to Scotland at about this time. Disembarking at Newcastle, Cameron wrote a coded letter to M'Ward telling of his safe arrival, while Hog made his way northwards to Glasgow. Hog was to remain there, preaching privately, for a further two years before returning once again to Holland, and he took no further active part in the course of events in Scotland.

On leaving Newcastle, Cameron made his way towards the western borders, to his favourite haunts in Nithsdale and Annandale, where he had enjoyed so much success the previous year. News of his coming had preceded him and attempts had once again been made to prejudice the local people against him. These had clearly been unavailing for, as he later reported to M'Ward, 'I was received with more affection and joy than ever before.'

Cameron's motive in going to these parts was not, initially at least, to start field-preaching, for M'Ward had strictly enjoined him to take the advice of the most faithful field-preachers before embarking on any work on his own. His visit to the south-west was therefore basically in the nature of a reconnaissance, aimed at judging the situation after five months' absence from Scotland and ascertaining the views of some whom he had come to trust. What he found gave him cause for moderate satisfaction: the people had, it is true, been cowed into submission by the severity of the persecution after Bothwell — indeed, one of the notorious circuit courts was sitting at Dumfries at that very time — but they had by no means lost their desire for the preaching of the Word. A similar desire manifested itself as Cameron made his way northwards through Clydesdale towards Edinburgh. When he arrived at Tinto Hill — a renowned preaching-spot in earlier days — the local people urged him to wait among them, and to preach in the fields.

Cameron, however, was firm in his resolve. Much as it must have grieved him to refuse, he had given his word to M'Ward that he would not resume field-preaching until he had consulted the older field-preachers, and this he was determined to do. Already, however, he could not have cherished a great deal of hope; he had learned when at Tinto Hill that John Dickson, one of the most indefatigable of the field-preachers in earlier days, had been there only three weeks earlier but had refused to preach in the fields.

When he eventually reached Edinburgh, Cameron's suspicions were only too fully confirmed. Of all the field-preachers formerly active, Cameron was able to find only two. One was Dickson himself; the other was Thomas Hog of Kiltearn, in Ross-shire, who had been imprisoned for some two years on the Bass Rock and had recently been released under the terms of the indemnity granted after Bothwell. Dickson was a close friend and frequent correspondent of M'Ward, and Hog for his part had gained a reputation throughout Scotland for his fearless resistance to the episcopal order in the north and his championing of the cause of Presbyterianism. He had also given much encouragement to John Welwood in the latter's visits to the north and had been a close friend of the Collace sisters who, as we saw in an earlier chapter, had links with Falkland and, quite possibly, with the Cameron family.

However, if Cameron had expected support from either of these sources, he was doomed to disappointment. Both men made clear to him that, in their view, field-preaching had become too dangerous and should not be contemplated. They pointed to the greatly increased severity of the persecution, and the risks to which Cameron would be exposing his hearers. They stressed that the resumption of field-preaching could be seen as a particular provocation at a time when the Duke of York, the King's brother, was shortly due to visit Scotland. Such action, they argued, could well occasion an even greater intensity of the persecution, and bring down the wrath of the government on the nonconforming Presbyterians as a whole.

The discussions left Cameron in a state of agonizing perplexity. He had returned from Holland with high hopes. He had been ready to heed the call of M'Ward to 'lift the fallen standard, and display it publicly before the world'. He had seen for himself the eagerness of the people for the preached Word. Yet here were two men, the most respected of the field-preachers in Scotland — two men, indeed, for whom M'Ward himself had the highest regard — advising him not to proceed. Cameron wrestled with the problem in his own mind, but could find no solution.

At length, on 30 October, he wrote to M'Ward, giving him an account of the consultations he had held and earnestly seeking his guidance. His words clearly testify to the agonized state of his mind: 'This is the greatest strait and sharpest trial I ever yet met with, for their arguments do not satisfy me; my conscience telling me that the opportunity of a testimony is not to be slighted, as also I find that by forbearing it some are stumbled, others hardened, and many take occasion to say that all the ministers are going one gate. I intend tomorrow out to the country again and to consult the people; what I may do I know not. Oh for wisdom…! I expect your writing to me as soon as possible, as also that you will write to Mr Dickson.'[2]

Cameron no doubt fulfilled his intention of going again to seek the advice of the people, though it is doubtful if he contemplated any action until he had heard from M'Ward. As

Edr 30 octr 1679

Sr

I came but ys week to ys toun else I had sooner by a line signified my sense of ye singular kindnesse you & your wife showed to me in a strange land. I cannot requite it. but thinks my self bound to wish you & yours weel. o yt need is yt of living nigh god in ye so sad a time. I'm now straitned & intends to write afterward at more lenth. my respects to your mother in law & mr gordon

I am Sr

yours much obliedged to serve you in the lord

R. C.

Sr youl doe me ye favour as to present my service to madam Besshopie & to deliver ye inclosed to our friend. be pleased to tell my other intimats as you have occasion yt I intend shortly to write to ym

Cameron's letter of thanks to his friends in Holland (see note 2, page 315)
By permission of the Keeper of the Records of Scotland

it was, he was not left long in suspense. On 11 November M'Ward replied in full, giving him the most complete guidance he could have wished.

By this time, M'Ward had heard from John Dickson of the meeting of ministers — the so-called 'General Assembly' — in Edinburgh on 16 September, which had voted in favour of accepting the Third Indulgence. M'Ward was, understandably, extremely dismayed by this event, and he used it to add force to his response to Cameron. 'Brother,' he wrote, 'you know that great Mr Brown's judgement and mine was that preaching in the fields now was the holding up of the testimony against the enemy, but I might add that since I have heard of the procedure of that new assembly, I judge that way of preaching no less necessary as a testimony against them, than against the professedly stated enemy.'

M'Ward went on to tell Cameron of accounts which had reached him of people being turned away from house-meetings lest the numbers swell above what the house could contain, and the meeting be therefore reckoned a field-meeting.

> I must tell you, my brother, I have heard of practices which I am sure that great field-preacher, the Prince and Saviour, will never approve, that when some had travelled far to hear sermon, and the room being full ere they came, so that there was no place for them, after all their wandering they were forced to return. For my own part, I had rather have obtained the mercy of dying for preaching in the fields, than have so offended one of these little ones. Alas, alas that the people of God should in that matter particularly see us walk as men, and not rather as those who so preach and persuade the things pertaining to the kingdom of God as not regarding our own lives; yea, as rejoicing to be offered upon the

> sacrifice and service of their faith. But, brother, because you have spoken with those great men, Mr Hog and Mr Dickson, that I may not seem to rush you into a contradiction to their advice for the present, which I should account rashness in me, I shall offer you my opinion in the case; and I durst not do otherwise, be the consequence what it might.

M'Ward then went on to give Cameron a series of detailed instructions. These showed not only considerable forethought, but a keen appreciation of the sensitivities which were particularly troubling the younger man at this time. These were, of course, known to M'Ward from his earlier discussions with Cameron in Holland, and M'Ward made full use of his knowledge to counsel his young friend as freely and affectionately as he could. M'Ward's advice was important, and it is worth quoting at some length, since there is every evidence that Cameron acted upon it when preparing for what was to be the decisive and culminating period of his life's work.

> First [advised M'Ward], wherever you come, show all readiness and cheerfulness among the people to preach in the fields upon a call to it, nay the necessity that is now upon you, not to decline it in point of testimony. Secondly, when you have thus appeared ready and willing, to prevent their stumbling I would have yourself and some of the more judicious in the bounds where you are called to preach, set some time apart seriously to seek the Lord for light and leading how to appear with most advantage to his work. Then thirdly, after serious seeking of God, I would have you acquaint your friends that you are to preach at such a place and house; if any house will thereabout be willing to receive you, and able

to contain such as come, then preach in the house; but if not, then look on yourself as called of God to imitate him who gave you the commission, by preaching in the fields, yea, and as called by that deed to witness against that stated enemy to the work of God, and those assemblers.

M'Ward went on:

If people should resolve to come from so many airts [i.e. directions] to hear, and this were evident to you by such as called you, I could never scruple to appoint any place in the fields where these judicious persons thought it most convenient; yea, I would do it, and bless him that he hath put it upon the hearts of the people to come and own him in the face of so much hazard from a fierce and furious enemy. As this would stop the mouths of such as are ready to reproach, as if you affected the fields in opposition to a house that you might be reputed singular, so it would prevent the people's stumbling, yea, endear you to them, and, as I am persuaded, Christ will look upon it as your testimony to him, so you shall have peace, peace, sweet peace, yea, peace swelling over at its banks arising to the height of joy unspeakable and glorious in your own soul amidst the worst of what can befall you from the stated enemy and these assemblers...

Dear brother, live near God; let him be your all; make him so by believing, and he shall be so to you; he shall never disappoint you, but by doing unto you above all you can ask or think. In the meantime, be busy instructing and teaching from house to house, and then I hope the success shall be such as will quickly determine the question, and force you to the fields.

Cameron could not fail to be moved by this fervent and stirring appeal. M'Ward's words found a strong echo in his own conscience, and helped to resolve his remaining doubts. His way was now clear. He must now offer himself to the people of God in Scotland as their minister; as one who, now that he was ordained, carried the full authority of the ministerial office; as one who would stand for faithfulness to the Reformation standards and Covenants in the face of all compromise, opposition or persecution.

Cameron well knew that such a testimony would not carry universal appeal. Adherence to it would involve difficulty and danger. For his hearers, it would mean exposure to the full fury of the law. But he had been given his commission; and he believed that, as it was his duty to preach, so it was the duty of others to hear. And he believed too that his offer of himself would discriminate between those who were prepared to make that sacrifice and those who were not.

But there was an essential prerequisite, as M'Ward indeed had emphasized: he must first of all have the call of the people. Even as an unordained preacher, Cameron had never preached without an invitation from the people. As a committed Presbyterian, he well knew that it was that call alone which validated his ministry, and gave him the full authority to preach. That was the case in the present unsettled condition of the church, just as much as it had been in her more settled days. Indeed, at a time when his hearers would be exposed to particular danger and hazard, the need to secure that call was all the more compelling.

Cameron appears to have been in Edinburgh at the time M'Ward's letter reached him. His reaction to it was decisive. At the earliest opportunity he returned to the south-west, to the area around Dumfries, where he knew that the firmest support awaited him. It was there, if anywhere, that he could expect to put M'Ward's advice into action.

17. Field-preaching resumed

Cameron's hopes were not disappointed. On his earlier visit to Nithsdale, just after his return from Holland, he had been welcomed warmly, but had encountered some reluctance on the part of the people to resume field-meetings. Now there was no such problem. It may be that the intensity of the persecution in the south-west had to some extent subsided, and the authorities' attention was taken up at this time with the imminent arrival of the Duke of York, the king's brother, who was expected in Edinburgh in mid-November. The news of Cameron's vain efforts to interest the older ministers had also, no doubt, reached the people, and had aroused their sympathies in his favour. At all events, Cameron found, when he consulted the people as M'Ward had counselled, that not only was there a strong enthusiasm for him to minister among them, but evidence of support on such a scale as would be satisfied only by his preaching in the fields.

Cameron needed no further encouragement. On the following Lord's Day he convened a meeting in the fields near Glencea, some six miles north of Dumfries, and just a mile from the mansion occupied by Sir Robert Dalzell, who was the local Member of Parliament and a noted agent of repression on behalf of the government.[1] The results appear to have surpassed even his expectations. Some three thousand people assembled from all parts of the surrounding countryside, and the evidence of their support was unmistakable. For Cameron, it was the vindication he had been seeking. Here, if not from his fellow-ministers, then at least from the people of God in Scotland, was the evidence of God's seal of approval on his mission. And having been once convinced of that fact, he was not to look back.

Cameron could no doubt have continued preaching in Nithsdale for considerably longer. As it was, however, he was anxious to test opinion in other parts of the country, and he was also concerned not to expose his hearers in one place to unnecessary danger. When therefore his day's preaching was over, he made his way back into Clydesdale, where he had earlier found evidence of popular support in his favour. The results here were even more encouraging: once again he was welcomed with great enthusiasm on the part of the people, and on the following Lord's Day at Tinto Hill he preached to an audience of between three and four thousand.[2] The next week found him at Crawfordjohn, another centre of popular support in Clydesdale, where he stayed for some time with loyal sympathizers.[3]

Inevitably, reports of Cameron's preaching soon began to circulate widely through central and southern Scotland. As might have been expected, reactions were varied. On the part of some, the news that a witness had once again been raised to the persecuted gospel was greeted with profound thanksgiving to God. But others deeply and bitterly resented Cameron's mission. By none was he more strenuously opposed than by the moderate Presbyterians. They remembered how he had been a cause of division before Bothwell, and they feared that he would once again stir up the fires of division at a time when, they believed, it was essential to preserve unity and to avoid aggravating the authorities.

Cameron was accused of rashness and impetuosity, of thrusting himself forward without regard for the consequences and of exposing his hearers to needless difficulty and danger. These attacks were, in their own way, a reflection of the decline that had taken place in the church's witness since Bothwell Bridge, and an evidence of the corrosive effect of compromise. Cameron, needless to say, was untroubled by them, and he pressed on with his ministry regardless. Taking full advantage of an unusually mild, settled winter,[4] he yielded himself unstintingly to the invitations he received from the people, and preached with increasing frequency both in houses and in the fields. On 8 December he was able to write, in a coded letter to his friend Andrew Russell in Rotterdam, 'I have got a far better market than was expected when I came from you; our wares vend well, both in open markets and in houses through the country.'

Not surprisingly, Cameron's activities had by this time come to the attention of the government. For some time, however, he continued to enjoy remarkable freedom from harassment — a state of affairs which may have been, in part at least, the result of the authorities' preoccupation with the visit of the Duke of York. Indeed, while his activities were widely known, and debated, in Edinburgh, no plan of action appears to have been decided against him by the Privy Council.

The episcopal clergy, understandably enough, found such apparent indifference hard to tolerate. Bishop Paterson of Edinburgh, writing on 1 January 1680 to the Duke of Lauderdale, noted with some asperity: 'Great promises were made to His Royal Highness for bringing in Cameron to justice, but as yet no performance.' He added, with sound insight: 'If the feat were done, it is easy to see that the indulged Presbyterian party and even Welsh, etc. should be more obliged thereby, than the king or the church.' Events were to prove Paterson a true prophet.

While remaining intent on his preaching activity, Cameron was by no means forgetful of the concerns of his immediate family. His father Allan still languished in prison, steadfastly refusing to pay the fine of 100 merks which would have purchased his freedom. His mother, now very frail, and his brother Andrew were at home in Edinburgh. It is likely that Cameron had made frequent visits to them since his return; at least, the evidence suggests that he was in Edinburgh fairly often during this time, trying unsuccessfully to gain some support from his fellow-ministers.

Andrew, the youngest of the family, had recently finished his preliminary training as a 'writer', or lawyer, and his father, fearing the corruptions of the Scottish universities, was anxious to send him to complete his education in Holland.[5] From the available evidence, Allan Cameron had already been in touch with Robert M'Ward when Richard had gone over to Rotterdam the previous summer. He now took the opportunity to renew the correspondence in the hope that M'Ward would be able to help find a place for Andrew at one of the Dutch universities. His letter, dated 24 February 1680, also gave M'Ward some revealing insights into his own family situation and into the circumstances in which his son Richard was now placed.

One point which is clear from Allan Cameron's letter is that he shared the strong principles of his eldest son. He had, he explained, refused to pay the fine because to do so would have been an acknowledgement of the authorities' right to impose it, and an admission of a guilt which he did not accept. He had also, he told M'Ward, refused to hear any minister who had accepted the Indulgence, or had petitioned for licence from the Privy Council. This had brought him much reproach, but he was determined to maintain a clear conscience.

Allan Cameron went on to commend to M'Ward his son Andrew, whom he was sending over 'for breeding at your colleges'. Andrew had, he noted, 'been bred a writer here', but, he added significantly, he was 'now being looked upon with an evil eye, because of his relations'. The most notorious of these relations was, of course, his brother Richard, of whom his father went on to speak. Allan Cameron's words may at first sight seem harsh, but they clearly carry all the love and longing of a father's heart:

> Sir [he wrote], my poor foolish ignorant son, as he is reproached by enemies for going to the fields at this time, so he is little encouraged by the best of friends, because they say he thereby exceedingly endangers the people and himself also. That young man went not to the fields after he came home till he had the earnest call of the Lord's people thereto, who declared they did very well consider the hazard, and that they would own none for their lawful ministers but such as were as clear and ready to avouch Christ Jesus and his standard by preaching in the fields as well as in houses. The Lord has helped his poor people and him hitherto, and hid them in being about their duty out of season and in season; and if ministers be commanded to preach, surely people are commanded and warranted to hear.

Allan Cameron went on, in words which showed the depth of his feelings for his son: 'He has great need of your prayers, for his life is in jeopardy every day, and there is a multitude waiting for his halting. Blessed be our merciful Lord, his mother and I both have desired freely to offer him up to his Lord and Master, in whatsoever service he has for him.' He ended:

> This is a day of great darkness and wrath from the Almighty upon this church and land, and they are like to be few that shall hold their feet; therefore I humbly and earnestly beg the help of your prayers, with any others

> of the Lord's servants and people that are with you, that I and my poor family may find grace, and be helped of God in this time of so great need.

The strength which Richard Cameron derived from his immediate family has perhaps not been given the attention it should. The influence of godly parents has often been crucial to the witness of a man of God. Allan Cameron's letter — unfortunately the only one from his pen which has survived — shows that in Richard Cameron's case that influence was both decisive and strong.

Cameron had in the meantime also been continuing his own correspondence with M'Ward. While little of this has survived, it is fairly clear from the sequel that M'Ward had started to urge him, with increasing insistence, that the time to make a more formal public testimony had now come. M'Ward could not forget that in his parting commission to Cameron he had told him 'to lift the fallen standard, and display it publicly before the world'. While he welcomed the news of Cameron's preaching, M'Ward made it plain that he did not regard this commission as being fulfilled until the cause which Cameron represented had been carried to the very heart and centre of public affairs in Scotland. M'Ward saw this being done in two ways: first, by convening public meetings, or fasts, in which the sins of the land would be plainly and unambiguously declared; and second, by making public declarations affirming Reformed and Presbyterian principles in the face of the apostasy and tyranny of the church and nation.

That was very much Cameron's view too. Indeed, in a postscript to his letter of 30 October quoted in the previous chapter, he had expressed his regret that the terms of a testimony had not been drawn up before he left Holland, and that the causes for calling a fast had not been stated. However, while he was prepared to undertake the preaching ministry unsupported, he was less willing at this stage to take on the responsibility which a formal public testimony would entail. It seemed to him that, if such a testimony were to carry authority, it should be seen as the collective work of the church and not merely that of one individual.

And that, of course, was the problem: there was no one with whom Cameron could share the effort, and he naturally felt that since he had been unable to persuade any of his fellow-ministers to join him in preaching, he was even less likely to induce them to join him in a public testimony. For a time, therefore, he continued to demur at M'Ward's promptings, notwithstanding his deep respect for the older man's judgement. M'Ward, for his part, appears to have grown increasingly restive at Cameron's attitude, and he was soon to give expression to his feelings in forthright terms.

What finally broke M'Ward's patience was the news which reached him, apparently early in 1680, of the extravagant reception given to the Duke of York in Scotland. To him, this seemed the final evidence of the degeneracy of his countrymen, and he reacted to it with shocked disbelief. That such a welcome should have been accorded a known Roman Catholic, and one whose claims to the throne had been rejected by the English House of Commons, was, in M'Ward's view, profoundly disgraceful. Nothing now could be added to the catalogue of Scotland's miseries, or to the judgements which awaited her at God's hand.

In a letter to Cameron, probably written in January 1680, M'Ward poured out his indignation at the news, and urged the younger man to action in the strongest terms:

> A new necessity is laid upon me to write this line unto you, by the account I have had of the solemnity of that reception decreed for the Duke of York in Scotland. Brother, I cannot hide it from you that I would have been

> less troubled if I had heard that he had marched down to Scotland with an army, made up of his English, French and Irish papists, than to have heard that by this very deed we have declared our abominable baseness in the sight of God, angels and men. Alas, whither have we not caused our shame to go! Oh, where is the spirit of our noble ancestors, zealous for the Lord God of hosts? Alas, where are our Knoxes, who said that one mass was more fearful to him, than if ten thousand armed enemies were landed in any part of the nation, to suppress the whole religion? All that made us famous and renowned among the nations was our love and loyalty to Jesus Christ, our former faithfulness and fixedness in his cause, our fervour in opposing kings when they did show favour to the popish party; that was that rich and radiant diadem which made us a renown among all the churches of Christ; but now, by this base, this abominable deed in the sight of all the nations, that beautiful crown is fallen from our head... We seem to have forgotten we have souls, and are so much beasts, as, with the faces of men, we can bow our neck to the yoke of bondage, and glory in being so base.

M'Ward went on to deplore the effect that the news would have on the friends of the Protestant faith in England, Holland and elsewhere, and the low opinion it would breed of Scotland among them:

> Will they look upon us as the successors of those who so contended for truth against Queen Mary of unhappy memory? Will they look upon us as the posterity of those who ventured the whole interest of the nation for the defence of true religion and just liberty? It is easy for you, dear brother, to judge what they must and will say

of us. It may be they will find names for it; but, I profess, I can find none expressive of its nature.

M'Ward now came to the point and purpose of his letter:

> Now, brother, if you would know what I intend by all this, I shall shortly tell you. You see how matters stand, and how the whole nation is ready to be looked upon as a company of poor, base, degenerate souls, having neither regard to religion nor any respect to the liberty of the nation; but as a miserable company who by this foolish frolic have declared to the world how easy it is for this declared enemy to Jesus Christ and his interest, the limb and instrument of Antichrist, to command their service and assistance... And therefore, to prevent this, I would have you forthwith, without any further demur, procrastination or delay, speak to some of your more zealous and serious brethren, and awaken them unto the due and deep consideration of these things; that they and you may excite and stir up the people to give such a present signification of their hatred at, and abhorrence of this deed, as may let the world hear that there are persons in that land of that love and loyalty to Christ, and of that regard to liberty, as they dare adventure at all disadvantages, yea, in the sight of death.

M'Ward did not hesitate to say exactly what he wanted of Cameron:

> There is something on your part now presently called for as indispensable duty... I would have you call all the godly, in all the several corners of the nation, to keep a day of solemn public humiliation, that an idolater was with so much solemnity and ceremony welcomed, in

> such a capacity as the presumptive heir to the Crown, into a land engaged, under the penalty of incurring the displeasure of God Almighty, to extirpate these abominations ... and as second branch of the cause of this fast, the grievous sin not calling to public mourning sooner ... but leaving you to sub-divide and branch out the causes of this public humiliation, according as you see reason, both from what is already suggested, and what will certainly occur to yourself, when you set yourself seriously before the Lord, to consider it.

M'Ward was, of course, well aware of the difficulties facing Cameron, and the opposition he was likely to encounter, not only from outside the church but from within. In the final section of his letter he strove to encourage him with words of strong reassurance:

> You know well, brother, that it would make many, who now sink into the depth of sorrow, weep for joy, to see you, as incensed with the true zeal of God, call to weeping and mourning for the madness of this mirth... You know beside, how this would contribute for the keeping up, or rather recovering the credit and necessary repute of the ministry, brought under contempt by our course and carriage... Up, dear brother, rise and be doing; call in your brethren to this weeping, this wrestling, this witnessing work; stir up yourself and others to a seriousness in this duty... So carry, so acquit yourself in this juncture, as it may be evident you can neither be dared nor daunted into forbearance of a duty of so much concernment to the cause, by the frowning or fear of this furious enemy, nor be demurred by your reluctant brethren... Let not the want of the company, or concurrence of such who have not the spirit of the day,

> and whose hearts are hid from understanding present duty, make you shrink, or shun so eminent an appearance for your God. Up and be doing; go forward, as not fearing what flesh can do unto you... Your own God shall be with you, and hold your hand in the undertaking, and make your single and serious essayings of this solemn duty successful beyond expectation, yea, to admiration... Grace in its plenty and power will be sufficient for the work, and make it appear that while you are in it, and about it, you are not alone; grace, great grace, from the God of all grace, be with you.[6]

It would have been difficult for Cameron to remain unmoved by this letter, and it was to prove extremely influential in his future work. However, for the moment he might well have been excused had he given way to feelings of frustration. He was being pressed into action by M'Ward — action which he knew was his duty, but which he felt unable to undertake without the support of his brethren in the ministry, none of whom had shown any inclination to help him. It was, for him, a time of considerable trial and perplexity.

However, relief was finally at hand, and it would come, not from within Scotland, but from outside it. In a postscript to his letter in the previous November, M'Ward had noted: 'Mr Cargill went hence today, pressed in spirit to go home to preach in the fields.' As events were to show, these words were to carry profound significance for Cameron in the following months.

Donald Cargill, whose life from now on was to be closely linked with that of Cameron, was the son of a local notary from Perthshire, and had been ordained to the Barony Church, Glasgow, in 1655. After seven years of ministry there he had been ejected by order of the Privy Council, and banished to the north of the Tay. His banishment was later revoked in the hope that he could be brought to conform, but he refused to accept the Indulgences offered by the government, and instead embarked on an active career of field-preaching, mainly in and around Glasgow. Following the battle of Bothwell Bridge, at which he was wounded, he sought refuge for a time in Rotterdam with M'Ward and Brown.

Alone among the older ministers, Cargill had supported Cameron's stand on the Indulgence, and indeed had preached with him on several occasions before Bothwell Bridge. It is possible that the two men had renewed their acquaintance during Cameron's stay in Holland, though there is no certain evidence of this. What is clear is that a strong bond of affection had developed between them, and that events were destined to cement this still further. Cargill admired the firmness and resolution of his younger friend, and his staunch adherence to Reformation principles; while Cameron, for his part, respected Cargill's faithfulness and diligence and his mature judgement on the controversial issues of the time. The friendship thus forged, between men of widely differing temperaments, was to usher in one of the most remarkable periods in the life of the persecuted church and to inspire the faith of many in the difficult and dark days ahead.

M'Ward's reference to Cargill's departure from Rotterdam, in his letter to Cameron the previous November, apparently did not mean that Cargill was returning to Scotland there and then; the evidence rather suggests that he did not return until around February 1680, having possibly spent some time in England on the way. Cameron, no doubt, awaited his arrival with some impatience. Knowing what he did of Cargill, he would have cherished high expectations that here at last was one whom he could trust to support him. And, as events were to show, he was not to be disappointed.

18.
Powerful preacher and faithful friend

While he awaited Cargill's return, Cameron continued with his preaching activity in the south-west of Scotland. His reputation had by now spread widely, and accounts of the power of his preaching multiplied.

Even some of the moderate Presbyterians, who were his bitterest critics, were silenced. One of them, Henry Erskine, who had himself suffered for his nonconformity, later confided to a friend that he had contemplated preaching against Cameron, but had been warned in the night by an audible voice: 'Beware thou call not Cameron's preaching vain.'[1]

It was also recounted how the lairds of Logan and Horsecleugh, Cameron's erstwhile opponents at Cumnock, had been so impressed by the evident tokens of divine power accompanying his ministry that they sought his forgiveness for their opposition to him. Cameron dealt with them faithfully. He forgave them with all his heart, he said, for the wrongs they had done him personally, but was persuaded that they would be punished for the wrong they had done to the cause and interest of Christ. Logan's family, he predicted, would be childless, while Horsecleugh would lose his property by fire.[2] Both predictions, it was recorded some fifty years later, had come to pass in the memory of many then living.

Patrick Walker records another incident from around this time which made a profound impression. Cameron and his hearers were gathered in a house, the weather at the time being unsuitable for assembling out of doors. His theme was the everlasting destiny of the righteous and the wicked, in which he sought to bring home to his hearers the solemnity of their situation, and to dispel the illusion that they could seek any middle course.

Among his hearers was Andrew Dalziel, a wild-fowler, who had been detained indoors by the weather and was present as an onlooker. Dalziel was known in the neighbourhood for his loose living, and Cameron's searching preaching aroused his indignation. At last he could restrain himself no longer. 'Sir,' he called out derisively, 'we neither know you nor your God.'

What followed is best told in Walker's own words: 'Mr Cameron, musing a little, said: "You, and all that do not know my God in his mercy, shall know him in his judgement, which shall be sudden and surprising in a few days upon you, which shall make you a terror to yourself, and all that shall be witness to your death; and I, as a sent servant of Jesus Christ, whose commission I bear, and whose badge or blaze is upon my breast, give you warning, and leave you to the justice of God."'

It is not difficult to imagine the solemnizing effects of these words on his audience — an effect which was heightened beyond measure some days later by the news of Dalziel's sudden death. Not surprisingly, Walker records: 'The report of these strange things occasioned calls to come to him for dispensing of public gospel ordinances, from all corners in the south and west of Scotland.'

There can indeed be no doubt that, for many who heard him, Cameron's preaching now carried a note of authority they had encountered in no other preacher. Cameron himself was increasingly conscious of a sense of God's presence with him, which not only invested his words with a particular power, but gave him an unusual insight into the will and purpose of God. As a result, he felt strengthened and equipped in a distinctive way for the work before him. Enemies might oppose, and professed friends disappoint him, but he was never to lose the assurance that his course of action was sanctioned by the Lord himself. And it was that assurance which was to carry him forward through the final, crucial stage of his life and ministry.

But however conscious he was of the Lord's presence, Cameron was never indifferent to the claims of human society. Companionable by nature, he constantly prized the fellowship of like-minded Christians. This had been clearly evident in earlier phases of his life and, now that he was an ordained minister, he did not allow the claims of Christian fellowship to go by default. His frequent preaching in the south-west had brought him into contact with many whose company he cherished, and who were a constant source of support and strength to him.

The area in north Galloway known as the Glenkens held a particular place in his affections. One of the most influential families here were the Gordons — Alexander Gordon and his wife Janet and their young family, of Earlston House, near New Galloway. The Gordons of Earlston had long been distinguished for their support of the Reformed faith, and one of their ancestors had been credited with bringing the Reformed teachings to Galloway even before the advent of the Reformation itself.[3]

Alexander Gordon's father William and his grandfather, another Alexander, had both been friends and correspondents of Samuel Rutherford. When William Gordon had heard, the previous summer, of the Presbyterians being in arms at Bothwell Bridge, he had promptly set out to join them, but being an old man, and able to travel only slowly, he had not arrived on the scene until the action was over. Government troops, scouring the roads and lanes for stragglers, came upon him as he travelled and, after the briefest of questionings, shot him without mercy. His son Alexander, who was involved in the action, very narrowly escaped a similar fate and was compelled to go into hiding for his own safety. On 19 February 1680 the High Court in Edinburgh condemned him to death in his absence and declared his lands and estates forfeit, though his wife and family were apparently allowed to remain on at Earlston.

Janet Gordon — known commonly as Lady Earlston the younger — was a sister of Robert Hamilton, and it seems that Cameron had been acquainted with her in earlier days.[4] Her plight now stirred him to sympathy, and soon after the sentence was passed on her husband he wrote to her in affectionate terms, recalling his past fellowship with them both and exhorting her to steadfastness in the face of trial.

> I am bound while I live [he wrote] to remember with thanksgiving the Lord's condescendence and kindness to me in Earlston, where I am sure we had some good days, not to be forgotten. I am more and more refreshed with my thoughts of the Laird [i.e. her husband] and of what God hath done and is doing to him. I am hopeful that the Lord shall carry him and you through your tribulations, which may be great for a little time. And now you may be sure that your steps shall be more observed than any forfeited family in Galloway; therefore I hope you will not be high-minded, but fear.

Cameron went on to impart some rich words of comfort:

> Happy is the man that feareth the Lord always; you should also trust in him at all times, for in the Lord Jehovah there is everlasting strength. There is enough in

> him for bearing your charges. You have now a notable opportunity of giving proof of your love to our sweetest Lord Jesus, who hath done so much for us. Praise, praise to him that hath pitched upon you to witness for him, and that he is still keeping possession of that family of which you are now a mother, and that the honour thereof is screwed up to so high a pitch in your time. This is the Lord's doing; his ways and thoughts are not as our ways and thoughts.

He concluded: 'I desire to remember your son and daughter. I entreat that your Ladyship and sister may remember me; you know what need there is for praying for one another. The Lord be with you all.'[5]

Shortly afterwards, on 22 March 1680, Cameron addressed a letter to Alexander Gordon himself. In it, he speaks of plans he currently had in hand, and of his desire to meet his friend to discuss them. He was deliberately vague about these plans, no doubt for fear of his letter being intercepted by the authorities. Enough was said, however, to show that by this time Cameron was coming to firm decisions on what his future testimony should be, and that he had fully counted the cost of these decisions for the persecuted church in Scotland, and not least for himself. Indeed, it is impossible to read this letter and not to realize that Cameron now regarded himself as a willing sacrifice — an offering ready to be laid on the altar, once the work that his Lord entrusted to him had been done.

'I was this day within five miles of Nith,' he writes, 'in order to meet with your Honour; but one is come to me from other friends who has made me turn my head to another airt [i.e. direction]; the business is of moment, of which you may after this (if the Lord will) be informed.' He goes on to mention his brother Andrew's intended departure for Holland, and that he himself will be going to Edinburgh to make arrangements for his brother's journey. While there, he writes, 'We are to have considerable things in hand,' and, he tells his friend:

> I will be content, if business will permit, and counsel sought from the Lord, that yourself were there; but if you cannot win [i.e. manage] I'll make all the haste I can to see you and friends with you…
>
> I entreat you to signify this to our friends in Dalry, Kells and Glencairn; I hope the Lord has some work for them yet, though I were gone, which will not be while my Master has work for me. Oh to be ready to be bound, yea, and to die! I dare not sit [i.e. decline] this call, whatever be the hazard. The Lord will carry on his work, mauger [i.e. despite] all opposition. The daughter of Zion shall yet arise and thresh — Micah 4:13…
>
> I hope to meet in heaven with not a few out of the house of Earlston… Oh how refreshing will it be to see in that day several who lived in the Glenkens, together with some from Balmaghie and Crossmichael. The Lord be with you all; I doubt not but you mind me in your prayers. My respects to both your ladies, sisters, not forgetting the young Laird, as sure as any I know, and my own mistress Ann. Referring other things till meeting, Sir, I bid you farewell.

Apart from other things in this letter, the final greeting is notable. Cameron was referring to the Gordons' young son William, and their infant daughter Ann. This man, who could stand his ground fearlessly against any opposition, could yet speak tenderly and affectionately of little children. This is a trait which also appears in his sermons. Cameron's work among children, in his earlier days, had clearly been close to his heart.

19.
The bond is drawn up

Although some problems remain, many of the obscurities in Cameron's letter to Gordon, quoted at the end of the last chapter, are clarified by the subsequent course of events. Indeed, the letter itself helps to put in context the actions in which Cameron was now to be engaged, and which were to dominate the remainder of his life and ministry.

It is clear that by the time the letter was written Cameron was conscious of a significant increase in support for his cause in comparison to what had previously been available to him. On no other basis, indeed, could he have felt sufficiently confident to lay plans for the future on the scale he now envisaged. The inference is that, not only had Cargill now returned and pledged his support, but that Cameron also had backing from other sources which encouraged him to press forward in a way that he would not have ventured to do on his own account. There was now the prospect of being able to act in concert with others whose contribution would make it possible for him to be seen to be acting, not merely as an individual, but as a representative of the true persecuted church of God in Scotland.

The consultations which Cameron held in Edinburgh had two main outcomes. The first was a decision, based on M'Ward's advice, to organize public fasts for the state of the country, and particularly for the Duke of York's reception in Scotland. The second decision was more far-reaching. It involved the drawing up of a bond, or covenant, pledging the signatories to mutual defence and, in effect, constituting them as a party opposed to the established order in church and state. The terms of the bond were as follows:

> We under-subscribers bind and oblige ourselves to be faithful to God, and to be true to one another, and to all others that shall join with us in adhering to the Rutherglen Testimony, and disclaiming the Hamilton Declaration, chiefly because it takes in the king's interest, which we are loosed from by reason of his perfidy and covenant-breaking both to the Most High God, and the people over whom he was set, upon the terms of his propagating the main end of the Covenants, to wit, the reformation of religion; and instead of that, usurping to himself the royal prerogative of Jesus Christ, and encroaching upon the liberties of the church, and so stating himself in opposition both to Jesus Christ himself the Mediator and the free government of his house; as also in disowning and protesting against the reception of the Duke of York, a professed Papist, and whatever else has been done in this land (which was given to the Lord) in prejudice of our Covenanted and universally sworn-to work of reformation. And although (as the Lord who searcheth the hearts knows) we be for government and governors both civil and ecclesiastic, such as the Word of God and our Covenants allow; yet by this, we disown the present magistrates who openly and avowedly are doing still what lies in them for destroying utterly our work of reformation from popery, prelacy, Erastianism [i.e. state supremacy over the church] and other heresies and errors. And by this we declare also, that we are not

> any more to own ministers indulged, and such as drive at a sinful union with them; nor are we to join any more with ministers or professors of any rank that are guilty of any of the defections of this time, until they give satisfaction proportionably to the scandal or offence they have given.

The bond was almost certainly drafted by Cameron, and it bears some unmistakable marks of his authorship.[1] For him, it marked the start of a radical new departure in his public ministry. Hitherto, generally speaking, he had concerned himself with public affairs only to the extent that these affected the ministry and testimony of the church. True, he had previously denounced the corruptions of the king and government, but this was the first time that he had lent his name to a statement directly disowning their authority. It is noteworthy that the grounds stated for doing so were specifically cited as their breach of the Covenant. There could, of course, be no doubt whatever that the king — and those under him — had violated the Covenant. Even those most opposed to Cameron would have conceded that. What was more open to question was whether their breach of Covenant constituted grounds for disowning their authority. It was precisely here that the bond touched on an issue which was to be of crucial importance for Cameron and his supporters in the weeks ahead, and indeed which was ultimately to cost him his life.

As Cameron well knew, the doctrine of a mutual compact between king and people was well established in the Scottish Reformed tradition. It had first been propounded by George Buchanan, tutor to James VI, in his book *De Jure Regni Apud Scotos*, published as early as 1579. Its most notable exponent had been Samuel Rutherford, in his *Lex Rex*, which had caused a major controversy on its publication in 1644. Later writers, such as John Brown of Wamphray in his *Apologetical*

Relation (1665), and Sir James Stewart and James Stirling in *Naphtali* (1667) and *Jus Populi Vindicatum* (1669), had developed the doctrine further and applied it to the prevailing situation in Scotland in their own day. These works, naturally enough, had angered the authorities, who saw them as a challenge to the established order of absolute government, and they had ordered the public burning of Rutherford's book and the others named above. However, it proved easier to burn the books than to answer their arguments, and despite some plausible attempts, these were never successfully refuted.

In propounding the idea of a mutual compact, the various writers had addressed the situation arising where either party failed to honour their part of the bargain. Buchanan had asserted on this point: 'There being a mutual compact between king and people, he who first recedes from what is covenanted, and doth counteract what he hath covenanted, he looses the contract; and the bond being loosed which did hold fast the king with the people, whatever right did belong to him by virtue of that compact, he looses it, and the people are as free as before the stipulation.'[2]

The authors of *Jus Populi Vindicatum* had been equally plain: 'When the prince doth violate his compact, as to all its conditions, or as to its chief, main and most necessary condition, the subjects are *de jure* [i.e. as of right] free from subjection to him, and at liberty to make choice of another.'[3] And they had gone on to claim that, if in the ordinary course of events there was understood to be a compact between king and people, then how much more was this the case where the king had come under the specific and binding obligations of the Covenants![4]

But there were dangers here, of which Rutherford, for one, was well aware. The view that kings could be deposed because of heresy or differences in religion was a well-known Roman Catholic doctrine, and one of its leading exponents had been the Jesuit Cardinal Bellarmine. Rutherford had been careful, in *Lex Rex,* to distance himself from this view. 'Far be it from me', he wrote, 'to argue, with Bellarmine, that any prince who is spiritually leprous and turned heretical, is presently to be dethroned. Nothing can dethrone a king but such tyranny as is inconsistent with his royal office.'[5] And John Brown had drawn a distinction between disowning a king and resisting him. 'The Scots plead not', he wrote, for deposing or dethroning of kings, but only for resisting and withstanding them, when they carry a hostile mind against them ... they plead only, that in that case the people may, and are bound before God, to defend themselves when their religion is sought to be taken away, or altered.'[6]

Judged against this background, the bond to which Cameron set his name could, arguably, be seen to be going further than was justified by traditional Scottish Reformed opinion. But the difference was more apparent than real. It was certainly implicit in the bond, though it may not have been stated openly, that the grounds for disowning the king and government were precisely that tyranny which Rutherford had seen as a justification for a king's exclusion from the throne. What constituted tyranny was, of course, a matter of subjective opinion, and it was here that Cameron parted company with many of his contemporaries. The authors of *Jus Populi Vindicatum,* which Cameron appears to have taken as his particular guide, were certainly in no doubt on the matter:

> This king hath not, as he ought to have done, maintained the true religion, nor right preaching, and administration of sacraments; neither hath he, according to his power, abolished and withstood all false religions contrary to the same; neither hath he ruled us according to the will of God, but rather persecuted us for adhering to the Word of God; nor hath he ruled us by the laudable

> laws and constitutions of the realm, but hath overturned our laws and liberties, and hath framed and established iniquity by a law... Who then can blame a people standing to their own defence, when oppressed and tyrannized over by his emissaries, who hath thus violated the principal and only conditions of the compact, and is forcing them to the same excess of wickedness and perjury?[7]

Cameron was not therefore proposing anything that was basically new in Scottish Reformed thought. But it was one thing for such views to be propounded in works such as *Jus Populi Vindicatum;* it was quite another for them to become the rallying-point of a resistance movement against an established order of government. For this is basically what the bond was intended to be. The grounds for that resistance had not yet been defined in detail; that was to come later. But it was as an initial rallying-point that the bond was to serve its purpose. The time was not yet ripe for a public declaration. Cameron well knew that to proclaim such principles openly would invite certain retribution. While he would not flinch from this when the time came, he clearly saw a need at this stage to prepare the ground. The bond therefore appears to have been designed, at least in part, to test the strength of support which Cameron could expect, and to gain agreement privately for what would, in process of time, be declared publicly. As such, it was to play a vital part in paving the way for the public work which Cameron — and his co-signatories — would soon undertake.

For the rest, the bond showed clearly the influence of M'Ward, in its denunciation of the usurpation of the rights of the church, its repudiation of the reception given to the Duke of York and its opposition to those ministers who had received the Indulgence. However, in its determination not to own 'such as drive a sinful union' with those ministers, and to exact satisfaction from those 'guilty of the defections of this time', it went further than M'Ward had been prepared to go. This particular commitment was to work itself out among the ranks of Cameron's own followers before many weeks had passed.

The number of initial signatories of the bond has not been recorded, though it eventually contained twenty-seven signatures in all.[8] Surprisingly, the first signature was not that of Cameron but of Thomas Douglas, who had been a member of the 'presbytery' which met to discipline Cameron at Dunscore in 1678. Douglas, who had been at Bothwell and afterwards in Holland, had recently returned to Scotland — possibly in company with Cargill — and had now allied himself with Cameron. While in Holland he had been involved in a controversy with the adherents of Robert Hamilton, because of his acceptance of an invitation to preach in the Scots Church in Rotterdam, then pastored by Robert Fleming, who had argued against separation from the ministers who had accepted the Indulgence.[9] Douglas did, however, enjoy the favour of Robert M'Ward, who held him in some esteem, and who appears to have persuaded him to support Cameron on his return to Scotland. Given his previous experience of Douglas, the fact that Cameron was prepared to accept him — and to yield to him pride of place in signing the bond — can be seen as an evidence of Cameron's Christian charity. It was a trait which others on his side were not, in the event, prepared to share.

20.
The movement gains impetus

With the drawing up of the bond, Cameron now had a committed nucleus of support. Those who signed, at least initially, included some who had been with him in earlier days, and had supported him in his confrontations with Welsh and the older ministers. Most of them, including his brother Michael — inseparable from him as ever — were to remain with him to the end.

The bond appears to have been kept open for signatures, and a number of others were added later. It is clear, however, that several of those who closely associated themselves with Cameron, both at this time and afterwards, did not sign the bond. No doubt there were various reasons why this should be so, not all of which can now be established.

One notable name missing from the list was that of Donald Cargill. Cargill was in full sympathy with Cameron so far as a testimony through preaching was concerned, but he is known from other evidence to have felt that the issue of disowning the king's authority required more careful thought and argument than had yet been given to it. Cautious and deliberate by nature, he was clearly reluctant to commit himself publicly to a particular view until he had thought the issue through to his own satisfaction. In the meantime, as it later became plain, he was working on his own theories of how the issue should best be addressed.

As the terms of the bond made clear, the group which now formed itself around Cameron was motivated solely by considerations of defence — defence of themselves, certainly, against attack by enemies, but primarily to allow the preaching of the gospel to proceed unhindered. To enable them to provide an effective defence, several of them carried arms. For that reason, some present-day writers have likened them to a guerrilla movement, but that is to do them a fundamental injustice. The aims of the group were stated clearly by Cameron himself in an address later recalled by Archibald Alison, who was to suffer for his faith:

> My friends [he had told them], we are not to compare ourselves with Gideon's three hundred men, no, not at all; our design is to have you examined, how ye are, and what ye are; to choose two or three of the foot, and two or three of the horse, that are found fittest qualified for elders, to try your principles, to try your life and conversation, and to have you being Christians. Our number was more the last day, and we gave them free leave to go home, and only but a few handful to stay; for we design not to fall upon any party of the forces, except they be few in number and oppose us in keeping up the gospel in the fields, for I am persuaded that one meeting in the fields has been more owned and countenanced by his presence with his people than twenty house meetings, as they are now bought; and therefore make no strife among yourselves about officers, because they are but men; yea, I think there is not a man among you all meet for it; we are not meet to be a minister to you, only we are to wait till the Lord provide better; and ye that are not satisfied to stay in defence of the gospel, good-morrow to you, whatsoever ye be.[1]

Whatever else these words show, they certainly demonstrate that Cameron did not see his following as having any aggressive intent. On the contrary, he saw them as a responsible community of Christians — a Christian army, in effect — and, as such, subject to standards of both church order and military discipline. But while he looked for commitment from each man, there was no coercion. As his words showed, no one was forced to stay against his will. This was an army of volunteers, not of conscripts. And it was an army bound together by the highest of motives — the defence of the preached gospel in the fields, and the upholding of the honour of Christ in covenanted Scotland. Cameron was never to allow his men to forget these high aims, just as he was ever to keep mindful of them himself. And it was on that basis that he and they now went forward together.

It is likely that Cameron had preached on several occasions with Cargill since the latter's return, and this work was given further momentum by the arrival of Douglas. The combined efforts of three men naturally attracted more widespread attention than Cameron could have achieved on his own, and there were already signs of awakened interest in many places. Soon, the focus of the field-meetings began to move out of the relatively narrow confines of the south-west into the major heartlands of west and central Scotland.

Once this had been done, the stage was set for a move which Cameron had long contemplated — the holding of a public fast for the nation's sins, and particularly for the reception accorded to the Duke of York the previous year. Cameron was, no doubt, only too conscious of the delay on his part in following out M'Ward's instructions, but now that at last the conditions were right he lost no time in putting his plans into action. On a day in April — probably early in the month — he, Cargill and Douglas convened a public fast at Darmead, a traditional preaching-spot on the borders of Lothian and

Clydesdale.[2] It was the first such meeting since before Bothwell Bridge, and for Cameron it marked the start of a new and decisive phase in his public ministry. It would scarcely have been surprising had he ventured on the occasion with some apprehension. But the meeting was undisturbed, and Cameron and his fellow-preachers appear to have taken this as a sign that so long as they remained faithful in their callings, they could expect the Lord's protection, both of themselves and of their hearers. From that point of view, the Darmead meeting was crucial to much that followed.

Unfortunately, little of what was said at Darmead has been preserved, and what remains of Cameron's preaching is no more than fragmentary. However, enough has survived to show the general tenor of his message that day. Taking as his text Malachi 3:1, 'Behold, I will send my messenger, and he shall prepare the way before me; and the Lord, whom ye seek, shall suddenly come to his temple,' he applied the words to God's coming in judgement, to reckon with the land, and especially the church, for the unfaithfulness of ministers and people.

The specific sin which had prompted the meeting was the reception given to the Duke of York, and Cameron was unsparing in his denunciations of those responsible:

> He will punish them that with so much solemnity received that popish prince among us, who is a declared and an avowed enemy to the Protestant interest. That has done much to put the copestone on our disgrace. Would England have thought that Scotland would have done it? In England not only the prelatic party but also indifferent formalists wonder at it, and the episcopal folk in England may think themselves much better Protestants than the Presbyterians in Scotland.

But no less guilty were those who had complied with the government, particularly those who had bonded for ministers:

> He will punish them that received favours of our king and rulers when their hands were reeking hot with the blood of the saints at Bothwell; and gentlemen gave in money to take in bonds for them. Oh let not this be told in Gath! I would not be in the lives of these professing gentlemen that have received favours, or connived at them, be they who they will, for all broad Scotland.

He was equally unsparing in his denunciations of a host of other public sins. These included what he saw as the compromising conduct of Welsh and his party in framing the Hamilton Declaration; the widespread acceptance of payment of the cess (the tax levied specifically for the purpose of raising forces to suppress the field-preaching); the standing reproach of the Indulgence; and the attempts to silence faithful ministers. All these had provoked God's wrath against the land and the church. 'What will they say', he asked, in an obvious reference to his own experience, 'that have sat down to depose ministers for faithfulness and freedom?' And there was one sin above all others of which the land was guilty: 'We and our fathers have sinned in bringing the king back again, that murderer, that enemy to God and his work.' Cameron clearly did not view this as extravagant language, for 'By his falsifying that oath [i.e. the Covenant] we are bound to look upon him and his family as the stated enemies of our Lord Jesus Christ.'

But, as so often, Cameron also had words of counsel and comfort for those who remained faithful, for those who mourned for the afflictions of Zion:

> Are there any that are groaning under the burden of sin, sighing and mourning for the abominations of the

> land? Come and enter into the bond of the everlasting covenant; we know no better shelter … as you have received Christ, so walk in him, have your eyes towards him; he will have a remnant, and they will be a people of one language; they will be a piece of cleanly leaven, that leaveneth the whole lump … when he begins to set all things in order in his house, he will make his remnant to shine. Quit not your prayers; quit not secret prayer, enter into your chamber and shut the door; if you quit your duty ere he come, you will think shame to make him welcome. Quit not your confidence, for he will come suddenly to his temple, and do great things. Flee unto him, for there is no shelter, but under his shadow.

This was a message which was to set the tone for many others like it in the memorable months ahead.

While the Darmead meeting had been unmolested, it was inevitable that the increased level of field-preaching activity should attract the attention of the authorities. Field-preaching had been carried on, in a few remote corners, ever since Bothwell Bridge, but this was the first time that it had re-emerged in the central heartlands where the bulk of the population lived.

The extent of the Privy Council's concern was reflected in a letter they addressed to the king on 8 April, in which they proposed a series of measures against the 'fanatics' who were 'running out again to field-conventicles in several places of the kingdom'. These included the appointment of special judiciary commissions to try offenders, and instructions to the armed forces to attack those who attended field-meetings 'wherever they can be found' and to kill them in case of resistance.

This was followed on 6 May by a decision to garrison detachments of troops at various places in the western shires, which, as always, were considered the main centres of disaffection to the government. Clearly, the fear of a further rebellion was now very real. The Duke of York, now back in England, confided on 24 April to the Duke of Lauderdale: 'By letters I have received I find the field conventicles increase, which generally have been the fore-runners of a rebellion.'[3] And a Roman Catholic priest, writing from Edinburgh on 13 April, noted that 'The conventicles are great everywhere.' The same writer, two weeks earlier, had informed his correspondent of rumours that the 'Whigs [i.e. the Presbyterians] are rising'.[4]

While some of these reports were no doubt overdrawn, they do suggest that the movement associated with Cameron and his colleagues was already beginning to make an impact. Cameron was determined to make that impact even greater. Throughout April and May he preached constantly with Cargill and Douglas, attracting ever larger audiences, and prompting many who had up to now been waverers to side with him, irrespective of the danger to themselves. While Cargill and Douglas — particularly Cargill — could command respect from their hearers, it was undoubtedly Cameron who carried the greatest popular appeal. This was not merely a matter of personality — though that was no doubt a factor — but of the remarkable preaching qualities which were now so evident in him and which discerning Christians had come to recognize as very special gifts of the Spirit. It was these qualities, above all, which were to become his hallmark in the tumultuous weeks ahead.

By mid-May, Cameron felt that the tide of popular feeling was such as made it fitting to plan for another day of public fasting and prayer. This was fixed for Auchengilloch, a remote spot in the moors south of Strathaven, on Friday, 28 May. Cameron alludes to this meeting in a letter he wrote to Alexander Gordon of Earlston on 22 May, in which he also imparts some rich spiritual comfort to his friend:

> If you know nothing to obstruct our appointment on Friday next, I am willing, in the Lord's strength, to keep it... We must go on in the strength of the Lord, whatever be the difficulties and discouragements in our way; our Lord's ends are well worth the pursuing, he is coming, his reward is with him, and his work, to wit of judgement, is before him. Eye hath not seen, nor ear heard, what he hath prepared for them that wait for him; yea, blessed are the eyes who shall see what he will do for the remnant that are in this land, and for his church throughout the earth. Happy are they whom he is now chastening, that he may hide them from the day of evil. A large share of present sufferings is well worth the having, for the consolations of such shall much more abound. The Lord will make our hearts glad, according to the days wherein he afflicted us, and makes us to see evil.[5]

Cameron could not have counselled his friend in this way unless he himself had reached the point of complete resignation to God's will. This note of acceptance, coupled with confidence in God's ultimate deliverance of his church, was to become a familiar theme of Cameron's preaching in the weeks that followed. The ultimate deliverance — the end of the long night of persecution — was the hope that he constantly held out to his hearers. It was a hope that he would not live to see realized himself, as he well knew, but it would certainly be fulfilled in God's time. The fact that he would not share in it was immaterial. What mattered to him supremely was his obedience to the call and commission of God, and its outworking in his life and witness. And if the price of that obedience was to be his life, he was now fully prepared to make that ultimate sacrifice in the fulness of God's time.

21.
The fast at Auchengilloch

The preaching places used during the persecution were chosen not only for their security — the protection they afforded from attack — but for their strategic location. Since the field-preachers depended on invitations from particular parishes to preach (and Cameron, for his part, was always careful not to preach without such a call), it was necessary to choose the part of the parish which offered the greatest strategic advantage. Auchengilloch, the scene of the projected fast, was such a place. Though in itself remote — situated as it was in the south-east corner of the parish of Avondale — it was readily accessible from a wide area of the surrounding country, ranging from Nithsdale and Galloway in the west to Lothian in the east. Auchengilloch also had the further advantage of being so located as to make it virtually impossible for horse-troopers to reach it — a vital consideration in planning a meeting of any size.

On the day planned for the meeting the weather proved fine and warm, and large numbers of people assembled. It had been agreed that Cameron, Cargill and Douglas would share the preaching. It fell to Cameron to begin the proceedings and, in accordance with custom, he started with a short 'preface', or introduction, before giving his sermon.

Cameron's opening words were typical, as he challenged his hearers in uncompromising terms:

> What are you doing here this day? There are several of you come from afar. Is it your zeal for the Lord of hosts that has brought you here? Oh how few can say, that the zeal of thine house hath eaten me up! As for you that have not this end before you, that Christ may come unto this land, and have the crown set upon his royal head, you have little to do here, and we would willingly be rid of you. And we take these hills around us to witness against you this day, if this be not your end to bring Christ back again unto this land.
>
> What are you come here for? [he continued]. Are you come to seek Jesus of Nazareth who was crucified? Last year about this time our Lord was, as it were, upon the Mount of Olives; he rode as it were triumphantly upon the head of a small party to the market cross of Rutherglen, and many cried, 'Hosanna to the Son of David' for a few days after. But since the 22nd of June 1679 how many have cried out, 'Crucify him, crucify him, away with him; we will have no more to do with him; Christ is too dear a Lord for us; these field-meetings of his are too costly for us; we wish there had never been any of these field-meetings in Scotland'? Are there none of you that were eye- and ear-witnesses of this grievous departure of Christ, June 22nd? And are there none of you crying out, 'I have not seen a sight of him since,' and also crying out, 'Oh, where shall I find him?'

This led him to speak, though fleetingly, of the movements of the Spirit he had seen since his return:

> But I will tell you, sirs, our Lord has appeared to some since. We can instance the day and particular place, wherein the Lord has of late appeared gloriously in this land, even as gloriously as ever heretofore, if ye will suffer us to say it without boasting or vanity. And may this not beget a longing desire in you, to get a sight of him too; as it is now more than a twelvemonth since you saw his power and glory in his sanctuary and his meetings? See if you will take him again to be your King; and see if you will put your hands to his crown which is now lying upon the ground, and do what you can to set it upon his royal head again, for it becomes him best of all to wear it.

After this introduction Cameron went on to give his sermon. His text, from Hosea 13:9, 'O Israel, thou hast destroyed thyself, but in me is thine help,' was intended to draw a parallel between the Israel of the prophet's day and the situation in contemporary Scotland. He began by powerfully applying this theme in a series of challenges to his hearers: 'We have it in commission to say to the Church of Scotland, "Thou hast destroyed thyself, O Church of Scotland; O ministers of Scotland, O commons and people of all sorts in Scotland, you have destroyed yourselves."' 'Who was charged here?' Cameron asked his hearers.

> It was even Israel, a people near unto the Lord. The most of heathens will not do this. Nay, animals of the brute creation will not do it. And yet men, yea men that are called Christians, will do it; many who are baptized in the name of Christ will do it. But if there be any place of destruction in the caverns of hell, hotter than another, as we doubt not that there is, many of those who call themselves Christians will not rest until they have cast

> themselves into that place… There is that in the heart of man that would destroy him. Oh, but man is a blind darkened creature! He has a great aversion to that which is good, and a great proneness unto that which is evil. There is no creature upon earth so mad and wild as man.

He then proceeded to enumerate the sins of which the land was guilty, basing his remarks on the words of the prophet: 'By swearing, and lying, and killing, and stealing, and committing adultery, they break out, and blood toucheth blood.' This was not, however, a mere denunciation of sin without an understanding of the temptations which faced many of his audience. 'I confess,' he said, 'folk are much to be pitied at this time who take a liberty to lie, especially when soldiers come to the house and ask if such a man was there.' But, even making all allowances, there was no room for compromise:

> It is true, you are not bound at the very first (if you can without sin shift it) to tell them; but beware of lying on any account; rather tell them that such a one was there, though you and your house should be ruined by it; yea, though it should tend to the prejudice of the best ministers in Scotland. God will not give you thanks for saving one's life by a lie. Let us be strict and ingenuous, both with God and man.

He went on to speak of ministers, and their betrayal of the interest of Christ:

> There are many ministers in Scotland (it is true I am but a young man that says it) that shall not be any ministers, if there were no more ministers to be had in it. We must speak against ministers, and we must cry for the sins of the ministers of Scotland, that have betrayed

> the work of Reformation; and even gone beyond curates and bishops in betraying and destroying it. The Lord will lay that woe unto their charge.

But Cameron was to bring the lesson of his text nearer home still and apply it to the remnant themselves, to those who continued faithful — even they were not without the need for warning and rebuke:

> But let all of us look unto ourselves, and see what we have brought upon ourselves. We will not get a field-meeting in Scotland but what is here at this time. Last year we had twenty or thirty, that carried the Lord's banner from one place to another in Scotland. It is not so now; but it is much that we have such a meeting as this. God be thanked for it. But we are brought very low, and our persecutors are greater than we; and they are now saying, 'We have got them under and let us keep them so.' They think they will get us all apprehended, and there is a great appearance of it. They will behead and hang us, and, if possible, eradicate us from the face of the earth. We look upon our right hand, and upon our left hand, and there is no man that knows or cares for us. We are a party on whom few look upon the right hand, few of the ministers and professors. The most part of them have got into towns and country places; and the best news they could hear would be that a party of the enemy had come and cut every one of us off.

Even among the remnant themselves, he said, there were the seeds of self-destruction. In a revealing comment which was later to prove only too accurate, Cameron remarked:

> Let us speak about the matters of God, we will scarcely agree together; not one speaks comfortably,

> nor agrees with another... We may say, 'Where will we cause our shame to go?' Our enemies laugh at us, and it is sad, that we have done it all with our own hands. If we had kept our hands free of sin, it had been otherwise with us; we might have defied all our enemies. But now we are scattered, like sheep without a shepherd, or like a leaf tossed and driven to and fro with the wind.

But Cameron's message was by no means one of despair. 'This is the way our Lord takes,' he had remarked earlier, 'first to wound, and then to heal.' It was now time for him to encourage his audience in the promises of God:

> There is help for us in him who brought Israel out of Egypt through the Red Sea. We are not in a more dangerous case than the Israelites were in when they came out of Egypt. They had as great an army pursuing them as our king can command; yet they passed through safely, while Pharaoh and all his host were drowned. We are not to look for miracles; but we may look for wonders; and the Lord will do great wonders for the people that own his cause. He is able to save all that come unto him.

However, something was required on the part of the people before the promised help could be given:

> Our Lord is saying, 'If you would have help from me, you must take me to be your King; you must take me to be head of the church.' Our Lord Jesus is, and must be King upon his holy hill of Zion. There is no king in the church besides him; the Lord has given him to be King to rule in you, and over you. Now, are you content to let the King of glory, the Lord of hosts, enter into your hearts and souls? And, oh, what say you in Galloway and

> Nithsdale? Will you take Christ to be your King, and to be the anointed King of the church? And what say you of Clydesdale and Lothian? Are there any of you here content to cast yourselves at his feet, and to enter your names in his list among his subjects? Come, and set down your names, and submit unto him, and give away yourselves unto him. There were hope in Israel concerning our case, if there were any this day crying, 'I am content to take him for my King, my Lord, and Saviour.'

Cameron had up to this point concentrated on the duties of his audience towards God. But his message was not yet fully delivered, and he had reserved the most portentous part of it until the last. It concerned the question of obedience to king and government. If his audience had been awaiting some radical pronouncement on this point, they were not to be disappointed. He told them:

> We must cry we will have no other king but Christ. If you would have him be for you, you must cut off this king, and these princes, and make able men be rulers, endued with suitable qualifications both of body and mind, that employ their power for the cause and interest of God. If we had the zeal of God within us we would not call him our king; and even with regard to the nobles and magistrates of this land, we would not acknowledge them to be magistrates. The Lord knows we are obliged to speak these things. I will tell you, if ever you see good days in Scotland without disowning the present magistrates, then believe me no more. I know not if this generation will be honoured to cast off these rulers; but those that the Lord makes instruments to bring back Christ, and to recover our liberties civil and ecclesiastic, shall be such as shall disown this king, and those

> inferiors under him, against whom our Lord is denouncing war. Let them take heed to themselves; for though they should take us to scaffolds, or kill us in the fields, the Lord will yet raise up a party who will be avenged upon them. And are there none to execute justice and judgement upon those wicked men who are both treacherous and tyrannical? The Lord is calling men of all ranks and stations to execute judgement upon them. And if it be done, we cannot but justify the deed; and such are to be commended for it, as Jael was.

Cameron was referring here to the biblical story of Jael, the wife of Heber the Kenite, who singlehandedly killed Sisera, captain of the host of Jabin, King of Canaan, when he had sought refuge among her people. Not surprisingly, some have claimed that in saying this Cameron was advocating the principles of assassination. Taken out of context, his words would certainly appear to lend at least an appearance of support to such a view. But he was careful, in closing his sermon, to explain exactly what he had meant:

> Let us fight against those wicked rulers with the weapons of the spiritual warfare, the arms of secret prayer. Let us pray unto the Lord to cut them off; and the Lord will raise up those that will contemn and despise them. The juncture of time is such, that we must state ourselves in opposition to those enemies. We must not trifle with them any more. We must be content either to quit them all, or comply with them. If we would resolve to quit all for Christ, he would return us all, and give us as much as we had, and twice as good and more.

It was, then, a spiritual warfare to which Cameron was calling his hearers — a warfare by prayer and witness-bearing, leaving the issue to God. He was not advocating private action without resort to divine guidance. Certainly, there might be instruments raised up by God to fulfil his will, and to them honour would be due. But it was not for men to take matters into their own hands, or to seek to anticipate God's purposes. However hard the road ahead, however severe the provocation, the call was for undeviating submission to God's will. God would be honoured by his people's trust that he would overrule all things for his glory.

22.
Cameron preaches at Crawfordjohn

Auchengilloch had been a climactic event for Cameron. It was a tribute to his strength of character that he had been able to preach so forcefully, for the threat of disturbance by the enemy had been very real. Indeed, with such large numbers congregating, it would have been surprising had the meeting not come to the notice of the authorities. General Dalyell, the commander of the government's forces, had his headquarters at this time at Kilmarnock, and was in a position to dispatch troops at short notice. But by the time he got word of the meeting, it was too late. The following day, he wrote to the Earl of Airlie, who was stationed with troops of horse and dragoons at Ayr, to 'Strive to get intelligence what the enemy's rendezvous has been for.'[1] By then, however, Cameron was well out of reach, and planning his next move.

On the following Lord's Day, 30 May, Cameron was engaged to preach in the parish of Crawfordjohn, in the southern end of Clydesdale. Because of the increasing risk of attack, the meeting was arranged for a particularly remote spot, known as Shawhead, deep in the hills south of Muirkirk. But, though remote, the place chosen was strategically situated near the point where four parishes converged — Crawfordjohn and Douglas in Clydesdale, and Muirkirk and Auchinleck in Ayrshire — so that hearers from a wide area could conveniently gather there. As at Auchengilloch on the Friday, the choice of site was to prove more than a match for the authorities.

Cameron, who this time was unaccompanied by either Cargill or Douglas, began the services for the day with a 'preface', or introduction, in his usual challenging style:

> Do any of you know, whether the Lord will be here this day? How many of you have been endeavouring to wrestle with the Lord this last night, that he might come here to this meeting? Oh how many are come here today, that are as great strangers to him as they were that hour they were born! Oh how many are strangers to God in our Israel! But if you knew what communion and fellowship with him were, you would say all the world is but tasteless, and but loss and dung to you. If you get a taste of him this day, you will say that he is sweeter than the honeycomb: 'And whom have I in heaven but thee? And there is none upon the earth that I desire besides thee.' If this frame were amongst you, how pleasant it would be! It is likely the Lord will, in less or more, countenance this despised meeting gathered here today, whatever be amongst us, for indeed we are black with persecution; but there is a remnant, and they being in our Lord Jesus Christ, are comely and desirable.

He drove home the challenge:

> Now stir up yourselves; and since you are assembled, you shall have an offer of him this day. Prepare for it; we are in some hopes that we shall get him offered to you. It will be much if ever you get a time or season for receiving him again in this world. It may be you shall never see him till all the world see him at the last day,

> when you shall see yourselves on his left hand. He is now upon the door threshold, so to speak; and he is loth to go from Scotland. And will you deal with him not to go away? For if he go away, our meeting will be but a heartless one. Then be earnest with him in prayer, and so call upon his name.

After a 'lecture', or exposition, based on Psalm 92, he went on to give his sermon. He took as his text the words of Christ in John 5:40: 'And ye will not come to me, that ye might have life.' That sermon was to prove memorable in the experience of all who heard it. Confronting his hearers with the claims of Christ as the only Saviour, he went on to apply the words of his text with extraordinary power. Few sermons, it has been said, ever preached in Scotland have been attended with such a remarkable outpouring of the Spirit.[2]

Three hundred years and more have passed since that sermon was preached, but it is still possible to catch something of the spirit of the occasion from the written record, as Cameron faced his hearers with the realities of sin, death and judgement:

> It is very hard to convince men of sin. Many come to hear preaching and read the Bible; but those that are not convinced of sin have never come to Christ. They cannot hear them that are free in telling them their faults. It is true, they will hear of sin in general, but how hard it is to get folk to particularize their sins. Some are brought to ordinances, and some to read the Word, and some even to conviction of sin, but will they quit it? It is true, you may be grieved for sin; but have you grieved and hated yourself for your sin? Oh if you got but a view of the saints on Mount Zion, clothed with righteousness, even that of Christ, and a sight of the terror of God, you

> would know that it is a bitter thing to depart from the living God; you would abhor nothing like sin. Consider how few are prevailed with to resolve and endeavour to forsake sin. There are many folk will be convinced of sin, and grieved for it; but they cannot quit it. Many a man that has even paid that wicked cess, will acknowledge it an evil and a sin. And likewise they will acknowledge the Indulgence is a sin; but they must not leave it; it is so sweet a cup, you must not take it from your heads; but you must drink it, if it should be your death. Woe's me for Scotland this day, for its public sins! The days were in this land, when men had much zeal for Christ; they thought themselves happy to be zealous for God's name; and now we have the same opportunity that our fathers had, who put all in hazard for the doctrine, worship and discipline and form of the laws of the house of God. They put themselves into the state of the quarrel to get the gospel in its purity transmitted to posterity in succeeding generations. But oh how few men now will quit anything for Christ!

He went on to deal even more searchingly with the consciences of his hearers:

> There are some that think it is as easy to believe as to take a piece of bread in their hands, or a drink out of a man's hand. Alas, you came over-easily by your religion in the west of Scotland. You may think of yourselves as you will, but if you have not some kind of a law-work within you, you will no more come to heaven than devils will do. It is good indeed to be moved; but it does no good without some law-work. O sad to think upon the west of Scotland! It may be you think you have enough, and stand in no need of preaching, or persecuted

gospel-ordinances; and yet you are the people in all Scotland that are in the worst condition. He has been crying to you in the parishes of Muirkirk, Crawfordjohn and Douglas, that 'Ye will not come unto me that ye might have life.' And what say you to us? Are there any here that say, 'We will not'? Shall we go away, and tell our Master that you will not come unto him?

Cameron was now ready for his fervent, climactic appeal. He preceded it with a word of prayer, then went on:

Our Lord is here this day saying, 'Will you take me, you that have had a lie so long in your right hand?' What say you to it? You that have been plagued with deadness, hardness of heart and unbelief, he is now requiring you to give in your answer. What say you, 'Yes' or 'No'? What think you of the offer? And what fault find you in him? There may be some saying, 'If I get or take him, I shall get a cross also.' Well, that is true; but you will get a sweet cross. Thus we offer him to you in the parishes of Auchinleck, Douglas, Crawfordjohn, and all you that live thereabout; and what say you? Will you take him? Tell us what you say, for we take instruments before these hills and mountains around us, that we have offered him to you this day. You that are free of cess-paying, will you take him? You that are free of the bond now tendered by the enemies, will you accept of him this day? Oh will you cast your eyes upon him? Angels are wondering at this offer; they stand beholding with admiration, that our Lord is giving you such an offer this day. Nay, those that have gone to hell many years ago, who are now crying out in the agonies of torment, may be saying, 'Oh that we had such an offer, as yonder parish of Auchinleck!' Oh come, come then to him; and

> there shall never be more of your by-past sins; they shall be buried...
>
> Now what say you to me? And what shall I say to him that sent me to you? Shall I say, 'Lord, there are some yonder saying, "I am content to give Christ my heart, hand, house, lands and all I have for his cause"'? Now if you can make a better bargain, then do it. Look over to the Shawhead, and these hills, and take a look of them, for they are all witnesses now; and when you are dying they shall all come before your face. We take every one of you witness against another; and will not that aggravate your sorrow when they come into your mind and conscience, saying, 'We heard you invited and obtested to take Christ, and we were witnesses; and yet you would not'?

The fervour and solemnity of his words made a powerful impression on his audience, and some of them were deeply affected. Cameron took notice of this, and went on:

> There is some tenderness amongst you now, and that is favourable to look upon. But yet that is not all; the angels will go up to report at the throne what is everyone's choice this day; they will go up to heaven, and report good news, and thus they will say, 'There were some in the parishes of Auchinleck, Douglas and Crawfordjohn that were receiving our Lord in the offers of the gospel, and he is become their Lord,' and this will be welcome news. Many in hell will be saying, 'Woe's us! There are some going away, and will not come here; they are taking the alarm, and flying from the wrath to come, that is now devouring us. Oh we had the offer, but will never get it again.' 'But stay,' says the devil, 'we will set the troopers and dragoons upon them, and they

> shall be taken, and their minister shall be killed.' Yes, they shall be taken, and imprisoned, banished and all ruined; but we defy him and them.
>
> You will not come [he concluded], you that live hereabout, for fear of this; and some, it may be, have not come here on that account. Oh dreadful stupid fear that has come upon you! But our Lord has come to your door. Will you take him, yea or not? Will you take him home with you? It is a great wonder that anyone in Scotland is getting such an offer this day. But take him, and change your minds. Give up with banning, cursing and swearing; give up with cess-paying; give up with the Indulgence; and give up with all the ministers that take not up the cross of Christ which we are bearing at this day; take the glorious person who has occasioned our coming here this day into this wild place. What, shall I say that any of you were content to take him? I would fain think that some will take him; and if you from the bottom of your heart have a mind to take him, you shall get the earnest of the Spirit; he will in no wise cast you out. And you that have taken him, walk worthy of him; and when our Lord returns to this land, they shall be the persons that shall be most eminent, that abide by him now; they shall be most eminent about the throne.

As these extracts show, and as other occasions were to prove, Cameron's preaching powers were now unquestionably at their height. His development as a preacher had been quite extraordinary. From a relatively inexperienced probationer he had progressed in a few months to become the pre-eminent field-preacher in Scotland — and that at a time of the bitterest repression and persecution. All his life up to this point had been a preparation for this great work. He had not, of course, embarked on the work alone; and for Cargill and

Douglas — particularly Cargill — there was a devoted and attached following among the people. But it was Cameron supremely who commanded their allegiance. The power of his personality, his natural eloquence, the forcefulness of his preaching style, the note of authority which bespoke a closeness of communion with God — all combined to produce an unforgettable impression.

To his hearers — several of whom were later to suffer for their faith — these few weeks in the early summer of 1680 were to prove a veritable heaven upon earth. 'I am sure', wrote one of them, John Malcolm, 'the gospel preached by Mr Richard Cameron especially, was backed with the power and presence of Christ. As much of Christ and heaven were found, as finite creatures on earth were able to hold; yea, and more than they could hold. The streams of living waters ran through among his people at these meetings, like a flood upon the souls of many, who can witness if they were called to it that they would not have been afraid of ten thousands… The fathers will be telling the children of it, when they are old men, that in the year 1680 there were great days; upon the mountains up and down the west, it was then that I got the real impression of God on my soul.'

Another, John Potter, wrote in his last testimony, 'And now when I am stepping out of time into eternity, I declare that I adhere to all the doctrines that ever I heard Mr Richard Cameron or Mr Donald Cargill preach; and my soul blesses God that ever I heard either of them; for my soul has been refreshed to hear the voice and shouting of a king among these field-meetings, wherein the fountain of living waters has been made to run down among the people of God, in such a manner that armies could not have terrified us.'

Patrick Walker, who had the benefit of first-hand accounts from some of Cameron's hearers, gives a similar testimony, in his own inimitable style:

> The power and presence of the Lord going along with the gospel ordinances dispensed by him in those six months, wherein he ran fast, his time being short, he was taught and helped of the Lord to let down the net at the right side of the ship, where there were on every public day many caught, to their conviction, confirmation, comfort and edification, according as their various cases were. Our martyrs, sufferers, and other Christians had to tell to the fearers of the Lord, what he did for their souls at such times and places; these signal manifestations of the Lord's love and pity in these sun-blink days of the gospel, not only of clear enlightening light, but also of vehement heat, to thaw, warm and melt their hearts in such a flame of love to the Lord Jesus Christ, and such a zeal upon their spirits for the concerns of his glory, that made them willing and ready to spend and be spent, and rejoice that they were counted worthy to die for the name of the Lord Jesus Christ; which deserves to be recorded to all generations.[3]

This was the motivation that drove Cameron as he entered on what were to prove to be the closing weeks of his life.

23.
The Queensferry Paper

It had been one of Cameron's ambitions, ever since his return to Scotland, to publish a declaration of the principles of the non-complying Presbyterians. Indeed, he had expressed his regret to Robert M'Ward that such a declaration had not been prepared before his departure from Holland. It is fairly clear that the bond that Cameron and his supporters had drawn up in March 1680 had been intended as a prototype for a public declaration. However, various circumstances had conspired to delay the undertaking, and Cameron appears to have felt that he was not fully equipped for the task of skilled drafting which a formal declaration would involve.

With Donald Cargill's return from Holland, that difficulty had in a measure been laid to rest. Cargill, the son of a Perthshire notary, had himself been trained for the law, and was well versed in legal forms and styles. He was also a logical and clear-headed thinker, and so was in a marked degree qualified for the task in hand. To him, therefore, the work of drawing up a formal statement mainly fell.

While it is clear that most of the work on the declaration was done by Cargill, it is less certain how far he personally endorsed the sentiments to which it gave expression. He knew, of course, that the declaration was intended as a manifesto of the non-complying remnant as a whole. It had therefore to seek to reflect varying shades of opinion. That was no easy task. Cameron himself had referred, in his sermon at Auchengilloch, to the difficulty of securing agreement even among his own supporters and adherents. When that task was extended beyond Cameron's immediate circle, the difficulty became even more palpable.

Cargill appears to have started work on the declaration soon after his return to Scotland.[1] Working with his usual meticulous care, he had virtually completed a first draft of the document by the end of May. The sequence of events at this point is not altogether clear. It would seem, however, that before the draft was considered in any detail by Cameron and the rest, a decision was taken to send it over to Rotterdam to be shown to Robert M'Ward. The messenger chosen for this purpose was Henry Hall, who had earlier shown himself to be a staunch supporter of Cameron, and who had spent some time in Holland after Bothwell Bridge.

On Thursday, 3 June, Cargill accompanied Hall to Queensferry, where he was hoping to embark for Holland. While waiting there in an inn they were suddenly surprised by the Governor of Blackness Castle, and commanded to surrender in the name of the king. A fierce struggle ensued, in which Hall was mortally wounded, while Cargill managed to make good his escape. In the confusion a travelling-bag was seized, containing various personal papers, among them the draft of the declaration.[2]

The seizure of the declaration was a serious and embarrassing loss. Much work had been expended on it, probably by various hands, and it had been expected to undergo further revision before being published to the world. Now all these plans had gone awry. For Cargill the loss was particularly distressing. He had framed the declaration in terms which no doubt reflected the views of several for whom he had a regard, but it is fairly certain that he would not have been prepared to see it published without submitting it to the scrutiny of others, such as M'Ward, whose judgement he particularly valued. Now that opportunity had been for ever lost. The declaration was fixed irretrievably in the form in which it was found. Unrevised as it was, it would now inevitably be seen as a definitive statement of principle on the part of those whom Cargill and Hall represented.

The authorities were quick to see the propaganda value of the discovery. Orders were speedily given to have the document printed, so as to cause its authors the maximum embarrassment, and to let everyone see the pernicious nature of the principles against which the government were contending.[3] There can be no doubt that, in a measure at least, these tactics achieved the desired effect. In particular, they served to isolate Cameron and Cargill still further from the main body of Presbyterians in Scotland and to stigmatize them as holding principles which the great majority saw as subversive of good order in church and state. The grounds for such a view were of course rooted in the document itself, and some acquaintance with it is necessary to an understanding of the reception it met.

The document — or the Queensferry Paper, as it came to be called — started with a ringing affirmation of purpose:

> We under-subscribers, for ourselves, and all that join with us, and adhere to us, being put to it by God, our consciences, and men, do bind our souls with a solemn and sacred bond ... we judged it our duty again to covenant with God, and one another, and to publish this Declaration to the world of our purposes, that men may know our most inward thoughts, the rules that we walk by, and the outmost ends that we have before our eyes, for this intent, that these who are lovers of God, zealous of his reigning in glory, and desirous of Reformation, and the propagation of his kingdom, may have occasion

> no more to be jealous [i.e. suspicious] of our intentions, and others may have no ground to load us with odious and foul aspersions.

There followed seven articles, or statements of intent, pledging the subscribers to specific courses of action. The first was a commitment to God and to the authority of Scripture. The second was a commitment to 'advance the kingdom of Christ throughout the land, and the true reformed religion, and free the church of God from the thraldom, tyranny, encroachment and corruption of prelacy on the one hand, and Erastianism on the other'.

The second article went on to pledge that 'We shall to our power relieve the church and subjects of this kingdom of that opposition that hath been exercised upon their consciences, civil rights and liberties, that men may serve him holily, without fear, and possess their civil rights in quietness, without disturbance.' The reference here to 'civil rights and liberties' was noteworthy. Here was a document which was not limiting itself narrowly to the rights of the church. It recognized that with the rights of the church was bound up the liberty of the people. This had been a fundamental tenet of the Reformation church. The authors of the paper were using terms which may have a modern ring to them, but they were stating a principle which was as old as the Reformed church itself. It was an evidence of their loyalty to, and understanding of, the very principles of Scottish Presbyterianism which they had been accused of betraying. And it effectively gave the lie to those who sought to depict them as actuated only by a narrow factional interest, divorced from the mainstream of the Reformed tradition.

The third article committed the signatories to extirpate 'idolatry and superstition' — by which was meant the relics of Romanism — and prelacy, as pledged in the Covenants.

With the fourth article the paper ventured onto more contentious ground:

> Seriously considering that the hand of our kings has been against the throne of the Lord, and that now for a long time, the succession of our kings and the most part of our rulers with him hath been against the purity and power of religion and godliness, and freedom of the church of God, and hath degenerate[d] from the virtue and good government of their predecessors into tyranny; governed contrary to all right laws, divine and human, exercised such tyranny and arbitrary government, oppressed men in their consciences and civil rights, used free men with less discretion and justice than their beasts; so that it can no more be called a government, but a lustful rage, exercised with as little right reason, and with more cruelty than in beasts, and they themselves can be no more called governors, but public grassators [i.e. terrorists], and public judgements, which all men ought as earnestly to labour to be free of, as of sword, famine or pestilence raging amongst us; and instead of rewarding the good, hath made butcheries and murders on the Lord's people, sold them as slaves, imprisoned, forfeited, banished and fined them, upon no other account but for maintaining the Lord's right to rule consciences against the usurpations of men, and repelling unjust violence, which innocent nature allows to all...
>
> Being assured of God's approbation and men's, whose hearts are not utterly biased, and their consciences altogether corrupted, and knowing assuredly that the upholding of such is to uphold men to bear down Christ's authority and to uphold Satan's, and the depriving of men of right government, to the ruining of religion

> and undoing of human society; we then seeing, if we shall acknowledge their authority, the endless miseries that will follow, and siding with God against his stated and declared enemies, do reject that king, and these associate with him, from being our rulers, and declare them henceforth to be no lawful rulers, as they have declared us to be no lawful subjects, upon a ground far less warrantable, as men unbiased may see; and that after this, we neither owe, nor shall yield any willing obedience to them, but shall rather suffer the utmost of their cruelties and injustice, until God shall plead our cause; because they have altered and destroyed the Lord's established religion, overturned the fundamental and established laws of the kingdom, taken altogether away Christ's church and government, and changed the civil government of this land into tyranny; so that none can look upon us or judge us bound in allegiance to them, unless they say also we are bound in allegiance to devils, they being his vice-regents and not God's.

This was uncompromising indeed, and in an age nurtured in the divine right of kings it was calculated to have a startling effect. Yet there was nothing in it inconsistent with what Reformed writers such as Buchanan, Rutherford and Brown had clearly taught. Tyranny in a ruler was a just ground for disclaiming allegiance. The principle was familiar enough. What was new was that, for the first time, the principle was being given practical expression. That, no doubt, accounted for the lack of understanding with which the paper was viewed by the main body of Presbyterians. Almost universally, the authors were seen as deviants from the principles of Presbyterianism. Much was made of the article in the *Westminster Confession* which states that 'Infidelity or difference in religion doth not make void the magistrate's just and legal authority, nor free the people from their due obedience to him.'

This, however, as Rutherford had shown, did not tie the subject to obedience to tyrannical rulers. There was obviously room for debate over exactly what constituted tyranny, but the authors of the paper could certainly claim, with all show of reason, that they had clearly proved the premises on which their action was based. And, that being so, they could claim with equal fairness that by disowning their allegiance they had not done anything which broke faith with the principles of historic Presbyterianism.

But the paper went further still. Its fifth article began:

> We then being made free, by God and their own doings, he giving the law, and they giving the transgression of that law, which is the cause that we are loosed now from all obligations, both divine and civil to them, and knowing that no society of men that hath corruption in them can be without laws and government, and desiring to be governed in the best way that is least liable to inconveniences and tyranny, we do declare that we shall set up over ourselves, and over all that God shall give us power, government and governors, according to the Word of God, and especially according to that word, Exodus 18:21: 'Moreover, thou shalt provide out of all the people able men, such as fear God, men of truth, hating covetousness'; and that we shall no more commit the government of ourselves, and the making of laws for us, to any one single person, and lineal successor, we not being tied as the Jews were by God to one family, government not being an inheritance but an office, which must be squared not to the interest and lust of a man, but to the good of the Commonwealth; and this kind of government by a single person being most liable

> to inconveniences, as sad and long experience may now teach us, and aptest to degenerate into tyranny. Moreover, we declare that these men whom we shall set over us shall be engaged to govern us principally by that civil or judicial law given by God to his people of Israel, especially in matters of life and death, and in all other things also, so far as they teach.

Here was something entirely new, revolutionary indeed. What was being advocated was the rejection of hereditary monarchy altogether, and the adoption of a republican form of government.

None of the Reformed writers had come this far. Admittedly, Calvin had remarked that 'Monarchy is prone to tyranny,' and had expressed his personal preference for aristocracy — that is, rule by several. But he had also said, 'Should those to whom the Lord has assigned one form of government take it upon them anxiously to long for a change, the wish would not only be foolish and superfluous but very pernicious ... for if it has pleased him to appoint kings over kingdoms, and senates or burgomasters over free states, whatever be the form which he has appointed in the places in which we live, our duty is to obey and submit.'[4] Knox, despite his well-known view that tyrannical rulers could be dethroned, had not advocated the overthrow of the monarchy as such. Rutherford, in his *Lex Rex,* had certainly accepted that there were other forms of divinely appointed government besides monarchy, but even he had not gone so far as to repudiate monarchy as an institution. These principles were popularly associated only with those known as 'fifth monarchy men', who believed in setting up the kingdom of Christ by force and repudiating allegiance to any other government.

The authors of the declaration well knew they would be stigmatized as such: 'We know', they wrote, 'that men of malignant and perverse spirits will raise an ignorant clamour upon this, that it is a fifth-monarchy, and we fifth-monarchy-men, and will labour to amuse the people with strange terms, and put odious names on good things to make them hateful, as their way is; but if this be their fifth-monarchy, we both are, and ought to be such, and that according to his Word.'

Given this disclaimer, it must remain something of a mystery how these principles came to be advocated in the declaration. But perhaps there is a key. In his sermon at Auchengilloch on 28 May, Cameron had said, 'We must cry, we will have no other king but Christ. Say you, are you against all monarchy and civil government? We are not much taken up with that, if God let pure government be established, that is most for the good and advantage of civil and ecclesiastic society… If you would have him be for you, you must cut off this king, and these princes, and make able men be rulers, endued with suitable qualifications both of body and mind, that employ their power for the cause and interest of God… Our Lord will set up other magistrates, according to his promise.'

There is, to say the least, a passing resemblance between these words and the text of the declaration. In advocating the abolition of the monarchy, the declaration was certainly expressing a view strikingly similar to what Cameron had already proclaimed in public. It seems a reasonable inference that, although the declaration may have been penned largely by Cargill, Cameron played an influential part in its composition. How he arrived at this particular view is another matter. There is nothing to suggest that he was indebted to anyone else for it. Rather, the evidence would point to the conclusion that, having debated the issue fully in his own mind, he had come to the personal conviction that nothing short of this radical step was justified. This was a view which, as events were to show, he was not prepared to press, and its inclusion in the document may well have been designed merely to test the opinions of those to whom the draft was to be shown. Be that as it may, circumstances had dictated that an opinion which may have been intended as purely speculative was now to be judged as the authoritative view of the parties to the declaration. And that judgement was to have important consequences.[5]

The final two articles of the declaration were concerned with the ministry. Once again, they were nothing if not radical in tone. They began by restating the objections to the Indulgence, which they described as 'ministers departing from the court of Christ, and of the ministers of Christ are become the ministers of men'. Then the document went on to avow that:

> We neither can, nor will hear preaching, nor receive sacraments from these ministers that have accepted of, and voted for that liberty; and declare all who have encouraged and strengthened their hands, by hearing and pleading for them, all those who have trafficked for a union with them, without their renouncing and repenting of these things, all those that do not testify faithfully against them, and after do not deport themselves suitably to their testimonies, and all who join not in public with their brethren, who are testifying against them; we declare that we shall not hear them preach, nor receive sacraments from them.

This was a radical view of separation, extending not only to the ministers who had accepted the Indulgence and their supporters, but also to all those who could not bring themselves to condemn publicly what these ministers had done. As such, it went beyond the practice of all but a very few. Cargill, for example, was known to have associated with Alexander Peden, who, though firmly against the Indulgence himself, could not find it in him to condemn the ministers who had accepted it. One is left to assume that here again the paper shows the influence of Cameron, though in this instance there is nothing quite comparable to be found in his preaching. As with the reference to the monarchy, it appears likely that this statement was included in the paper only speculatively, and further deliberation might well have seen it modified or omitted. It is certainly very doubtful whether M'Ward, whose own practice lay in another direction, would have been content to allow such a view to be given any prominence.

The document concluded with a resolution on the part of the authors 'that none of us shall take upon him the preaching of the Word, or administering the sacraments, unless called and ordained thereto by the ministers of the gospel,' and 'that we shall go about this work in time to come with more fasting and praying, and more careful inspection into the conversation and holiness of these men that shall be chosen and ordained; the want of which formerly hath been a great sin, both in ministers and people, which hath not been the least cause of this defection'.

This resolution, if followed to the letter, would have disqualified even licensed probationers from preaching the gospel, and subjected candidates for ordination to much more rigorous examination. Here again, the reasons for such an extreme view are difficult to find. From the sequel, however, it would appear that they may have reflected some dissatisfaction on the part of Cameron's associates with certain of their own party. If that is so, the evidence of that dissatisfaction was soon to come to light.

24.
The Sanquhar Declaration

Whatever influence Cameron may have had on the content of the Queensferry Paper, the capture of the document in its unfinished form was no doubt as frustrating for him as it was for those who had drawn it up. He had, of course, long advocated the issue of a public declaration, and he had probably awaited the completion of this document with some impatience. Now it appeared that the whole enterprise was to go by default. The enemies had seized not only the paper, but with it the initiative. It was they who now would give the world the document on which so much labour had been spent. It was they who would reap the propaganda value from its publication. The paper would be presented, not as a rallying-point of resistance to tyranny, but as the ravings of a group of fanatics opposed to the public peace. The truths it contained would be held up to ridicule. And any impact it might have made on the public conscience would be neutralized.

This was an outcome Cameron was not prepared to contemplate. He had come to see a declaration as a vital part of the public testimony, and he could not accept that the opportunity for it might be lost. He was certainly not prepared to concede the initiative to the enemy. But time was short. If the situation was to be retrieved, even in part, urgent action was called for. And, he concluded, that action was for Cameron himself to take.

The result was to prove memorable. On Tuesday, 22 June 1680 (the first anniversary of Bothwell Bridge) Cameron and a group of twenty horsemen rode in procession into the small town of Sanquhar, in Nithsdale, and made their way to the market cross. There, after drawing up in order, they constituted their proceedings with the singing of a psalm. Cameron's brother Michael then publicly read a document which, with due ceremony, he affixed to the cross. Others of Cameron's party posted up copies in other prominent places in the town. This done, they sang another psalm, and then departed in the same way as they had come.

The document they left was in these terms:

The Declaration and Testimony of the True-Presbyterian, Anti-Prelatic and Anti-Erastian, Persecuted Party in Scotland

It is not amongst the smallest of the Lord's mercies to this poor land, that there [have] always been some who [have] given a testimony of every course of defection which we were guilty of, which is a token for good, that he does not as yet intend to cast us off altogether, but that he will leave a remnant, in whom he will be glorious, if they (through his grace) keep themselves clean still, and walk in his way and method, as it hath been walked in, and owned by him in our predecessors (of truly worthy memory) in their time, in their carrying on of our noble work of reformation, in the several steps thereof, from popery and prelacy, and likewise from Erastian supremacy, so much usurped by him, who it is true (so far as we know) is descended from the race of our kings; yet he hath so far deborded [i.e. deviated] from what he ought to have been, by his perjury and usurpation in church matters, and tyranny in matters civil, as is known

Obelisk marking the spot where the market cross formerly stood to which the Sanquhar Declaration was affixed.

by the whole land, that we have just reason to believe, that one of the Lord's great controversies against us is, that we have not disowned him, and the men of his practices, whether inferior magistrates, or any others, as enemies to our Lord and his crown, and the true Protestant and Presbyterian interest in their hands, our Lord's espoused bride and church.

Therefore, although we be for government, and governors, such as the Word of God, and our Covenants, allows, yet we for ourselves, and all that will adhere to us, as the representatives of the true Presbyterian church, and Covenanted nation of Scotland, considering the great hazard of lying under such a sin, do by these presents, disown Charles Stuart, who hath been reigning, or rather (we may say) tyrannizing on the throne of Britain these years past, as having any right or title to, or interest in the crown of Scotland or government thereof (forfaulted several years since by his perjury and breach of Covenant with God and his church) and usurpation of his crown and royal prerogatives therein, and many other breaches in matters ecclesiastic, and by his tyranny and breach of the very *leges regnandi* [i.e. basics of government] in matters civil; for which reasons, we declare that several years since he should have been denuded of being king, ruler or magistrate, or having any power to act, or to be obeyed as such. As also, being under the standard of Christ, captain of salvation, we declare war against such a tyrant and usurper, and all the men of his practices, as enemies to our Lord Jesus Christ, his cause and Covenants, and against all such as have strengthened him, sided with him, or any ways acknowledged him in his usurpation and tyranny, civil and ecclesiastic, yea, and against all such as shall strengthen, side with, or any ways acknowledge any other in the like usurpation and tyranny, far more against such as would betray or deliver up our free reformed mother church, into the bondage of Antichrist, the Pope of Rome.

By this we homologate the testimony given at Rutherglen, the twenty-ninth of May 1679, and all the faithful testimonies of these that have gone before us, as of these also that have suffered of late; and we do disclaim that declaration published at Hamilton, June 1679, chiefly because it takes in the king's interest, which we are several years since loosed from, because of the foresaid reasons, and others, which may after this (if the Lord will) be published. As also, we disown, and by this resents the reception of the Duke of York, a professed Papist, as repugnant to our principles and vows to the Most High God, and as that which is the great (though alas too just) reproach of our church and nation: we also, by this, protest against his succeeding to the crown, and whatever hath been done, or any are essaying to do in this land (given to the Lord) in prejudice to our work of reformation.

And to conclude, we hope none will blame us for, or offend at, our rewarding these that are against us, as they have done to us, as the Lord gives the opportunity. This is not to exclude any that hath declined, if they be willing to give satisfaction to the degree of their offence.

Given at Sanquhar, the 22 of June, 1680[1]

The model for the Sanquhar Declaration was clearly not the Queensferry Paper — similar as it was in some respects — but the bond which Cameron and his associates had drawn up some months before. And as that was Cameron's work, so was this. The traces of his hand are unmistakable: the intensity of

Close-up of inscription on monument commemorating the publication of the Sanquhar Declaration and a later one by James Renwick. The inscription reads:

In commemoration of the two famous Sanquhar Declarations which were published on this spot where stood the ancient cross of the burgh, the one by the Rev. Richard Cameron on the 22nd of June 1680; the other by the Rev. James Renwick on the 25th of May 1685.
'The Killing Time'
If you would know the nature of their crime
Then read the story of that killing time
1854

the style, the eagerness of the composition, the repeated use of 'as also' to connect sentences. Several of the expressions in the bond were imported direct into the declaration. Notable among these was the section beginning, 'Although we be for government and governors…', which was an expanded version of a similar section in the bond. The bond also gave precedent for the avowal of the declaration at Rutherglen and the disclaiming of the one issued at Hamilton.

But there were also significant differences. The bond had disowned the king for his breach of Covenant, and usurpation of the rights of the church; the declaration did so too, but coupled this with his tyranny in matters of state. Underlying the declaration was the Reformed understanding of church and state as distinct but complementary institutions, both divinely appointed, the one dependent on the other. This was a concept with which Cameron had been familiar since his earliest days, and one which lay at the very heart of the Scottish Reformed tradition. But in a strange way, its very relevance had seldom been as strikingly displayed as in the persecution. It was the king's usurpation of the rights of the church which had led directly to the denial of his subjects' right to worship according to their conscience, and then to the deprivation of their civil rights as citizens. The one followed inexorably from the other. To that extent, it was impossible to disentangle the rights of the people from the rights of the church. Here again was a basic Reformed concept. The Scottish Reformation had not merely been a deliverance from spiritual darkness and superstition. It had been a movement towards the ideal of a nation-state governed by the laws of God. That ideal had been reinforced by the Covenants. And it was to that ideal that the declaration looked back.

The declaration also differed from the bond — and from the Queensferry Paper — in its total silence on the issue of the Indulgence, and indeed on the ministry generally. This was significant. Since his return from Holland, Cameron had concentrated noticeably less on matters concerning the ministry. It was not that he thought these matters less important than before. But he saw it as his priority to expose and denounce the tyranny which had established itself over both church and nation and which had been the prime cause of the defections and compromise which had so weakened the ranks of the ministry. And it was this emphasis which had been reflected in the declaration.

The declaration was also silent on the idea of the abolition of the monarchy which had been advocated in the Queensferry Paper. If Cameron had been the author of this idea — and there is no conclusive evidence that he was — he clearly did not think it crucial enough to warrant mentioning it in the declaration. Or, perhaps more probably, he had accepted that it was too revolutionary a concept to command support even from some on his own side and that its inclusion would merely distract attention from the more pressing matters which the declaration sought to address. At all events, nothing further of this idea was heard.

The declaration did, however, contain two features that were new. The first was its claim to speak on behalf of the 'true Presbyterian church and Covenanted nation of Scotland' and its designation of its authors as the 'representatives' of that church and nation. What Cameron meant by this was not altogether clear. According to one view, he and his supporters were assuming to themselves the magisterial authority which had hitherto resided in the king and council; they were implementing, in effect, the declared intention of the Queensferry Paper when it had spoken of setting aside the monarchy and declaring a Christian republic. In later years the United Societies[2] under James Renwick felt obliged to explain, in their *Informatory Vindication,* that the authors of the declaration had intended no such thing; they had merely meant that they saw themselves as adhering to the best traditions of Presbyterianism and the Covenants. There is no reason to doubt that this was indeed all that Cameron had intended. But the expressions left room for a different interpretation, and the authors of the subsequent Lanark Declaration in 1682 were to go so far as to term the authors of the Sanquhar Declaration a 'Convention of Estates' who had authoritatively repudiated the jurisdiction of the king. Renwick was to term this 'very exceptionable'. [3]

But the most contentious feature of the declaration was undoubtedly its 'declaration of war' against the king. Here indeed, it seemed, was clear proof of the hostile intentions of Cameron and his followers, and sufficient warrant for the authorities to take action against them. Here, in unmistakable terms, was rebellion — not merely a casting off of authority, but a positive raising of the standard against the government. So, indeed, it seemed to many. Here again, the United Societies later felt obliged to issue a disclaimer. Cameron and his followers, they argued, had not intended 'a declaring of a hostile war and martial insurrection', but simply 'a war of contradiction and opposition by testimonies'. Again, there is sufficient evidence that this was in fact what Cameron had intended; his sermon at Auchengilloch, after all, had summoned his audience to 'fight against these wicked rulers with the weapons of the spiritual warfare, the arms of secret prayer'. But, once again, the term lent itself to different interpretations. James Skene, who suffered for his faith in the following December, was in no doubt that since there was a declared war against the king, it was lawful to kill him. And, predictably enough, this was later to lead to one of the standard questions put to suspects by the Privy Council in order to trap them.

Cameron was in some measure prepared for the widespread hostile reaction to the declaration. He had expected it to be opposed by the ministers who had accepted the Indulgence, the church establishment and, of course, the government. But there is some evidence that not even he was prepared for the resentment which it aroused among the moderate Presbyterians, including several of the ministers who had not themselves profited by the Indulgence. These made it their business to discredit the declaration in every way possible and to pledge their loyalty to the king and government. Their greatest fear was that as Presbyterians they would all find themselves brought into disrepute with the authorities as a result of having the views expressed in the document attributed to them, and so they strove with might and main to prove that the principles of the declaration were not those of historic Presbyterianism. Indeed, opposition to the declaration was to become virtually a test of orthodoxy on the part of those who claimed to represent the Presbyterian tradition.

Despite what he knew of the moderate Presbyterians, Cameron appears to have expected better of at least some of them, and he reacted to their opposition with genuine dismay. He had not, it seems, expected to have to justify the declaration publicly, but the bitterness of the opposition on the part of those whom he saw as his natural allies impelled him eventually to write a short vindication of it. This, dated 15 July 1680, was produced in the form of an open letter, which was circulated widely at the time, but appears never to have been published. It was in these terms:

> As it doth not move us what malignant prelates say, so it doth not a little grieve us that any of our Covenanted brethren should deny our late declaration published at Sanquhar, when it is most consonant to our Covenants and Presbyterian principles, which tie only to Charles Stuart in defence of and subordination to religion, as this kirk *anno* 1648 expressly says; by which we must expone [i.e. interpret] that so much obtested

chapter 23 of the Confession of Faith which was accepted by this kirk only in so far as it was applicable to our Covenants, which certainly allows not a man to be supreme above our religion, as he at London now pretends. So that our Lord's diadem is as it were pulled off his head, and cannot be set on again without disowning at least the said Charles Stuart, the head of malignants and malignancy now in these lands, and therefore to be brought to condign punishment according to the Covenants, or at least to be deposed as one who hath openly defied Christ. At Newcastle his father was disowned because he would not take the Covenant, therefore now the son may be rejected for open breach thereof. For if the kirk of this kingdom *anno* 1648 disowned his father so far as to protest against releasing him out of prison, because of not taking the Covenant, may not we, the true representatives of the kirk, disown him who hath openly broken the Covenant after the taking thereof? If an uncovenanted king must lie in prison, what shall be done to a perjured king of whom there is no hope, and who can give no security for the future, he having broken all those ties which use to bind men?

Honest *Lex Rex* pleads that the people are free if the king break the Covenant made betwixt him and them. Now the said Charles Stuart hath broken the Covenant by which the land was married to the Lord, and without subscribing whereof this land would not have brought him out of Holland, so that it was made a fundamental of his right to succeed to the Crown, and, as *Naphtali* says, the Magna Carta of our religion. Therefore his open breach of it doth fully warrant his rejection by us, who are the followers of our old resolute Reformers who forced Queen Mary to depose herself. These worthies stood not on the *primores regni,* as some nowadays do.

> We are indeed private persons, but these arguments which have been used for the *primores regni,* or Parliaments resisting the king, have been fully answered, as you may see in loyal *Naphtali.* And we think that deposing is not more, but rather less than martial opposing, and that it is less to disown Charles Stuart than to appear against his father in the fields, with sword and pistol to kill him, as our Covenanters did formerly without being condemned by any but malignants and such like. And was not reformation from prelacy begun by a company of private women the year 1637, and who knows but we may be instrumental in a more glorious reformation wherein all of you will partake when accomplished, notwithstanding of your present whispering against us? Therefore to conclude, you must either renounce Presbytery and your Covenants, otherwise you must own us in our declaration and Covenants.

The document is interesting as showing the considerations which were uppermost in Cameron's mind when making the declaration. He was not so much concerned with debating the constitutional issues — though his references to *Lex Rex* and to *Naphtali* are significant — as with proving that his action was consistent with the actions of the earlier Covenanters and Reformers. Indeed, his whole emphasis is to show the continuity between the acts of the earlier Reformers and his own. He well knew that his action would be criticized as the work of a few fanatics or extremists who were outside the pale of historic Presbyterianism.[4] In a very real sense, indeed, he was anticipating much of the criticism which was to be levelled at him both in his own day and since. He was not introducing something new. He was walking in the footsteps of those who had been honoured in their day to witness against tyranny, superstition and persecution. Very significant is his description of himself and his party as 'followers of the old resolute Reformers'. It was with them — Knox, Melville, Rutherford and Gillespie — that he wished to be identified. And, when the declaration is set alongside their writings, it is difficult not to concede his claim.

Typical too is his reference to the women — Jenny Geddes among them — who led the protest in St Giles in 1637 against the new Service Book and Canons being imposed on the church. Once again it is characteristic of Cameron that he should choose an example of direct, unsophisticated action to support his case. Like the women of St Giles, he was not so much concerned with debating issues as with acting upon them. He believed that his own times called for an equally direct form of demonstration and that, if, like those women, he was found faithful, he too would be honoured to usher in a time of deliverance for the church. It was some time before that vision was to be accomplished, but there could be no doubt that a notable blow for liberty had been struck. The Sanquhar Declaration, Cameron was to say, would shake the throne of Britain. And in due time, and in its own way, it did.

25.
A price on his head

As might have been expected, the events at Queensferry and Sanquhar infuriated the government. Their narrow failure to capture Donald Cargill at Queensferry was a particular irritation, and the declaration at Sanquhar had taken the edge off the propaganda victory they had hoped to achieve by giving the world the Queensferry Paper. Making the most of the situation, they decided to publish the paper and the declaration together, and these were duly published in Edinburgh and London in the course of July.[1] To Cameron fell the doubtful honour of being described on the title-page as 'the notorious ring-leader of, and preacher at, their field-conventicles' and as having been accompanied at Sanquhar by 'twenty of that wretched crew'.

At the same time, the Privy Council took drastic steps to avenge the affront which had been done to the government's authority. Their reaction to the affair at Queensferry had been somewhat less than urgent, and they felt obliged to excuse themselves to the king's Secretary of State, Lauderdale, by explaining that the paper had been detained by General Dalyell and that they had been obliged to send to him specially for it. No such excuses could serve in the case of the Sanquhar Declaration. Unlike the paper, the declaration had been formally published; its publication was a calculated act of defiance against the government; and the council well knew that they would be called seriously to task unless they were seen to be actively taking steps to track down those responsible.

Nor could the council plead lack of information as an excuse on this occasion. Dalyell, who had learned from his experience, brought the declaration in to them as soon as he had laid hands on it. At the same time, Robert Carmichael, the Provost of Sanquhar, sent a copy to Edinburgh with a petition stating that he and his fellow-councillors had not been in any way responsible for the declaration and pleading that they should not be held to account for it.[2]

The council, predictably, spared no words in their condemnation of the declaration. This 'execrable paper', this 'villainous schedule', this 'most treasonable and unparalleled paper' — so their denunciations ran. Words were backed up by action. On 30 June the council issued a proclamation of unprecedented severity, describing the authors of the declaration as 'open and notorious traitors and rebels' and offering substantial rewards for their apprehension. Cameron was the prime target; a price of 5,000 merks was set on his head, with rewards of 3,000 merks each for his brother Michael, Thomas Douglas and Donald Cargill, and 1,000 merks for each of the others. Orders were addressed to the sheriffs and magistrates of every county and burgh in Scotland, urging them to take the most stringent steps for apprehending the rebels. In seventeen parishes in the south and south-west, the heritors, or local landowners, were required to summon all the people over sixteen years of age within their bounds, to put them on oath that they had not seen any of the rebels within the parishes, and to report the results to the nearest sheriffs and magistrates, under pain of being proceeded against as 'connivers at, and concealers of, the said traitors'. These measures caused extreme hardship to many innocent people, and greatly intensified the sense of oppression under which the country was suffering.

But the main instrument at the council's disposal was, of course, the army, which was under their direct control. The army commander, General Dalyell, had already sent them a note reporting 'that he has discovered there is a party in arms of these villains, consisting of about seventy horse ill-clothed and ill-mounted, and most of them ruffians and the scum of the people, in prosecution of whom he has sent several parties, whereof an account is expected'. The council thought Dalyell in need of even more encouragement, and at the same time as they issued their proclamation they wrote to him to 'recommend to and authorize your Excellency to command three or more parties of the forces, as you think fit, to search for and apprehend those traitors, and to secure them and their accomplices that they may be presented to justice, and to bring them in dead or alive, and that you call such noblemen and gentlemen of the country to be assisting, as you shall judge fit'.

Dalyell scarcely required any prompting to act. From his headquarters at Langside, near Glasgow, he issued a series of commands to his officers, urging them to use the utmost diligence to track down the rebels. The main forces at his disposal were under the command of the Earl of Airlie, stationed at Ayr, with a supplementary force under the Earl of Linlithgow at Dumfries. Following issue of the council's instructions, these forces were deployed over a wide area where Cameron and his party were known to haunt.

On the very day of the proclamation — 30 June — Dalyell heard from one of his commanders of dragoons, John Strachan, that 'Cameron was past Sanquhar with twenty horse', and was believed to be heading towards Clydesdale. He immediately ordered Airlie to march from Ayr with his entire force of horse and dragoons to Cumnock, in an attempt to cut Cameron off. Airlie had just been ordered by Dalyell to march to New Galloway to rendezvous with Linlithgow, who was marching there from Dumfries, and expressed his irritation at the sudden change of plan.[3] Nevertheless, in deference to Dalyell's orders he duly marched to Cumnock, from where he sent out parties in search of Cameron. One such party, led by the ensigns John Livingston and John Creichton, reported on 5 July that Cameron's party was believed to have disbanded, and to have split itself into 'twos and threes'. Another report the following day suggested that Cameron and his men had gone to the north of England.[4]

Conflicting reports of this kind illustrated the difficulty facing the armed forces. Though many of the local people had little sympathy with Cameron and his cause, they could not be persuaded to co-operate with his pursuers. Indeed, there were instances of the soldiers being deliberately misdirected in their searches by those who clearly knew of Cameron's whereabouts. A similar reluctance characterized the local landowners and gentlemen, whose assistance Dalyell had been specifically asked to enlist. One of the army commanders, writing to Airlie on 5 July, complained: 'I told your Lordship by my last that I feared the gentlemen in that country would give you but little intelligence, for all their pretences.'[5]

There can be no doubt that this reluctance to co-operate with the authorities enabled Cameron and his men to avoid detection, despite all the diligence of their pursuers. And, as time was to show, for as long as that state of affairs persisted, the authorities' prey would continue to elude them.

As the search intensified, Cameron himself continued in the company of those he had gathered round him since the signing of the bond. It is clear from Dalyell's information, which there is no reason to doubt, that the numbers of his adherents had grown considerably since the spring. While not all of these were signatories of the bond, many of them were to show, in no uncertain way, that their commitment and loyalty to Cameron were beyond question.

Cameron also continued to preach regularly with Cargill

and Douglas. Cargill had not been involved in the Sanquhar Declaration, and he was to declare later that he had not seen it before it was published. From contemporary evidence there is more than a hint that he had his reservations about the declaration, and particularly about the way in which the disowning of the king's authority had been gone about. For him, the issues were less clear-cut than they were for Cameron. To judge from his later actions — particularly the excommunication which he was to pronounce at Torwood — Cargill believed that the repudiation of the king's authority must be seen as a consequence of a spiritual sanction which must first of all be imposed for Charles' usurpation of the crown rights of Christ as head of the church, and for his breach of the duty which, as king, he owed to God. To Cargill, this order of things reflected the essential character of the monarchy as a divinely appointed institution. He certainly did not differ from Cameron on the principle of what had been done at Sanquhar, but on the emphasis. Nor did this difference prevent him from sharing regular preaching duties with his younger friend, whom he continued to hold in high regard.[6]

Thomas Douglas — unlike Cargill — was one of those who had signed the bond and he had supported Cameron loyally since returning earlier in the year from Holland. He had been one of the party at Sanquhar, and had preached regularly with Cameron before and since.[7] Cameron was, of course, aware of the controversy in which Douglas had been involved in Holland, in which Hamilton and others had been critical of his action in assisting at a communion at Rotterdam in the pulpit of Robert Fleming, who had argued in favour of union with the ministers who had accepted the Indulgence. Cameron had evidently seen no reason to make this an issue, nor for there to be any difficulty as a result of it about Douglas being one of his company. Nor, up to this point, do any of Cameron's supporters appear to have raised any objection to Douglas. However, all that was now to change.

Following the defeat at Bothwell Bridge the previous year, several of the leaders of the army, including Robert Hamilton, had sought refuge in Holland. Among the refugees was David Hackston of Rathillet, a country gentleman from Fife who had played a prominent part in some of the tumultuous events of the time. Hackston had been present at the death of James Sharp—though he had taken no direct part in the action—and had been a commander at Drumclog and at Bothwell Bridge. A staunch supporter of Robert Hamilton, he had written a lengthy defence of Hamilton's conduct at Bothwell.[8] He had also sided with Hamilton in the controversy in Holland involving Thomas Douglas.

Hamilton himself was to remain on the Continent until after the revolution of 1688, but Hackston, after remaining in Holland for some months, decided in the spring of 1680 to return to Scotland. It was an audacious venture, since a large price had been set on his head, but clearly he had found it impossible to endure exile any longer while his friends and former companions-in-arms were exposed to the full fury of the government. It was a move which was to have momentous consequences, both for them and for himself.

Hackston's journey back to Scotland was not without incident; he suffered shipwreck *en route,* and was rescued by a ship from Leith whose master had later to answer to the Privy Council for this act of mercy.[9] Arriving in Edinburgh in mid-June, he set out for the west to rendezvous with Cameron. Though in disguise, Hackston was recognized at Lesmahagow by one of the government's numerous spies, who reported his presence to the authorities.[10] He succeeded, however, in avoiding capture, and joined Cameron and the others shortly afterwards.

The course of events at this point is not altogether clear, and much has to be deduced from circumstantial evidence, but it would appear that, soon after joining Cameron, Hackston took exception to the latter's associating with Douglas. It would also seem from the sequel that Hackston was able to persuade a goodly number of Cameron's followers — and perhaps Cameron himself — to side with his view, after giving them more details of exactly what had occurred in Holland. As a result, a general meeting was held, at which Douglas was asked to express his repentance for his alleged offence. When he refused to do so he was, in his own words, 'silenced and necessitate to depart', and his relationship with Cameron and the rest was consequently at an end. Douglas retired to England, and later to Holland, and took no further part in Scottish affairs until the 1688 revolution.

The loss of Douglas' support was an undoubted setback for Cameron, and it left him with Cargill as the only fellow-preacher to whom he could turn. But it did not, so far as is known, occasion any breach among his own following — or if any such breach did occur it must have been quickly healed.[11] Nor did it prejudice his relations with Hackston, who quickly assumed a position of influence among Cameron's following, and became his most trusted lieutenant. As Cameron had seen no difficulty in working with Douglas, so he now found it equally acceptable to work with Hackston. His ability to rise above party disputes of this kind is one of the most interesting features of his career.

26.
New Monkland and Cumnock

Cameron was now the most sought-after person in the kingdom. From the authorities' point of view, as they had made clear in their proclamation, he was the most notorious traitor and rebel still at large — the one to whose capture the energies of all the forces and powers in the country must be directed. But in another way he was sought after no less keenly by a very different class of people. His reputation as a preacher was such that many hundreds — thousands, indeed — of discerning hearers were willing to brave all the dangers of the persecution to attend on his preaching. And he was determined not to disappoint them.

The main arena of his ministry remained the upland area of southern Clydesdale and the areas to the south and west around Cumnock and Sanquhar, where he could find not only the greatest physical security, but also the most loyal popular support. On occasion, however, and with greater frequency as his reputation grew, he ventured further afield.

On the Lord's Day after the publication of the Sanquhar Declaration he was in the parish of New Monkland, to the east of Glasgow, where he preached on what Patrick Walker called 'that sweet, soul-refreshing text': 'A man shall be an hiding-place from the wind, and a covert from the tempest.' It was, says Walker, writing in 1727, 'a desirable, confirming and comforting day, to the sweet experience of some yet alive'. 'In his preface that day', Walker goes on, 'he said he was fully assured that the Lord, in mercy to this church and nation, would sweep the throne of Britain of that unhappy race of the name of Stuart, for their treachery, tyranny and lechery, but especially their usurping the royal prerogatives of King Christ; this he was as sure of, as his hand was upon that cloth, yea more sure; for he had that by sense, but the other by faith.'

The next Lord's Day, 4 July, found him at the Grass Water, near Cumnock, where he again ventured to give a prediction concerning the fate of the house of Stuart and the providences and judgements awaiting Scotland. By this time, Cameron had an increasing presentiment of his own approaching death, and a note of special solemnity and pathos entered his preaching. Walker gives his very words, in the graphic vernacular in which they were obviously reported to him by a hearer:

> There are three or four things that I have to tell you this day, which I must not omit, because I will be but a breakfast or four-hours to the enemies some day shortly, and my work will be finished, and my time both. The first is this: as for that unhappy man, Charles II, who is now upon the throne of Britain, after him there shall not be a crowned king in Scotland of the name of Stuart.[1] Secondly, there shall not be an old Covenanter's head above the ground, that swore these Covenants with uplifted hands, ere ye get a right reformation in Scotland. Thirdly, a man may ride a summer day in Galloway, the shire of Ayr and Clydesdale, and not see a reeking house [i.e. a house with a smoking chimney], nor hear a cock crow; and several other shires shall be little better, ere ye get a right and thorough reformation in Scotland. Fourthly, the rod that the Lord will make use of, shall be the French and other foreigners, together with a wicked party in this land joining with them...

> But ye that stand to the testimony in that day, be not discouraged with the fewness of your number; for when Christ comes to raise up his work in Scotland, he will not want men enough to work for him; yea, he may chap upon the greatest man in Scotland, and he may be a great malignant, and say, 'Sir, let alone this Babel-building of yours, for I have another piece of work to put in your hand,' and he will gar him work for him, whether he will or not. It may be he'll convert the man, and give him his soul for a prey. And there are some of you that are hearing me, may live for age to see these things accomplished. And after these defections and judgements are over, ye may see the nettles grow out of the bedchambers of noblemen and gentlemen, and their names, memorials and posterity to perish from the earth.

Whatever other interpretation may be placed on Cameron's words, they can certainly be taken to mean that the persecuted church in Scotland was destined to undergo a period of even more severe trial before the day of ultimate deliverance came. This was also a theme which was often on the lips of Donald Cargill, with whom Cameron preached with increasing frequency in these final days.

On Thursday, 8 July, Cameron was with Cargill at Carluke, in northern Clydesdale, where they observed another public fast for the sins of the land and church. Cameron preached that day on the words in Isaiah 49:24: 'Shall the prey be taken from the mighty, or the lawful captive delivered?' He used them to illustrate the apparent impossibility of the persecuted church escaping from the all-powerful tyranny which surrounded her, and yet the absolute certainty of her deliverance when God himself would intervene on her behalf: 'For *I* will contend with him that contendeth with thee, and *I* will save thy children' (Isaiah 49:25).

In a word, are we not made a prey? We are in captivity according to their law that is established by iniquity. They have many of our Lord's servants in prison, and all according to their law. We must not take it ill that it is so. The Lord has warned us, 'If any man come unto me, he must deny himself, and take up his cross.' And through many tribulations, we must enter into the kingdom of heaven.

That was not all:

Not only is the church sometimes a prey to the mighty; but the people of God will be just on the point of despairing that ever they can be delivered. Shall the prey be taken from the king; from the Council; from the forces and soldiers? How can it be? It cannot be. When we look to our right hand, there is none to care for us; all refuge faileth us. There is a question here which I desire all the ministers of Scotland to answer. Ask them, will yonder prey be taken from the mighty? Nay, say they, we need not attempt it; and we ourselves who know it, are on the point of despairing. We begin to think it needless to preach, pray, fast, weep or fight; for when we attempt to rise, or to use the means, the Lord comes, and gives us such a blow, that we are made to sit down, and cleave faster to the ground than ever before.

But Cameron quickly put this into perspective:

Between God's giving a promise to his people, and the accomplishment thereof, there may follow such things as may make us think it will never be accomplished, but rather the contrary. Never think that you will get salvation, till God come and contend with his enemies. Many would invert the Lord's order and method; they would first have salvation, and then contending with enemies; but that is not God's way. When he comes to execute justice and judgement on the land, he will make all know that he is the Redeemer of his people, and that his lovingkindness has been remaining with them all along.

But was this not an encouragement to lethargy, to abandoning any effort until God himself would act? Cameron was ready for this objection: 'We may say, we need not trouble ourselves about it, since the Lord will do it. Indeed the Lord will do it; but we must be in the use of the means that are incumbent on us.' He proceeded to explain what these means were and gave particular emphasis to making a testimony. The Sanquhar Declaration was no doubt uppermost in his mind as he spoke:

> It is a shame for this generation that they are so much for silence, and against a testimony, when the Lord is extorting it from them. And if any appear for a testimony, the rest are afraid and offended thereby. We have often said in the fields, that our chief ruler is a traitor to God, and our mother-church; and when we go to the market-crosses, to declare it by papers, the most part are offended in our Lord at this time. But I will tell you, I desire not to take the praise to myself, but I say that if that testimony be adhered to, it will give them a sore blow.

No less important than public testimony was the renewal of Covenant obligations. Cameron did not spare his words in applying this to the circumstances of the day, quoting from Psalm 76: 'Vow, and pay unto the Lord your God. He shall cut off the spirit of princes: he is terrible to the kings of the earth.'

> Would you have the Lord cut off the spirit of princes — cut off that base and abominable family, that have been tyrannizing over these kingdoms? Would you have him terrible to King Charles, James Duke of York, and the Duke of Monmouth too? Then vow, and bring yourselves under engagements to the Most High. Let us never imagine that ever a party in Scotland will thrive, or that our Lord will give success unto them, even using other lawful means, except they vow to the Lord, and endeavour to perform.

As always, Cameron did not hesitate to declare his own position:

> I do not desire to reflect upon our fathers for bringing home Charles Stuart to get the crown; indeed some of them did regret and go mourning to the grave for it. Yea, his actions since, and the connivances of those who had his favour, or any power under him, evidence that it is impossible to manifest or maintain the royal prerogatives of Jesus Christ, and yet maintain the king's civil rights. Since it is so declared that we must either quit him as king, or Christ, indeed for my part I am for no king but Jesus Christ, since they will have none but Cæsar. When Christ is seated upon his throne and his crown upon his head, let such magistrates be appointed in every particular station as will employ their power for the advancement of his kingdom, and for destroying the kingdom of darkness in this land, and in every place where Christ shall reign; and then let them be owned.

Cameron was here harking back to the idea of a Christian republic, which he clearly still hankered after, though it had not found a place in the Sanquhar Declaration.

He ended, as he so often did, with words full of encouragement for his hearers, bidding them at the same time beware of putting their trust in ecumenical solutions, which were as popular then as they are now:

> Some may think, 'Oh but it would be a hopeful business, if all the ministers, professors and people would join in one!' Indeed, if I saw them all coming to join in one as matters now stand, I would think it good wisdom to run away from that union; it would be a black mark. He will not give his glory to another; he will have few means, that his glory may the more conspicuously appear. Oh to wait on him for counsel, wisdom, courage of every sort for doing and suffering anything he may be calling us to. His and our enemies are laughing at us! Well, go to the Lord, and put him to make out his word: 'Thus hast thou said, and be as good as thy Word. Thou hast heard the blasphemy of thine enemies.' Plead with him; you may plead more familiarly with him than with any man in the countryside. Oh that we were but groaning to the Lord, and telling him what he has promised! We would get wonderful things made out by him. There are as great things to be got from the Lord now, as ever; he never said to the seed of Jacob, 'Seek ye my face in vain.' What have we to fear? Is not the Lord on our side? And if so, it matters not who is against us. Shall the prey be taken from the mighty, or the lawful captive delivered? Now go with the answer to this question from the Lord, believing that he is to arise and contend with them that contend with his people.

27.
Cameron's last sermon

Cameron appears by now to have reached the clear conviction that his work was done. He had fulfilled the commission which had been given him, on that memorable day in Rotterdam, to 'lift the fallen standard, and display it publicly before the world'. He had vindicated the honour of God by bringing the preached gospel, in all its purity, once again before the people of his native land. He had defied the persecution which had sought to overthrow the Reformation heritage of the Church of Scotland and to prevent its members from worshipping God according to their consciences. He had made a public testimony against the tyranny which oppressed both church and state. It now only remained for him to render himself up, as a willing sacrifice, to the God who had called him.

The picture of Cameron in these final days is of one who was wearied of the world and its tribulations, and who longed eagerly for the enjoyment of the eternal reward. Patrick Walker puts it like this: 'He had got such a large earnest, that made him have a soul-longing for a full possession of the inheritance, that seldom he prayed in a family, or sought a blessing, or gave thanks, but he requested to wait for patience till the Lord's time came; as several of my very dear acquaintances, who travelled much with him, told me.'

However, Cameron did not allow his anticipation of his eternal reward to impair his usefulness in God's service for so long as he might be left in the world. Immediately after the public fast at Carluke he made his way south to Crawfordjohn, in southern Clydesdale, in readiness for yet another Lord's Day's preaching.

Coming to the house where he was to lodge, he spent the whole of the Saturday, 10 July, in prayer and meditation alone. The mistress of the house, concerned at his long seclusion, and having tried several times to gain his attention, at last made so bold as to enter the room where he was. She found him in a state of despondency, and anxiously asked the reason. He replied, in his own graphic way: 'That weary promise that I gave to these ministers has lain heavy upon me, for which my carcass shall dung the wilderness, and that within a fortnight.'

Joy and despondency were both always part of Cameron's character. But there was nothing here incompatible with his faith in the future. It was as he contemplated that future that he was filled with a greater sense of his own unworthiness — which, for him, was epitomized in the undertaking he had given, several months earlier, to refrain from speaking on the Indulgence. He well knew that, since that time, he had been enabled to do great things for God. But it was an evidence of the high state of spiritual maturity he had reached that he should now think only of his shortcomings, and see his death as a chastisement for unfaithfulness rather than a gateway to glory.

When he came to give his sermon the following day — the Lord's Day, 11 July — he preached again from what had become one of his favourite texts: 'And ye will not come unto me, that ye might have life' (John 5:40). It was without doubt one of the most memorable sermons of his life. Nearly fifty years later, when Patrick Walker was collecting his reminiscences of Cameron, the memory of that sermon remained fresh in the minds of those still alive who had heard it.[1]

In the course of the sermon both Cameron and his hearers were overcome with emotion, so that for a time he was quite unable to continue. To quote Patrick Walker: 'He fell in such a rap of calm weeping, and the greater part of that multitude, that there was scarce a dry cheek to be seen among them; which obliged him to halt and pray, where he continued long praying for the Jews' restoration and engrafting again, and for the fall of Antichrist, and that the Lord would hasten the day, that he was sure was coming, that he would sweep the throne of Britain of that unhappy race of Stuart.'

In the course of the following week Cameron was engaged on drawing up his vindication of the Sanquhar Declaration, which he completed and signed on Thursday, 15 July. He then prepared for the preaching on the following Lord's Day. This time the preaching-place was the Kype Water in the parish of Avondale, on the western fringes of Clydesdale. He was to share the day's preaching with Donald Cargill. For Cargill, and for most of the others present, it was to be their last meeting with Cameron on earth.

Cameron's chosen text was one that he had made his own — one that he had taken as his guide in many a testing trial and circumstance. It was: 'Be still, and know that I am God' (Psalm 46:10). The text was only brief, but inexhaustibly profound. 'Many', he remarked, 'are the mysteries that are contained and wrapped up in the shortest sentences of Scripture.' He went on to expound the text in a closely ordered way, dealing, in catechetical style, with what was forbidden, what was required, the reasons annexed and the use, or application, of the text.

What was *forbidden* was murmuring against God, no matter what circumstances he might be pleased to send into the lives of his people: 'Beware of it, for it is a dreadful thing to quarrel with God. Who may say to him, "What doest thou?" Let us then, while we bear the yoke, sit alone, and keep silence, and put our mouths in the dust, if so be there may be hope.'

What was *required* was composure of spirit: 'It is taking well with the providential dispensations of God, because he alone has done it, and if you cannot see through them, you hope against hope, that God will bring good out of them. We should not limit, nor set bounds to him; but let him take his own way in granting that which is most upon our spirits, and fulfilling the desires of our hearts.'

It was when he came to the *'reasons annexed'* to his text that his sermon was to reach its climax. It was as if his whole view of God — his sovereignty, his unchangeableness, his infinite wisdom and majesty — had been condensed into one memorable utterance:

> He is God still. Think not that he is, in any respect, less God than he was many years ago. It is true, he appeared more visibly to men twenty or thirty years since, in this land, than he does now; but he is the same God now, that he was then when his work flourished. He is the same God yesterday, today and for ever. Oh for high and honourable thoughts of him; for though he be unchangeable, yet oh how often do our thoughts change of him! Our good thoughts of him ebb and flow as his dispensations towards us. Sometimes folk have good thoughts of God, and at other times they begin to think he has forgotten the earth. How dangerous is such a thought, for he has as much power for managing and governing his affairs now as ever; he is always sitting in the assembly of the gods, and rules in the midst of his enemies. All the angels that are beholding him, in the greatness of his glory, and the brightness of his countenance, cannot tell the hundredth, nay the thousandth part of him. But we may know much of him by his works of creation and providence. At this time, the present providences may supply the want of preaching. The dispensations of this time have much in them. By these dispensations we may know many things that our fathers

> knew not; they had not the means of knowing many of the mysterious secrets of God's nature, that we may see by the dispensations of the time.

God had promised that he would be exalted among the heathen; he would be exalted in the earth. Cameron had a glorious vision of the future of God's cause in Scotland, which he went on to share with his hearers:

> The day has been, when Zion was stately in Scotland. The terror of the Church of Scotland once took hold of all the kings and great men that passed by. Yea, the terror of it took hold on popish princes, nay on the pope himself; but all this exalting that we have seen is nothing to what is to come. The church was high; but it shall be yet much higher. The church of Christ is to be so exalted, that its members shall be made to ride upon the high places of the earth.

Cameron was careful at this point to deny any association with the views of the fifth monarchists, which had been charged against him, and who looked for a thousand-year reign of Christ on earth.

> But [he went on] we are of the opinion that the church shall yet be more high and glorious, and the church shall have more power than ever she had before; and therefore we declare avowedly in opposition to all tyrannical magistrates over Protestants and over Presbyterians, magistrates that are open enemies to God. We declare we will have none such acknowledged as lawful magistrates over us; we will have none but such as are for the advancement of piety, and the suppression of impiety and wickedness. Let all the world say as they will, we have the Word of God for it. The work begun shall be

> carried on in spite of all opposition; our Lord shall be exalted on earth; and we do not question much but that he shall yet be exalted in Scotland.

But if this glorious vision were to be realized, the people of God in Scotland would need faith. He applied this truth in a striking way:

> I assure you that we in Scotland have need to take heed to ourselves. I am very much afraid that we may even have done with good days in Scotland for all this. But let us stir up ourselves, and take hold of him by faith; for I assure you, if you be not delivered, and made a free and purified people, we shall be no more a free corporation, nation, or embodied people, than the Jews are this day.

There followed some words of remarkable power:

> I say not this to disquiet you, but to stir you up to take hold of Christ, and his standard on which it shall be written, 'Let Christ Reign.' Let us study to have it set up amongst us. It is hard to tell, where it shall be first erected; but our Lord is to set up a standard, and oh that it may be carried to Scotland! When it is set up, it shall be carried through the nations; and it shall go to Rome, and the gates of Rome shall be burnt with fire. It is a standard that shall overthrow the throne of Britain, and all the thrones in Europe, that will not kiss the Son lest he be angry, and in his anger they perish from the way.

As he drew the sermon to a close, his thoughts continued to dwell on the glory and majesty of God. It was as if in these final moments he could not tear himself away from this great theme.

> Labour to have much of the awe, fear and dread of God upon your spirits. Oh that you would set the Lord always before you. It is neither lord, laird, general, nor forces that can stand in thy sight, O Lord, if once thou be angry. If this were on our spirit, looking to and fearing of men would much disappear; if this consideration were on our spirits, man's greatness would not be once named by us. If we looked to the greatness, sovereignty and power of God, and could say, 'The Lord of hosts is with us, the God of Jacob is our refuge,' we would have composure of spirit.

His final words were almost subdued in comparison with what had gone before. But after the forcefulness and power of his earlier utterances there was a special solemnity about these parting words of quiet counsel and consolation, the last his hearers were ever to hear from him:

> Would you be still? Then strive to have faith in exercise all the time. The least faith in exercise, has more strength than thousands of men and armies. Oh but faith has a strange power with God! Try if you have faith; and if you have it, cry, 'Lord, I believe, help thou mine unbelief.' Deny it not, though never so small. If you have any, use the little you have, and you may get more; and this will tend much to establish and compose your heart in an evil time. For without being still, there is no right going about duty. Without it, we cannot wrestle, pray or praise. How can ministers preach, or people hear? How can there be reading or praying aright without being still? The man that is disquieted and fearful is unfit for any piece of duty; he is a prey to every temptation. We say, it is good fishing in troubled waters; the devil first labours to confuse men, and then he easily

> catches them; then he will bait his hook, and take them by one temptation or another. So that the thing to be understood here is to be patiently waiting on God, and to beware of grudging, murmuring, despondency, fearfulness, and disquiet of mind.

With these words, Cameron's preaching ministry was ended.

28.
The last days

It is difficult to believe that in exhorting his hearers to 'be still' Cameron did not have in mind the particular relevance of these words to himself. Outwardly his circumstances were threatening in the extreme. As he well knew, the forces of authority were gathering themselves against him. But this was by no means the only threat. Cameron and his party were now deeply and bitterly resented by the moderate Presbyterians, who were represented among a number of the landed gentry of the west. For so long as he had confined himself to preaching, without touching on affairs of state, they had been content, in the main, to let him alone; but now that he had publicly thrown off the king's authority, and been declared an open traitor and rebel, any countenancing of him on their part would be liable to be construed as rebellion. Even so, there were few who were prepared to take the ultimate step of betraying him to the authorities. But the temptation to do so must have been strong, particularly for those whose own sympathies had previously brought them under suspicion by the government and who now saw themselves as exposed to even greater risk by Cameron's activities. In the end, it was this factor that was to prove decisive.

Meanwhile, the hunt for Cameron was being pursued with unremitting vigour.[1] A wide expanse of country, from

Clydesdale into Nithsdale and Galloway, and westwards towards Cumnock and Ayr, had become the scene of intense military activity. In response to reported sightings of Cameron, Airlie's troops were sent hither and thither in search of him. From Strathaven and Lanark in the north to Dalmellington and New Galloway in the south, and from Cumnock in the west to Douglas and Crawfordjohn in the east, there were few places which escaped the attentions of the soldiers. Spies and informers were recruited, and the whole area brought into a state of martial law. Around mid-July Dalyell himself moved from his base at Langside to Lanark to supervise operations.[2] By then, Airlie and his men had spent some three weeks fruitlessly searching for Cameron. But the net was closing around him.

Cameron was clearly not short of information about the enemy's movements, or the intensity of the search now being made for him. There is evidence to suggest that, as a matter of tactics, he and his followers had made it their practice to disband between public preaching engagements and only to come together, in mutual defence, when Cameron was engaged to preach. However, as the search for him intensified, Cameron saw safety in greater numbers, and in the week after his sermon at Kype Water he was attended by the full complement of his supporters, amounting to twenty-three horse and forty foot in all.[3] There is also evidence that, during this week, he was joined by several others for the first time. There appears to have been a prevailing mood that a confrontation with the enemy could not be long delayed, and some who had perhaps previously hesitated to throw in their lot with Cameron now rallied publicly to his support.

Moving around the countryside with over sixty armed followers, Cameron could scarcely have hoped to avoid detection by the many parties of troops sent in his pursuit. His position was made even more difficult by the presence of spies and informers, some of whom, sadly, were those who had formerly attended field-meetings and who now acted against him with the particular spite and virulence of the apostate. Notable among these was a certain Robert Cannon of Mandrogat, who had fought at Pentland, but now made himself useful in the service of the persecutors.[4]

Cannon had learned of Cameron's field-meeting at Crawfordjohn on 11 July, and had passed on the information to the authorities. There was, however, a delay in the information being acted on, and by the time it reached Airlie, then at New Galloway, on 19 July it was already well out of date. Airlie's staff, however, appear to have assumed that the information related to the previous day, 18 July, and on the strength of this assumption he immediately ordered out one of his lieutenants with a strong force of horse and dragoons, with orders to pursue Cameron 'to the uttermost' and to report back regularly on the progress he was making.[5]

The information on which Airlie had acted, mistakenly as it turned out, was that Cameron had been 'between Roberton and Crawfordjohn on Sunday last'. It was there, initially, that he directed his troops, with orders to stop the passes into Annandale and to the east. Cameron had in fact left the area several days before, and for some days the troops scoured the countryside without success. Indeed, by Wednesday, 21 July, Airlie and his staff had started to wonder what had become of them.[6] However, at some point, possibly on Thursday, 22 July, they appear to have come under fresh orders from Dalyell himself, now stationed at Lanark, to march westwards towards Cumnock. These orders, it seems, were prompted by information received from another quarter, which was ultimately to prove decisive.

The precise sequence of events at this point is uncertain, though the general picture is reasonably clear. According to one account, one of Cameron's own party had gone to Robert

Miller, the minister of Ochiltree, with a fabricated story that Cameron and his men had resolved to murder all the ministers in the west who had accepted the Indulgence (of whom Miller was one), and that the Sanquhar Declaration had been intended to herald this plan being put into action. Miller is said to have passed on the story to Sir John Cochrane of Ochiltree, who was a relative of his by marriage, and who was one of the most influential of the west-country landowners.

Cochrane, the second son of the Earl of Dundonald, was a moderate Presbyterian who had previously been in trouble with the government over his support for the Presbyterian cause, and had even fought on the Presbyterian side at Bothwell Bridge. He had also, in 1678, been part of a deputation to the king which had complained about the government's oppressive policies in Scotland.[7] Given his record, Cochrane was anxious not to be seen as a sympathizer with rebels and, whether Miller was involved or not, he scarcely needed the impetus of Miller's story to seek to ingratiate himself with the government.

In a letter written at Cumnock on 4 July, Airlie had told Dalyell that 'Sir John Cochrane hath been with me,' and though he could at that point give no certain account of Cameron's whereabouts, he and others had resolved, Airlie said, 'to be with me this day and tomorrow with what intelligence they can learn'. It seems that Cochrane had now discovered where Cameron and his party were to be found, and there can be little doubt that it was he who redirected the government party who were searching for Cameron.[8]

When he left Kype Water after preaching there, Cameron could have been under no illusions about the dangers to which he was now exposed. Accompanied by his armed followers, he made his way south and west to the area around Sorn, in the upper reaches of the Water of Ayr. For some time previously he and his party had made their base at Middle Wellwood

Farm, between Sorn and Muirkirk, where they worshipped regularly together and where they exercised from time to time in readiness for the confrontation which they expected soon.[9] It was to the area around Middle Wellwood that the bulk of Cameron's party returned after his preaching on 18 July.

Cameron himself meanwhile lodged at Meadowhead Farm, to the north of Sorn, with a sympathizer, William Mitchell, and his wife and daughter. It is uncertain how long he stayed at Meadowhead, but he was definitely there on the night of Wednesday, 21 July. The next morning, as he prepared to leave, the daughter of the house brought him water to wash his face and hands. When he had done so, and had dried them, he looked at his hands, put them to his face, and said solemnly, 'This is their last washing. I have need to make them clean, for there are many to see them.' The girl's mother wept when she heard these words, but he told her, 'Weep not for me, but for yourself and yours, and for the sins of a sinful land; for you have many melancholy, sorrowful, weary days before you.'

On rejoining his party, Cameron found that because of a sudden alarm the previous evening they had camped out on the moor all night. Hackston, who was in command, had sent out scouts to reconnoitre the situation, but they had returned that morning with nothing to report.

For the next few hours Cameron and his party remained together on the moor, keeping careful watch for the enemy. At length, between three and four in the afternoon, they lay down for some rest and refreshment. Scarcely had they done so when a local herdsman brought them the alarming news of the near approach of the government force, advancing rapidly from the east.

Decisions had to be taken instantly. According to one account, some of Cameron's men, fearful for his safety, urged him to make good his escape while the opportunity offered, but he resolutely refused.[10] Instead, he and Hackston threw themselves into organizing what defence they could. There was no time for discussion of tactics. Advised by the herdsman, who knew the ground intimately, they quickly took up posts some distance to the west, on the fringe of an extensive marsh, or morass, known as Airdsmoss. There, choosing the sole spot of advantage to be had, they turned to face the enemy.

Each man firmly declared his intention to fight. Cameron, gathering them all close around him, called them briefly to prayer. 'Lord', he said, and he repeated it three times over, in words which those who heard him would never forget, 'spare the green, and take the ripe.' He had time for two brief words of exhortation. First he spoke to his brother: 'Michael, come, let us fight it out to the last; for this is the day that I have longed for, and the death that I have prayed for, to die fighting against our Lord's avowed enemies; and this is the day that we will get the crown.' Then he addressed the rest and said, 'Be encouraged, all of you, to fight it out valiantly; for all of you that shall fall this day, I see heaven's gates cast wide open to receive them.'

The leader of the government force had by now come into view. It was Andrew Bruce of Earlshall. Years before, in Fife, the Camerons of Fordell and the Bruces of Earlshall had lived together as neighbours, on terms of intimate acquaintance. Allan Cameron had helped that same Andrew Bruce in a time of financial need. Now, in the mysteries of God's providence, the two families were brought together once more, in circumstances tragically different.

Behind Bruce rode several other men and officers from Fife. The foremost of the government troopers was David Ramsay, of St Andrews, a personal acquaintance of Hackston. The final act in the tragedy was about to be played out. The scene may have been a moorland in Ayrshire, but the chief protagonists were all men of Fife. For Cameron, the wheel had come full circle. Fife, some thirty-three years before, had given him his life. It was men of Fife who were now to end it.

The action began with Bruce ordering a party of some twenty dragoons on foot to attack the flank of Cameron's party, hoping to create an opportunity for his main body to advance. Hackston, on seeing this, despatched a party of foot-soldiers to meet them, and at the same time advanced all his horsemen to confront the government force. An initial exchange of fire brought down some of the enemy cavalry, but soon the horse of both sides started to become entangled in the morass. Several on each side, including Hackston himself, were forced to dismount, and to fight it out on foot. The action that followed was, according to Bruce's account later, 'very hot', with Cameron's party fighting 'like madmen' and refusing either to give way or take quarter. Indeed, for up to half an hour, the result hung in the balance. At length, however, the superior numbers of Bruce's troops took their toll. The foot-soldiers of Cameron's party, seeing their horsemen gradually worn down, gave up the fight as lost and fled the field, an action which they later bitterly regretted. Bereft of their support, the remaining horsemen were themselves forced to flee, or were made prisoner. By five o'clock, the action was over.[11]

The government troops, badly mauled as they were, were generous in praise of their opponents. 'They gave us all testimony', wrote Hackston later, 'of brave resolute men.' Years afterwards, some of them confided to Patrick Walker, as he was collecting materials for his *Life* of Cameron, 'that that handful were men of the greatest courage that ever they saw set their faces to fight, though they had been at battles abroad', and 'If they had been as well trained and armed and horsed as we were, we would have been put to the flight, and few of us escaped; their shots and strokes were deadly, and few recovered; though there were but nine of them killed, there were

Monument at Airdsmoss marking the battle site and commemorating the deaths of Richard Cameron and his companions

Close-up of inscription on the monument

Stone marking the grave of those who fell at Airdsmoss

twenty-eight of us killed dead, and died in their wounds in a few days.'

In addition to the nine dead on Cameron's side, there were four prisoners. Among these was Hackston, who had for some time been in the forefront of the action, then had engaged in hand-to-hand combat with David Ramsay before being cut down from behind by three of the troopers. Three others — William Manuel, John Vallance and John Pollock — the last of whom had acted as courier for Cameron's party and was not armed, were taken with him. Some of those who escaped, according to Patrick Walker, who knew several of them, 'wept thereafter that they died not there that day, for they were afraid that they would never be in such a case for to meet with death'.

Among the dead, inevitably, was Richard Cameron. He appears to have fallen in the thick of the action, fighting, as always, from the front. From Bruce's account, sent later that day, it appears that it had taken several of his men to overcome Cameron, and that they were unsure who he was until Bruce gave them some distinguishing marks by which to recognize him.[12] For Cameron, it was a death that he was prepared for, knowing that his work was done. His brother Michael died with him. Like the others who fell, he too was well prepared. 'These eight', wrote Patrick Walker, 'that died on the spot with him were ripe, and longing for that day and death.' Cameron's prayer, before the action began, had indeed been fully answered.

29.
M'Ward's words come true

For Bruce, there remained the formalities of victory. One of his men, Robert Murray, was paid a guinea to cut off Cameron's head and hands, to be presented as trophies to the Privy Council. A similar barbarism was intended for the body of his brother Michael, but was inflicted by mistake on the body of John Fowler, who had commanded the foot-soldiers. Bruce and his badly-mauled party then departed the scene with the prisoners, leaving the dead on both sides lying unburied.

It was essential that the prisoners — especially Hackston — be given early medical attention to ensure that they did not die of their wounds and so escape the vengeance planned for them by the authorities. Bruce therefore marched with the prisoners, and the heads of the slain, to Douglas, the nearest place where such attention could be had, and from where, late that night, he sent a dispatch to Dalyell, now at Lanark, reporting the news of his success. Early the next day the news was sent by fleet horse to Edinburgh, where it arrived in mid-morning. The result was sadly predictable. 'That dispensation', records Patrick Walker, 'of the fall and flight of these worthies at Airdsmoss, was a day of great joy and rejoicing, not only to the stated enemies, but also to the indulged and their favourites, telling it one to another as their joyful news, and some of them with loud laughter, whose names I could mention.'

Sir John Cochrane, meanwhile, had been to the field of action at Airdsmoss, where he had rescued a wounded government soldier, William Parker, who had been left behind by Bruce.[1] It would be gratifying to think that Cochrane had performed the last service of burying the dead but, though this is possible, it has not been recorded.

On the Friday, Hackston and the other prisoners were brought from Douglas to Lanark, where they were brutally interrogated by Dalyell and others of the military. The soldiers who had charge of the heads of Cameron and Fowler appear to have been left to themselves in the meantime, and they used the opportunity to devise their own act of barbarism at the expense of two of Cameron's local sympathizers. Patrick Walker recounts that 'They had Mr Cameron's and John Fowler's heads and hands in a sack; when they came to Lanark they carried them into the house of John Arcle, and enquired of his wife Elizabeth Hope, if she would buy calves' heads? They shook them out of the sack, and drave them up and down the house like footballs with their feet.' It can scarcely be supposed that such an act, if it really happened — and Patrick Walker vouches for the truth of the report — would have had the approval of Bruce, who of course had to deliver the heads to the Privy Council as proof of his victory, and indeed of his claim for a reward; but neither he nor other senior officers appear to have been present to prevent it.[2] The act appears therefore to have been a case of military indiscipline, of which, unfortunately, there were too many contemporary instances.

The next day, Bruce and his party started for Edinburgh. The Privy Council, at a special meeting that morning, issued instructions regarding the manner of their arrival. These have been preserved in their records:

> The magistrates of Edinburgh are appointed, as soon as the body of David Hackston of Rathillet is brought to

> the Water Gate, to receive him, and mount him on a bare-backed horse, with his face to the horse's tail, and his feet tied beneath his belly, and his hands flightered with ropes; and the executioner, with head covered, and his coat, lead his horse up the street to the Tolbooth, the said Hackston being bareheaded; that the three other prisoners be conveyed on foot, bareheaded, after him, with their hands tied to a goad of iron; ordain the said executioner to carry the head of Cameron on a halbert, from the Water Gate to the Council house.

By late that Saturday afternoon, 24 July, Bruce's party had arrived at the Water Gate of Edinburgh, at the foot of the Canongate, and adjacent to Holyroodhouse. What then took place is best told in the words of Patrick Walker, who had it from an eyewitness, whom he describes as 'my intimate acquaintance upwards of forty years, who had the experience both of imprisonment and banishment'. Walker describes how 'He was at the Water Gate at the foot of the Canongate, when the enemies came there with these prisoners' heads and hands; he saw them take Mr Cameron's head out of the sack; he knew it, being formerly his hearer, a man of a fair complexion, with his own hair, and his face very little altered, and put the point of a halbert in his blessed mouth, out of which had proceeded many gracious words, and turned Rathillet upon the horse, and tied a gade of iron upon William Manuel's and John Pollock's necks, and tied the rope to Rathillet's horse-tail, the hangman leading the horse with one hand, and holding up the halbert with Mr Cameron's head upon it with the other hand, up the street to the town-tolbooth of Edinburgh, crying, "There's the heads and hands of traitors, rebels."'[3]

Five years later, another ignominious procession was to make its way from the Water Gate to the Edinburgh Tolbooth. Once again a captured rebel was led by a rope by the common hangman. This time it was Sir John Cochrane of Ochiltree. Arrested for his part in the Earl of Argyle's rebellion against James II, he was brought to Edinburgh to stand trial. Cochrane, however, was sufficiently pliable to testify against those whom he had supported, and so escaped the fate which had threatened him. He lived out the rest of his life in obscurity, and even the year of his death is not known for certain. His mansion at Ochiltree had been burnt to the ground in October 1681, an event which many saw as a judgement for his betrayal of Cameron.[4] So far as is known, Cochrane remained unrepentant; in a letter written to the Chancellor of Scotland in 1683, at a time when he was being suspected of subversive activities, he asserted, as an argument in his favour: 'Upon all occasions I have been as active as any man to suppress all rebels, and particularly Cameron and his associates.'[5] Despite the efforts which have been made to excuse him, Cochrane stands self-condemned.

Cameron's death had deprived the Privy Council of the satisfaction of inflicting on him the vengeance they had long premeditated. They therefore concentrated the full force of their fury upon Hackston. Severely wounded, yet able to answer boldly and freely to his interrogators, he was condemned on 29 July to the most inhuman and brutal death that they could devise. The next day the sentence, in all its horrific details, was duly carried out.[6] Of the other prisoners brought in with Hackston, two — William Manuel and John Vallance — had in the interim died of their wounds. The third, John Pollock, was savagely tortured to extract information about Cameron's associates, and was eventually sent into banishment.

Though Cameron himself was beyond their reach, the council contrived yet more acts of callousness with regard to him. They had his head and hands brought to his aged father, who still languished in the Edinburgh Tolbooth, and asked the old man if he knew them. 'I know them, I know them', he replied. 'They are my son's, my dear son's. It is the Lord. Good is the will of the Lord, who cannot wrong me nor mine, but has made goodness and mercy to follow us all our days.' Amid the all-pervading evil, Allan Cameron's faith shone out as a clear light — a light which overcame the darkness of the hour, and which continued to burn brightly despite all the efforts of the powers of evil to extinguish it.

As a final act of ignominy, on Saturday, 31 July Cameron's head and hands were publicly displayed on the Netherbow Port of Edinburgh, with the fingers pointing upwards. The heads of Hackston and the others were also displayed with him. M'Ward's prophecy, made on the day of Cameron's ordination a year before, had finally been fulfilled.

Patrick Walker records touchingly how Stephen Cuthill from Bo'ness, whom he knew personally, went to Rotterdam to give M'Ward an account of Cameron's death. 'Come away, Stephen', said M'Ward to him, 'I longed to see you; give me an account of the murder of singular Cameron, and these other worthies with him.'

Cuthill gave a full account, not sparing any of the details. M'Ward was deeply moved: 'O worthy Cameron!' he broke out, 'highly honoured of the Lord, Cameron! O Covenant-breaking and burning Scotland, how many, long and great shall thy judgements be!'

Cuthill was keen to know the truth about what M'Ward had actually said at Cameron's ordination, and he took the opportunity to ask him personally. 'Indeed, Stephen', M'Ward replied, ''tis most true; and it was no foresight nor forethought in me; but when my hand was upon his head, I was as much persuaded of it, and as much affected with it, as if I had been at Airdsmoss, and seen his head and hands cut off, or as if I were standing at the Netherbow Port looking to it; I could be no more persuaded, affected and afflicted, than I was at that time.'

An eighteenth-century print of the Netherbow Port, Edinburgh
(which has since been demolished)
Reproduced by courtesy of Edinburgh Public Libraries

M'Ward died in May the following year, and with his death the persecuted church in Scotland lost a valued supporter and friend. With the capture and execution of Donald Cargill, just two months later, the 'suffering remnant' were left without a minister until the return of James Renwick from Holland in October 1683. For the next few years it was Renwick who upheld the standard of the persecuted church, until he too fell at the very dawn of the day of deliverance in 1688. Before that deliverance came, the church was called upon to go through a furnace of tribulation more intense than any she had experienced in her history. And throughout that experience she kept prominently before her the example of one who had given his all in the cause for which she contended — one who would ever be remembered by those left behind him and whose memory would be treasured as 'great Cameron'.

On 4 April 1689, after the era of persecution had finally ended, the Estates of Scotland issued a declaration stating that King James VII, the last representative of the Stuart dynasty, had forfeited the throne. The wording of the declaration bore a striking resemblance to an earlier declaration published in a small lowland town some nine years before. 'The Estates of the Kingdom of Scotland', it ran, 'find and declare that King James the Seventh hath invaded the fundamental constitution of this kingdom, and altered it from a legal limited monarchy to an arbitrary despotic power, and hath exercised the same to the subversion of the Protestant religion and the violation of the laws and liberties of the nation, inverting all the ends of government; whereby he hath forfeited the right to the Crown, and the throne is become vacant.' It was the final vindication of Cameron's action that day in 1680. The Sanquhar Declaration had shaken the throne of Britain.

30.
Cameron's place in history

It is scarcely surprising that a public career of such prominence and intensity as that of Richard Cameron should have led to widely differing assessments of his rightful place in history. Some commentators have seen him as a champion of civil and political liberties. Others have highlighted his defence of the rights of the church against the arbitrary claims of the state. Yet others have seen him pre-eminently as a preacher and evangelist. And there have always been some who, like the majority in his own day, have seen him only as a misguided zealot leading an unjustified revolt against lawful authority.

Cameron's career has, of course, to be viewed against the background of his own time. There were issues prominent in church and state which called forth from him a particular reaction suited to the needs of the hour. But, at the same time, there were elements in his response to these issues which are of permanent interest and relevance. It is on these, essentially, that his contribution to history must be assessed.

Cameron was first and foremost a preacher. Others, certainly, may have recognized his preaching abilities before he became aware of them himself, but once convinced that he had God's call to the ministry he embraced that calling with single-minded zeal. And it was a zeal which left no place for self. He had received his commission from the Lord. His work was to declare the whole counsel of God, without fear of man, and it was a task that he discharged faithfully at all times. Indeed, though his hearers were often challenged and chastened by his preaching, his faithfulness to his commission earned at once their attention and respect.

There is no question that Cameron had considerable natural abilities for the work of the ministry. He could communicate his message with energy and conviction. He could preach with outstanding eloquence and power. He could speak closely and searchingly to the conscience. His preaching style, though simple, was immensely effective. The fervency of his appeals, the penetrating questions, the graphic word-pictures — all were calculated to leave a lasting impression upon his hearers. These qualities were, of course, singularly suited to a situation where both preacher and hearers were often in danger of their lives and they invested his message with a peculiar solemnity and urgency. They also ensured that his words remained impressed on his hearers long after they had been spoken. It is notable that many of those whose testimonies are recorded in the *Cloud of Witnesses* bear witness to the power of Cameron's preaching.

It would be a mistake, however, to think that Cameron depended only on his natural gifts for the exercise of his ministry. Those sermons of his which have been published show signs of careful preparation. While they were no doubt delivered extempore, they follow a logical order of thought and application. They are obviously the product of a mind trained to think logically and to use his material to the maximum effect. They also show, interestingly enough, significant evidence of the didactic skills which he had learned in his earlier days and which he had no doubt had opportunity to develop in his teaching career at Falkland.

Cameron's message was essentially evangelical. The one great theme of his preaching was to point his hearers to Christ.

The most notable passages in his sermons are those appeals in which he pleads with sinners to look to Christ for salvation. But he was also careful to minister comfort and reassurance to the people of God. At a time when many were experiencing great hardship, and were in danger of losing their possessions, their homes and even their lives, his message was often one of encouragement to greater perseverance, of continued trust in God and of the blessings promised to those who would endure to the end.

Cameron's thinking was deeply rooted in the people. True, the minister had his calling from God, and that invested his office with a particular authority, but that did not in any way mean that he was divorced from the people. Cameron was always careful, notwithstanding his high sense of vocation to the ministry, never to preach without a call from the people. It was that call, indeed, which validated his ministry and confirmed his own call from God.

The right of the people to choose their own ministers was of the very essence of Presbyterianism, and Cameron was a Presbyterian through and through. For him church government was not a secondary issue, nor was Presbyterianism a mere option. It might have been supposed that, in the exceptional circumstances in which he was placed, Cameron would not have set much store by observing the forms of Presbyterianism. That was not at all the case. He took pains to ordain elders from among his followers, he carefully consulted the local eldership in places where he was to preach and he surprised the ministers at the Edinburgh meeting by faulting them for not having elders present. He was thoroughly familiar, too, with contemporary works in which the claims of Presbyterianism were presented. Even in the course of one of his most powerful sermons he could find time to counsel his hearers to study Samuel Rutherford's *Peaceable Plea for Paul's Presbytery in Scotland.* For Cameron, indeed, the structure and government of the Church of Scotland were an ideal not to be surpassed. In another of his sermons he gave it as a sign of future blessing on the church that 'All the neighbouring nations will come and take, as it were, a copy of the doctrine, worship and discipline of the Church of Scotland.'

In the latter part of his career, Cameron carried his testimony into a wider arena. It was not that he had decided to dabble in state affairs as distinct from those of the church; for him the two were inseparably united. As a true son of the Reformation, Cameron knew very well the strength of the link between civil and religious freedom. He was quick to see that the bondage of the church was a threat to the civil liberties of the nation. It was this insight which motivated his actions in the later stages of his life and particularly, of course, the declaration at Sanquhar. In those few months when he held the torch aloft he spoke not only for the liberties of the church, but for the liberties of the nation—a nation, indeed, whose bounds transcended those of his native Scotland and, in true covenanted fashion, extended also to the neighbouring kingdoms. It was not without significance that the Sanquhar Declaration spoke of Charles II as 'tyrannizing on the throne of *Britain*'. And in that respect, Cameron could claim to be a true herald of the deliverance which ultimately came to the people of Britain as a whole.

Cameron appeared on the scene at a time when the testimony of the church was being threatened with compromise. Later, when he returned from Holland, he rallied the spirits of the faithful when all seemed lost, and when the forces of persecution were well-nigh triumphant. It was largely due to his efforts that the final surrender never took place. His example of self-sacrificing service was to prove an inspiration to many in the dark days ahead. It invested his memory with a particular devotion and respect. To Robert Hamilton, who worked with him closely and perhaps knew him better than any man, he was always 'great Cameron'. And others too, who knew him and heard him preach, would carry to their dying day a treasured remembrance of him.

Much has been written about Cameron's temperament. He has been contrasted in this respect, not always to his advantage, with contemporaries such as Cargill and Renwick. Admittedly, Cameron can scarcely be advanced as a model of circumspection and prudence. He acted impulsively at times and he was, perhaps to a fault, impatient of obtaining results. His was, however, the impatience which comes from complete dedication to a cause. It was the same trait which caused him to be intolerant of error or compromise, no matter where he saw it. There were many who looked askance at his treatment of the Edinburgh ministers, many of whom were his elders and seniors. But for Cameron there was a higher allegiance, and a higher responsibility. If he appeared to treat the ministers with scant respect, it was because they had failed to honour the rights of the Master he loved and served.

But away from these confrontations, Cameron was capable of close and warm fellowship. Open and generous by nature, he attracted to himself a wide circle of friends and sympathizers. His correspondence with the Gordons gives an indication of the warmth of his friendships, and his particular closeness to children is evident in a number of ways. It is clear from his sermons that he was able to relate to people of varying classes and interests. This drew a response from his hearers, and was a vital element in his popular appeal.

It has been fashionable to decry Cameron as a deviant from the mainstream of Presbyterianism. Such claims were, of course, common in his own day. They do not, however, bear serious scrutiny. Indeed, it is a supreme irony that Cameron, of all men, should be so stigmatized, for few were more devoted in their attachment to Presbyterian and Reformation principles. Next to Scripture itself, Cameron was guided throughout his career by the standards of the Scottish Reformers, as reflected in the Covenants, and by the pronouncements of the post-1638 Assemblies. Far from being a deviant from Scottish Presbyterianism, he could claim to be one of its most orthodox proponents and defenders.

Ultimately, of course, critics of Cameron take their stand — as they did in his own day — on the fact that he was prepared to disown the authority of the king and magistrates. It is, however, a simplistic objection to say that this was contrary to the scriptural injunction to render obedience to rulers. Cameron well knew that the issues were more complex than that. He had perhaps not thought out the principles as carefully as his contemporary Donald Cargill, who was reluctant to act until he had clear guidance that the rulers had first been cast off by God, but Cameron was satisfied in his own mind. He could point to the views of older writers such as Knox and Buchanan, but he did not look so much to older authorities as to his own conscience, taught as it was by the Word of God. That, as always, was his supreme rule. He was perceptive enough to see that Scripture did not call for blind obedience to rulers, irrespective of their conduct and, while he may have been the first to give this principle practical expression, he was fully vindicated by events.

It is relatively easy to claim that in his views of civil government, in particular, Cameron was striving after an unattainable ideal. To the extent, certainly, that he saw the optimum form of civil government as an oligarchy patterned on the law of Moses – a concept he clearly favoured but which he did not press upon others – his views can best be described as visionary. But it was a vision with a purpose, and in bringing the issue to the forefront, Cameron performed a valuable service. For many of his contemporaries it was a startling thing that an established institution such as the monarchy should be called into question. But the very propagation of such a view was in itself a measure of how far the established institutions had become debased by those who occupied them. Whether consciously or not, the minds of Cameron's countrymen were being influenced in a direction which, in the end, was to prove decisive to the overthrow of tyranny and persecution.

One of Cameron's favourite words was 'honest'. He spoke of 'honest' *Lex Rex,* and of the 'honest' Acts of the Second Reformation Assemblies. It is a word that can be very aptly applied to himself. As he used it, it denotes a quality of testimony which is open and uncomplicated. It may not necessarily be the best-informed, but what it may lack in sophistication it gains in sincerity. It has in it, too, a quality which does not regard the cost. So it was with Cameron. Not that he was needlessly careless of his own life, or the lives of others; but he subordinated all other considerations to the honour of the Master he served. And when it became clear that the ultimate sacrifice was to be demanded of him, he went forward in complete submission to his Master's will.

Cameron has earned a distinctive place in history. In his native Scotland, his name has become synonymous with resolute and unflinching adherence to a cause. In his own day, that cause was surely the best of all possible causes — the right of his Master Christ to rule over his own house, and the right of the people to enjoy their civil and spiritual freedoms. These were principles for which Cameron thought it worthy to die. His contribution, at the time, may have appeared insignificant. But the passing of the years has enriched his memory, and today he has an honoured place in the gallery of Scotland's heroes. It is a place due to him, and one which he will surely retain.

Appendix I: Bibliographical notes

A brief biographical account of Cameron appeared in the first edition of the *Cloud of Witnesses* in 1714. A more extended *Life* was published by Patrick Walker in 1727 and has been several times reprinted, most recently in *Biographia Presbyteriana* (1827, reissued 1837) and *Six Saints of the Covenant* (1901), in the latter case copiously annotated by Dr David Hay Fleming. John Howie of Lochgoin drew largely on Walker's *Life* for his biographical notice of Cameron in the *Scots Worthies* (1775, many times reprinted).

Later biographies are by G. M. Bell (1833, 2nd edition 1843), Jean L. Watson (1880) and Richard Herkless (Famous Scots Series, 1896). There has been no further biography since Herkless' time, although Andrew Veitch drew on incidents in Cameron's life for a historical novel published in 1948. John L. Downie's *The Early Home of Richard Cameron* (1901) offers useful insights into Cameron's background in contemporary Falkland.

In 1733 William Wilson of Torfoot in the parish of Avondale published, under the title *Good News to Scotland*, Cameron's sermon at Carluke on 8 July 1680 on the text, 'Shall the prey be taken from the mighty, and the lawful captive delivered?' Wilson, who later became schoolmaster at Broomerside, near Douglas, was a staunch defender of the old ways and an admirer of the memory of the field-preachers and, like John Howie after him, he did valuable service in rescuing their work from oblivion. His *Good News to Scotland* was reissued in 1740 and on several later occasions.

In 1748 Wilson issued in two volumes the collected sermons of James Renwick (several times reprinted) and in 1751 he published his *True and Impartial Relation of Bothwell Bridge,* in which he strongly defended the conduct of Robert Hamilton and his supporters ('the honest party', as he termed them) in face of the compromise of John Welsh and his followers, whom he termed 'the Erastian party'. Wilson's account is valuable as it draws on some sources which are no longer extant and, while his sympathies are obvious, his work is at the same time an authoritative and detailed narrative of events. It was several times reprinted, and can be found appended to some early editions of the *Scots Worthies* and other works.

Wilson also had ambitions as a poet. It was he who penned the inscription on Samuel Rutherford's tombstone at St Andrews, and on occasion he devoted himself to writing acrostics on the names of his heroes. His effort on Cameron, which is appended to *Good News to Scotland* is as follows:

Most noble Cameron of renown,
A fame of thee shall ne'er go down;
Since truth with zeal thou didst pursue,
To Zion's King loyal and true.
Ev'n when the dragon spu'd his flood,
Resist thou didst unto the blood;
Ran swiftly, in thy Christian race,
In faith and patience, to that place
Christ did prepare for such as thee
He knew would not his standard flee;
A pattern of valour and zeal,
Rather to suffer than to fail,
Didst show thyself with might and main,
Counting that dross others thought gain;
A faithful witness 'gainst all those,
Men of all sorts did truth oppose;
Ev'n thou with Moses didst esteem
Reproaches for the God of heaven;
On him alone thou didst rely,
Not sparing for his cause to die.

Wilson died in 1757, firm to the end in his defence of the old paths and his opposition to the 'Erastian innovations' of his own time. His last testimony occupies no fewer than 170 pages in Calderwood's *Collection of Testimonies,* published at Kilmarnock in 1806. (See further on Wilson in J. H. Thomson, *The Martyr Graves of Scotland,* pp. 89-90.)

After Wilson, John M'Millan of Pentland published three of Cameron's letters (two to Alexander Gordon of Earlston and one to his wife Janet) in his *Collection of Letters* published in 1764. In 1779 John Howie of Lochgoin published two of Cameron's lectures and six of his sermons (including that published by Wilson) in his *Collection of Lectures and Sermons,* which was reissued in 1880 under the title *Sermons in Time of Persecution in Scotland.* A few of Cameron's sermons, some of them fragmentary, remain in various manuscript sources.

Appendix II: Mementoes of Cameron

Mementoes of Cameron are few. His signatures in the Matriculation Register in 1662 and in the Graduation Register in 1665 are preserved among the archives of the University of St Andrews. A few original papers, including his comments on the letter of the Dunscore ministers, his queries to Robert M'Ward about how to conduct himself on his return to Scotland, and his letter of 30 October 1679 to M'Ward, survive among the *Wodrow MSS* in the National Library of Scotland. His letter to Andrew Russell in Rotterdam, thanking Russell and his family for their hospitality during his stay in Holland, is preserved in the Scottish Record Office.

A plaque marks the Camerons' family home (much restored) just off the main square in Falkland. Nineteenth-century monuments record where Cameron preached at Darmead and Auchengilloch, and there is a similar monument at the market cross at Sanquhar commemorating the Declaration.

A memorial stone at Airdsmoss was in place as early as 1702 (J. H. Thomson, *The Martyr Graves Of Scotland,* pp.153-4) and was visited in 1723 by Patrick Walker who published the inscription in his *Life* of Cameron in 1727. The old stone, which still survives at the site, is inscribed around the sides with the words: 'Here Lyes the Corps of that famous and faithful preacher of the Gospell Mr Richard Cameron who with several others fell here in a rencounter with the bloody enemies of Truth and Godliness July 20 Anno 1680.' In the centre of the stone are the effigies of an open Bible and an arm with a drawn sword, and the words:

Halt, curious passenger, come here and read.
Our souls triumph with Christ our glorious head
In self defence we murder'd here do Ly
To witness 'gainst this Nation's perjury.

M
R. C.

Michael Cameron	Robert Dick
John Hamilton	Cap John Fuller
John Gemmel	Robert Paterson
James Gray	Thomas Watson

The initials 'MRC' stand for 'Mr Richard Cameron' and were commonly used to denote him in contemporary texts. An obelisk with a more modern inscription was erected in 1832.

Select bibliography

Cloud of Witnesses, 1714 and later editions.

Howie, John. *Scots Worthies,* Glasgow, 1775 and later editions.

Howie, John. *A Collection of Lectures and Sermons,* Glasgow, 1779, republished as *Sermons in Time of Persecution in Scotland,* Edinburgh, 1880.

Walker, Patrick. *Life of Mr Richard Cameron,* Edinburgh, 1727, republished in *Biographia Presbyteriana,* Edinburgh, 1827 and 1837, and *Six Saints of the Covenant,* London, 1901.

Bell, Gavin M. *The Scottish Martyr: Richard Cameron,* Edinburgh, 1833, republished 1843.

Herkless, John. *Richard Cameron* (Famous Scots Series), Edinburgh, 1896.

Downie, John. *The Early Home of Richard Cameron,* Paisley, 1901.

Veitch, Andrew. *Richard Cameron,* London, 1948.

Notes

Chapter 1 — The Cameron family

1. There are numerous variants of the name (see Johnston, *The Surnames of Scotland,* 1948, pp.128-9). The oldest form appears to be Cambrun; later forms include Campbroun, Cammeroun and Camroune.

2. 'Gilbert Cameroun', sometimes designated 'in Linlithgow', features in the *Accounts of the Lord High Treasurer* as a frequent supplier of horses to King James IV from 1495 onwards; the final payment to him is dated 6 June 1513, only three months before the tragedy of Flodden. It is possible that this Gilbert may have been the father of Patrick Cameron, the first of the Camerons identified with Birkenshaw (see note 3 below). The practice of naming the eldest son after the paternal grandfather was common in Scotland for many years and it may therefore be significant that Patrick named his eldest son Gilbert.

3. The *Protocol Book of Thomas Johnsoun* (no. 384) records 'Patrick Cammeroun' as having witnessed two instruments of sasine (i.e. documents relating to feudal property) at Linlithgow on 22 October 1526. Patrick is associated with Birkenshaw as early as 17 February 1538 (*Register of the Great Seal,* 5 March 1541: vol. 3, no. 2298). He appears as 'Patrik Cammroun' in the 1539-40 *Rental* of the Hospitallers' lands at Torphichen (see note 4 below). There is a reference to the appointment of a 'Patrick Cammeroun' as a royal messenger (*Registrum Secreti Sigilli,* 6 February 1549) but it is not known if this refers to the same Patrick; there is a possibility that it could be so, in view of the family's known royalist sympathies and the precedent of David Cameron (see note 16 below). Patrick must have died some time between 25 September 1563, when he witnessed a marriage contract at Linlithgow (*Protocol Book of Thomas Johnsoun,* no. 683) and 29 July 1564, when his son Thomas was described as 'son of the late Patrick Cammeroun' (*Ibid,* no. 703).

4. Apart from Birkenshaw the Camerons owned the two smaller estates of Bowcott (also known as Buchcott) and Woodend. Birkenshaw and Woodend were in the western part of Torphichen parish, known as the barony of Ogleface, while Bowcott was in Torphichen proper. The original feudal superiors of Torphichen were the Knights Hospitallers of St John of Jerusalem, who had held lands in the area since the twelfth century. As occupier of Bowcott, 'Patrik Cammeroun' featured in the Hospitallers' *Rental* of 1539-40 (*The Knights of St John of*

Jerusalem in Scotland, Scottish History Society, 1983, p.1). The Hospitallers also had rights to the 'teinds', or church tithes, in Ogleface, and relevant entries for Birkenshaw and Woodend appear in the *Rental* (*Ibid.,* p.5). The Hospitallers' jurisdiction ended in 1564 when their last preceptor in Scotland, James Sandilands, resigned all their lands to the Crown, receiving them back in his own name on consideration of a payment of 10,000 crowns and with the right to the title of Lord Torphichen (*Register of the Great Seal,* 24 January 1564: vol. 4, no. 1499).

5. *Registrum Secreti Sigilli,* 31 May 1568: vol. 6, no. 289.

6. The Camerons, however, even to a late stage, maintained their links with their West Lothian relatives. On 6 June 1678 Allan Cameron's youngest son Andrew was assigned a portion of the lands of Craigmarvie, near Birkenshaw, by virtue of a charter granted by Elizabeth Cameron, or Fleming, a granddaughter of the Andrew Cameron who had occupied Craigmarvie and Woodend at the beginning of the century and after whom Allan's son was apparently named (*Edinburgh Sasines,* 13 June 1678; cf. also note 8 below). The charter was witnessed in Edinburgh by Allan Cameron himself and by Andrew and Mungo Law, the Camerons' relatives from Falkland, and the event was clearly something of a family occasion.

7. In his will, Gilbert appointed Richard Muirhead of Alderston (later of Wester Inch, Bathgate) tutor to his eldest son Patrick and subsequently to his other children, none of whom had reached the age of majority. It is quite possible that Gilbert's son Richard was named after Richard Muirhead, who appears to have been a close family friend of the Camerons and whose children were later connected with them by marriage (see also notes 8 and 15 below). Patrick, who later married Muirhead's daughter Marion, was confirmed in his father's estate of Birkenshaw on 16 May 1575 (*Protocol Book of Andrew Ker*), when he was designated as *'pupillus'* (pupil), indicating that he had only then attained the age of fourteen (Erskine, *Principles of the Law of Scotland,* 1890, p.71). This would put Patrick's birth at around 1561, and since Richard was apparently the second eldest (he is mentioned second in the will) his birth can be placed at around 1563.

8. In his father's will Richard was left the estate or farm of Woodend (*Register of Confirmed Testaments, Edinburgh,* 6 October 1572). By the end of the century Woodend had passed into the ownership of Sir George Livingston of Ogleface, who sold it under reversion (i.e. subject to possible future redemption) to George Muirhead, merchant burgess of Edinburgh, and a son of the Richard Muirhead who had been tutor to Richard's brother Patrick (*Linlithgow Sasines,* 18 June and 3 July 1601). Muirhead in turn sold the property under reversion to Andrew Cameron of Craigmarvie, who was related to Richard and married Muirhead's sister Margaret (*Ibid,* 2 July and 9 September 1601). Though documentary evidence is lacking, it would appear that Richard had disposed of the property at some point before 1596. He certainly had sufficient funds by then to make substantial loans to some of his neighbours (see note 10 below).

9. Alexander Lindsay, a son of the tenth Earl of Crawford, was created Lord Spynie in the county of Moray in 1590 (*Scots Peerage,* VIII, pp.95-101). He continued, however, to live at the family seat at Kinblethmont in south Angus, where he had several other estates. It was there, no doubt, that Richard resided and where he may well have met his wife Elizabeth Carstairs. The Carstairs family were particularly numerous in and around St Andrews.

10. Richard is styled 'son to *umquhile* [i.e. the late] Gilbert Campbroun in Birkenshaw' in a bond which he granted on 4 November 1594 (*Register of Deeds,* 2 May 1604) and simply as 'Richard Camrone' in bonds of debt to him of 3 June 1596 *(Linlithgow Sheriff Court, Acts of Proper Confession).* By 10 July 1598 he had become 'servitor to my Lord of Spynie' *(Ibid.)* a designation used in subsequent references to him. Richard went on to lend further substantial sums to neighbours (*Linlithgow Sasines,* 21 June 1602; *Register of Deeds,* 2 May 1604), which would indicate that by then he was possessed of fairly considerable means.
11. *Fife and Kinross Sasines,* 2 September 1618. The charter of a third of the lands to Richard was granted at St Andrews on 29 November 1617. Later, when Carnegy had obtained the control of a larger part of Fordell (*Register of the Great Seal,* 10 July 1629: vol. 8, no. 1444) he granted a charter of half the lands to Richard (*Fife and Kinross Sasines,* 20 April 1632).
12. Richard acted as bailie, or attorney, for William Bruce of Earlshall and his son Andrew when they sold some of their lands to David Carnegie of Kinnaird (*Fife and Kinross Sasines,* 10 November 1626) and William Bruce's son John acted in a similar capacity when Patrick Cameron was invested in his father's property at Fordell (*Ibid.,* 19 November 1641). Together with the financial dealings between Allan Cameron and Andrew Bruce (see chapter 2), these contacts suggest a close familiarity between the Camerons and the Bruces extending over at least two generations.
13. There was a parish school at Leuchars before 1600 (James M. Beale, *A History of the Burgh and Parochial Schools of Fife,* 1983, p.7).
14. *Fife and Kinross Sasines,* 3 May 1646.
15. It is possible that Michael Cameron was named after the Rev. Michael Cranston, who married Agnes Muirhead, a daughter of Richard Muirhead of Wester Inch, Bathgate (see note 7 above) and who was later to acquire Birkenshaw from Robert Bartholomew, whose wife Marion (another daughter of Richard Muirhead) was the widow of Richard Cameron senior's elder brother Patrick (*Register of Deeds,* 1 December 1592; *Register of Confirmed Testaments, Edinburgh,* 12 April 1594; *Linlithgow Sasines,* 10 February 1601). Cranston was minister of Cramond from 1592 to 1631 (*Fasti,* vol.1, p.10). Another of Richard Muirhead's family, James, was minister of North Leith from 1599 to 1612 (*Ibid.,* vol.1, p.154; *Register of Confirmed Testaments, Edinburgh,* 26 January 1613). Interestingly, both Cranston and Muirhead resisted the episcopal innovations of James VI and I.
16. The *Accounts of the Lord High Treasurer of Scotland* record numerous payments to one 'David Cameroun, officiar and messenger' over a period from 1512 to 1526. Though his provenance is not recorded, the fact that Allan Cameron chose the name David for one of his sons suggests some evidence of a family connection.
17. The name of Allan Cameron's youngest son has been erroneously given as Alexander (Herkless, *Richard Cameron,* 1896, p.25; Smellie, *Men of the Covenant,* 1908 ed., vol. ii, pp.80-81). The mistake apparently derives from a reference in John Howie's *Faithful Contendings Displayed* (1780, p.332) which records the United Societies' decision to write to 'Mr Alexander Cameron' in Holland. (A copy of the societies' proceedings in the *Wodrow MSS,* collated in 1714 with the original manuscript, clearly has 'Andrew'.) Herkless (followed by Smellie) compounds the

error by describing 'Alexander' as a 'weaver', through a misreading of 'writer' in Allan's letter of 24 February 1680 to M'Ward. That his name was Andrew is clear from several documentary sources — for example, a deed signed by his father includes a statement that it was 'written by Andrew Cameron, my youngest son' (*Edinburgh Register of Deeds,* 7 August 1676). Andrew was apparently named after the Andrew Cameron who had occupied lands at Torphichen at the beginning of the century and whose granddaughter later endowed Andrew with a portion of her ancestral estates (see note 6 above).

18. R. Simpson, *Traditions of the Covenanters,* 1867, pp.117-20. The name Marion is to be found among the West Lothian Camerons; Marion Muirhead married Richard's elder brother Patrick in 1580 (*Register of Deeds,* 1 December 1592; see also note 7 above).

19. Andrew Bruce's brother Alexander was, however, a staunch Royalist and died fighting for Montrose at Kilsyth (*The Genealogist,* vol. VII, p.139). The fact that his brother John acted as bailie, or attorney, when Patrick Cameron was invested in his father's lands at Fordell (*Fife and Kinross Sasines,* 19 November 1641) could suggest that, if Patrick did fall at Kilsyth, he did so fighting for the same cause.

Chapter 2 — The early years

1. *Register of Deeds, Durie's Office,* 12 November 1662.

2. Cameron's signature in the matriculation roll is preserved among the muniments, or archives, of the University of St Andrews, as is his signature in the graduation register in 1665.

3. *Fife and Kinross Sasines,* 26 September 1660.

4. *Fife and Kinross Sasines,* 2 July 1662. In contrast to the later 'sale' of the Camerons' house at Falkland (see chapter 4), Fordell was sold *irredemabiliter, absque ulla reversione* (irredeemably, without any reversion).

5. *Edinburgh Register of Apprentices, 1583-1666* (Scottish Record Society, 1906), p.30.

6. A bond for a loan of 1,000 merks by Allan Cameron to the Bruces of Earlshall, dated 12 January 1663, designates Allan as 'now indweller in Kirkcaldy' (*Register of Deeds, Durie's Office,* 18 January 1664).

7. Herkless, *Richard Cameron,* pp.28-9.

8. There can be no doubt that Allan Cameron derived considerable social status from his marriage. His wife's father, George Paterson, was a burgess, and later bailie, of Falkland and a prominent member of the local community over many years (cf. *Fife and Kinross Sasines,* 14 April 1618; 2 August 1653; *Register of Deeds, Mackenzie's Office,* 26 May 1662; *Falkland Kirk Session Register,* 11 August and 3 November 1672). George Paterson's two other daughters were married influentially: Barbara to Andrew Law of Pittilloch, later bailie of Falkland and an elder in the local parish church; and Elizabeth to David Lundie of Drums, a prominent local landowner.

9. Allan Cameron first appears in the *Falkland Kirk Session Register* as a witness to a marriage contract on 13 November 1663. Later, on 2 September 1665, the *Register* records a payment of 20 shillings to him for the supply of nails for repairs to the parish church.

10. *Register of Deeds, Durie's Office,* 18 January 1664; *Dalrymple's Office,* 21 July 1669.

11. Kinloch married Isabel Lundie, daughter of David Lundie of Drums and his wife Elizabeth Paterson, who was Richard's maternal aunt (*Fife and Kinross Sasines,* 29 June 1665; see also note 8 above). In September 1663 he was appointed clerk to the Falkland Kirk Session, an appointment he held until February 1669 (see note 12 below).
12. Kinloch's medical attendant, James Pringle, 'chirurgeon and apothecary at Cupar', later brought proceedings against him for non-payment of medical fees (*Fife Inhibitions,* 11 July 1671). According to Pringle, Kinloch had 'in the month of April 1669 or thereby, received in his head two large and deep wounds'. Kinloch's handwriting in the *Falkland Kirk Session Register* stops abruptly at 14 February 1669.
13. Professor Herkless notes that the *Falkland Kirk Session Register* contains no note of Cameron's appointment as precentor, though, he goes on to say, 'The record from 1st April 1663 to 5th October 1667 has not been preserved.' The *Register* is, however, extant between these dates, having been merged with the *Parish Register* for the period. The precentor throughout this time was John Forbes, to whom there are frequent references. It must be assumed therefore that Cameron's work as precentor, for which the *Cloud of Witnesses* quotes his own authority (Thomson ed., 1871, p.497), was by way of temporary replacement for Forbes as the regular incumbent.
14. A bond granted on 27 July 1670 by Andrew Law and John Geddie to Alexander Watson, merchant of Kirkcaldy, was witnessed by 'Mr Richard Cameron, schoolmaster at Falkland' (*Register of Deeds, Mackenzie's Office,* 26 September 1671). This is a possibly unique contemporary corroboration of Cameron's tenure of the schoolmaster's post at Falkland, of which the earliest evidence is otherwise the biographical notice in the *Cloud of Witnesses* (1714).

Chapter 3 — Church and state in Scotland
1. T. M'Crie, *Life of Andrew Melville,* 1856, p.181.
2. *Naphtali,* 1667, Preface, p.2.
3. J. Kirkton, *The Secret and True History of the Church of Scotland,* 1817, p.49.

Chapter 4 — The Indulgences
1. *Register of the Privy Council,* 3rd series, vol. IV, p.40.
2. Kirkton, *History of the Church of Scotland,* p.343.
3. *Register of the Privy Council,* 3rd series, vol. IV, pp.229, 239.
4. A heritable bond of £493 Scots on the Falkland property was granted on 28 July 1669 to George Bayne, merchant burgess of Edinburgh, and in February 1670 the whole property was sold under reversion to David Ferguson, merchant burgess of Kirkcaldy, for the sum of £1175 8s 5d Scots (*Falkland Burgh Sasines,* 11 June 1700). On 22 August 1670 Bayne sold his interest to Ferguson *(Ibid.)* who thus gained control over the whole property. It is clear, however, that though the house was thus, in effect, mortgaged to Ferguson, Allan Cameron and his family continued to live there for several more years (see also note 5 below).
5. It has been assumed that by this transaction the Cameron family sold their Falkland property (cf. Herkless, *Richard Cameron,* pp.23-4). However, it is clear that the legal process involved what is known in Scots law as an 'improper wadset' (the term carries no pejorative implication) whereby the owner mortgages the

property to the creditor and undertakes payment of annual interest on the sum borrowed. It was usual for such arrangements to be accompanied by a lease-back, or 'back-tack', whereby the original owner continued to live in the property and paid a rent equivalent to the annual interest payment (cf. Stair Society, *Formulary of old Scots Legal Documents,* 1985, p.138). This explains, no doubt, why Allan Cameron and his family were still found living in Falkland in February 1674 *(Falkland Session Records)* and even as late as April 1675 (*Wodrow MSS,* fol. 33, f. 142).

6. David, second Earl of Wemyss (1610-79) had fought in the Civil Wars against Montrose and in later life became noticed for his enterprise in developing Methil Harbour for the export of coal mined on the Wemyss estate. It is not known when Allan Cameron entered the earl's service, but it was certainly before 4 August 1671, as he is designated in a bond signed on that date at Methil Harbour as 'servant to the Earl of Wemyss at Methil' (*Register of Deeds, Mackenzie's Office,* 30 January 1673). There is also a reference in a charter dated 23 February 1672 describing him as 'seneschal', or steward, to Wemyss (*Register of the Great Seal,* 23 September 1672). He had left the earl's service by early 1673 as he is described in a bond dated 13 March in that year at Wemyss as 'late servitor to the Earl of Wemyss at Methil'. Allan Cameron's financial troubles appear to have pursued him into the earl's service; the bond of 1673 obliged him to repay to the earl a debt of £902 7s 4d Scots (*Edinburgh Register of Deeds,* 11 January 1676).

7. As early as 9 December 1669 Geddie had been prosecuted for 'being lately at conventicles in Fife' (*Register of the Privy Council,* 3rd series, vol. III, p.104). His daughter Emilia, who died at sixteen, was noted for her remarkable spiritual insight and heavenly-mindedness; a memoir of her life (*The Life of Emilia Geddie,* 1774) was popular for many years and was commended by no less an authority than George Whitefield.

8. Geddie was appointed clerk to the Stewartry Court of Fife in May 1661 and factor to the second Earl of Atholl on 8 May 1665 (*Register of Deeds, Durie's Office,* 19 November 1667).

9. *Register of Deeds, Mackenzie's Office,* 26 September 1671 (see also chapter 2, note 14 above).

10. The legal document recording Rebecca Turner's entry into her inherited property in the Canongate (see note 15 below) was witnessed by 'Andrew Cameron, servitor to John Geddie, clerk of the burgh of Falkland' (cf. also *Register of Deeds, Mackenzie's Office,* 27 July 1674).

11. Hay was settled in Falkland in 1673 in succession to the deceased William Barclay (*Fasti,* vol. 5, p.153). Barclay had been an extreme episcopalian who was deprived of his charge in 1645 but was restored in 1663 following the introduction of episcopacy. It is likely that if Cameron assisted as precentor, he started doing so during Barclay's incumbency.

12. Jean Collace, unpublished memoirs (see chapter 5, note 2).

13. *Wodrow MSS,* fol. 33, f.142.

14. *Falkland Parish Register.* The parties were contracted on 20 October (*Falkland Kirk Session Register*).

15. *Edinburgh Sasines,* 23 January 1675.

16. By August 1678, when he was arrested for conventicle-keeping, Allan Cameron was living in a house in the Potterrow (*Register of the Privy Council,* 3rd Series, vol. VI, pp.11-12).

17. From a reference in a bond which he signed (*Register of Edinburgh Deeds,* 30 June 1676) it would appear that David Cameron spent some time trading in London before he settled in Edinburgh. There is no documented evidence of David after 1676; there may possibly be a connection with the fact that a shop belonging to a 'David Cameron' was one of several destroyed in a fire that year (*Register of the Privy Council,* 3rd Series, vol. V, p.113).
18. The *Edinburgh Register of Deeds* from mid-1675 onwards contains numerous transactions in the names of Allan Cameron and his sons Michael and David, all of them described as merchants in Edinburgh (and, in Michael's case, sometimes in Leith). Several of these were drawn up by the youngest son, Andrew, whose name is appended as 'writer hereof'. The earlier transactions were in many cases bonds for repayments of debts, usually relating to bulk purchases of merchandise which the Camerons apparently used to help them set up in business in the city.

Chapter 5 — The influence of John Welwood
1. Welwood was nothing if not a 'searching' preacher. Indeed, there must be few who have presented the claims of the Christian life in such uncompromising terms. Typical are these extracts from a sermon he preached in West Monkland on the words, 'If the righteous scarcely be saved,' in 1 Peter 4:18:

> Whence is it that several of you have the confidence that you shall be saved, since the righteous are scarcely saved? I think whoever is most godly will say that it is very much for him to get the hopes that he shall be saved. I remember a saying of a godly man in Ayr, when he was dying. 'For a long time', says he, 'I have not gone the length of the market cross without thoughts of God and Christ; yet I am in doubt now about my salvation.' What think you of that, sirs? It is reported of one who lived many years a retired life, wholly taken up with the matters of his salvation, that after so long a time's retirement, he was still in great vexation and perplexity about his soul's state. We speak not this to discourage you, as if the work of religion were a hard and intolerable work; but I tell you the even-down truth of the matter; the man that is saved goes through the severest trial, and it is well if he escapes with his life. It is a very great truth, a man who shall wrestle, weep and cry, and shall lie out of his bed when others are in it; shall keep at a distance from sin, and be humbled for it; shall have so much religion that all his neighbours shall wonder at it; when such a man has been many days, nights, weeks and years seriously taken up with the work of his salvation, minding nothing in comparison of it, daily mourning over sin, mortifying a body of sin and death, yet after all, it is much for that man who has taken all this pains, to attain unto the peace of God.

2. Katharine appears to have been the only one of the sisters to be married; an account of her spiritual experience appeared in 1735 under the title *Memoirs of Mrs Ross.* Jean's unpublished memoirs are preserved in *Adv MSS 34.5.19* and *Wodrow MSS* Oct.xxxi.
3. Alexander Shields accounts Welwood to have been one of the first to testify publicly against the Indulgence (*A Hind Let Loose,* 1687, p.122). A similar testimony is borne by Patrick Walker (*Six Saints of the Covenant,* vol. 1, p.333).
4. Shields, *A Hind Let Loose,* pp.117-18.

5. Welwood's surviving letters — all of them unpublished — include five to Richard Cameron, one to his father Allan Cameron, two to Thomas Hog of Kiltearn and twenty-six to Katharine and Elizabeth Collace. From references to 'Mr Richard' in his letters to the Collace sisters, it is reasonable to deduce that they were on terms of fairly close acquaintance with Cameron.
6. Interestingly, Welwood's letter was sent from Kinloch, the home of John Balfour, later the principal agent in the death of James Sharp. Welwood notes that he had asked Balfour to write to Cameron, implying a previous acquaintance between the two men.

Chapter 6 — Licensed to preach
1. *Records of the Presbytery of Jedburgh,* 5 September 1677 (cf. also Stewart, *The Covenanters of Teviotdale,* 1908, pp.252-3). The record notes that Cameron was 'but lately entered since Whitsunday last' (i.e. 3 June).
2. For an account of the hardships suffered by Lady Douglas see Anderson, *The Ladies of the Covenant,* 1855, pp.308-34, and Stewart, *The Covenanters of Teviotdale,* 1908, pp.102-10.
3. Welwood is buried in the churchyard of Dron, near Perth, where a tombstone with a poetic inscription marks his grave. The date of his death is commonly given as April 1679, following Patrick Walker (*Six Saints of the Covenant,* vol. I, p.206) and it is this date which appears on the stone. It is, however, incorrect; Alexander Brodie of Brodie heard of Welwood's death on 21 April 1678 (*Diary,* Spalding Club, 1863, p.399) and a similar date is given in a letter sent in 1716 to Robert Wodrow (*Wodrow MSS,* Qto 75, fol.13). Welwood died in the house of John Barclay, a merchant in Perth, whose wife was a sister of Thomas Halyburton, later Professor of Divinity at the University of St Andrews.
4. An account of Cameron written shortly after his appearance before the Edinburgh ministers in August 1678 states that he had been licensed some 'five months before'. It is not improbable that he was licensed with Thomas Hog the younger (see chapter 15, note 3) the date of whose licensing is given as 7 March 1678 (*Fasti,* vol. 7, p.551).
5. Patrick Walker (c.1666-1745) was Cameron's first biographer. He appears to have been a travelling bookseller, who had himself been a victim of the persecution, and in his later years resided in Edinburgh, where he brought out a series of lives of the foremost field-preachers. His *Life* of Cameron first appeared in 1727 and has been frequently reprinted (notably in *Biographia Presbyteriana* (1827 and 1837) and *Six Saints of the Covenant* (1901), with annotations by Dr David Hay Fleming). Walker does not appear to have known Cameron personally nor to have heard him preach, but he was on close terms with several who had done so and who gave him first-hand information, particularly on the closing stages of Cameron's life. (For further information, see M. Grant, *No King But Christ,* Evangelical Press, chapter 8, note 9).

Chapter 7 — Troubled times
1. Cf. Crichton, *Memoirs of the Rev John Blackader,* 1826, pp.182-9,195-9; *Testimony of Robert Garnock,* in J. Howie, *Scots Worthies,* 1870 ed., pp.459-60 (see also chapter 8, notes 1 and 3).

2. *Calendar of State Papers, Domestic Series,* 5 November 1677.
3. Robert Wodrow records that Kersland and other prisoners were rescued from the Glasgow Tolbooth during the fire which broke out in Glasgow in early November 1677 (*History,* II, p.331). This is at variance with an entry in the *Register of the Privy Council* (3rd Series, vol. V, p.287) which records that on 28 November 1677 the magistrates of Edinburgh were authorized to set Kersland free from their tolbooth. The *Register* entry is difficult to explain and may have been a case of mistaken identity. Wodrow notes of it: 'This liberation of Kersland I set down as I find it; how it came about I know not, and his friends know nothing about it, or that ever it came to his knowledge' (*History,* vol. II, p 361). Whatever the facts of the matter — and Wodrow's own account seems circumstantial enough — it is clear that Kersland was at liberty from about this time onwards.
4. *Register of the Privy Council,* 3rd Series, vol. V, pp.393-5.
5. Robert Hamilton was one of the six surviving children of Sir Thomas Hamilton of Preston by his second wife Anna Hamilton (G. Hamilton, *A History of the House of Hamilton,* 1933, pp.700-701). The eldest, William, succeeded his father in 1674, or possibly early 1675. Under a settlement of 9 May 1674 Robert Hamilton and his sister Janet each stood to receive 10,000 merks on their father's death, and their sisters Margaret, Jean and Anna 5,000 merks each (*Register of Deeds, Dalrymple's Office,* 14 July 1681). Among the archives of the Hamiltons of Preston is a receipt by Robert Hamilton for the last instalment of his patrimony of 10,000 merks, dated 24 November 1677. In November 1676 Janet Hamilton married Alexander Gordon of Earlston, a close friend and correspondent of Richard Cameron (see chapter 18). (For details of Hamilton's later life not covered elsewhere in this book, see *No King but Christ,* chapter 9, note 3).

Chapter 8 — Cameron speaks out
1. Crichton, *Memoirs of John Blackader,* pp.182-9. This version is not Blackader's original description, which has been preserved in the *Wodrow MSS* and is considerably less polished (for further details see *No King but Christ,* chapter 6, note 1).
2. *Andrew Russell Archive,* William Livingstone to Andrew Russell, 6 May 1678.
3. Crichton, *Memoirs of John Blackader,* pp.195-9. As in the case of the East Nisbet communion, the version recorded here is not original (see note 1 and *No King but Christ,* chapter 6, note 1).
4. This was Cameron's version of events, which there is no reason to doubt. According to another version of the Edinburgh meeting, it was alleged that the fast was due to be observed in the vacant parish of Fenwick, but that on arrival there Cameron and his supporters had deliberately — and provocatively — moved the place of meeting to Kilmarnock. This is not at all likely; Cameron was careful on all occasions not to preach without the clear call of the people.
5. Ross had not previously held a settled charge. He had, however, been active as a field-preacher for a considerable time, and in 1674 was the subject of a proclamation against him by the Privy Council. He was apprehended early in 1679 and sent to the Bass Rock, but was liberated in July of the same year. His subsequent career is uncertain, and he may not have survived the 1688 revolution (cf. M'Crie and others, *The Bass Rock,* 1848, pp.288-9).

Chapter 9 — The Edinburgh meeting

1. *Fasti Ecclesiæ Scoticanæ,* Edinburgh, 1866, vol.1, p.333. Mossman had not previously held a settled charge. Some time after the Edinburgh meeting he was apprehended by the authorities but on 4 July 1679 he and several others were ordered to be released from prison (*Register of the Privy Council,* 3rd Series, vol. VI, p.266). He became minister of Newbattle after the 1688 revolution.
2. *Register of the Privy Council,* 3rd Series, vol. IV, p.40.
3. *Fasti,* vol.2, pp.59-60. Jamieson became minister of Swinton in 1647 but was deprived of his office in 1661 and was subsequently outlawed for irregular preaching. After Bothwell Bridge he played a prominent part in persuading the prisoners in the Greyfriars Churchyard to take the bond for the peace, an action for which he is severely criticized by Patrick Walker (*Six Saints of the Covenant,* vol. 1, pp.53-4, 323).
4. Scott became minister of Hawick in 1657 but was deprived of his charge in 1662 and thereafter engaged in irregular preaching (*Fasti,* vol. 2, p.113). On 5 December 1678 he wrote to Robert M'Ward giving him a highly prejudiced account of the Edinburgh meeting which had interviewed Cameron. This was apparently designed to counter Cameron's own account of the meeting which had been sent to M'Ward some time earlier. Among other things Scott noted: 'In his narration he sets down the names of the ministers before whom he was called (yet he has missed several of them) and the names of the two ministers' houses where the meetings were kept, that thereby he might expose them to the fury of the civil magistrate.'
5. *Fasti,* vol. 2, p.327. Lidderdale had become minister of Tynron in 1644 but had been deprived of his charge on the introduction of episcopacy.

Chapter 10 — A mounting chorus of criticism

1. The *Privy Council Register* for 13 September 1678 refers to a 'numerous house conventicle' held in the house of Allan Cameron, 'merchant indweller in the Potterrow', on an unspecified date in August, at which Allan Cameron, his wife and several others were present, 'sundry of them being apprehended'. It continues: 'The said Allan Cameron being guilty of having a conventicle kept in his house, at which he was present, and having refused to depone as to others present, [the Council] fine him 100 merks, and ordain him to continue in prison until he pays the same and finds caution in 500 merks to live orderly and appear before the Council when called.' The precise date of the affair is given as 25 August in a later account by Allan Cameron himself, preserved in the *Wodrow MSS.* He refused to pay the fine as a matter of principle and, as is well known, he was still in prison at the time of his son's death. However, the *Privy Council Register* for 2 June 1681 contains the following: 'Allan Cameron being prisoner upon the account of a fine of 100 merks for having a conventicle in his house several years ago, upon payment of his fine to the town major as was formerly appointed, was dismissed.' This is not to say, of course, that Allan Cameron eventually capitulated; the fine could well have been paid by a sympathizer on his behalf.
2. Kersland died in Utrecht on 14 November 1680 (Wodrow, *History,* II, p.331).
3. Selkirk and Cameron may have been previously acquainted. Selkirk was chaplain to the Laird of Bonjedward, in the Borders, at the same time as Cameron was chaplain to Lady Douglas of Cavers (*Records of the Presbytery of Jedburgh,* 5 September 1677).

Chapter 11 — A formal indictment

1. McGoune later entered the ministry and was minister at St Boswells from 1691 to his death in 1696 at the age of forty-six (*Fasti,* vol. 2, p.192).

2. Michael Cameron and John Fowler fell with Cameron at Airdsmoss (see chapter 28). Robert Gray, who was from Northumberland, was executed in the Grassmarket on 19 May 1682. In his last testimony Gray wrote, 'I leave my testimony against these ministers that sat in a presbytery against worthy Mr Richard Cameron, that highly honoured martyr of Jesus Christ, and thought to have deposed him from his ministry; I also leave my testimony against that meeting that sat at Sundewal in Nithsdale, which I was a witness to. I am called to set to my seal to the faithfulness of that worthy man's doctrine, viz. worthy Mr Richard Cameron, who was the mean[s] that the Lord made use of to establish me in the faith. I bless the Lord that ever I saw him, or was honoured to be in his company' (*Cloud of Witnesses,* 1871 ed., p.234).

Chapter 12 — The work goes on

1. Irvine, described by Hamilton as an 'old minister', had been settled in Kirkmahoe in 1645 but was deprived of his charge on the introduction of episcopacy. He afterwards preached in the fields, for which he suffered his share of the persecution. Not long after Cameron's visit Irvine and several others were apprehended by John Graham of Claverhouse, and brought to Edinburgh where they were imprisoned. In a letter from Dumfries on 21 April 1679 Claverhouse wrote, 'I was going to have sent in the other prisoners but amongst them there is one Mr Francis Irvine, an old and infirm man, who is extremely troubled with the gravel, so that I will be forced to delay for five or six days' (*Letters of John Graham of Claverhouse,* Bannatyne Club, 1826, p.18). Orders were given, however, for Irvine's release from prison on 4 July (*Register of the Privy Council,* 3rd Series, vol. VI, p.266). Despite his affliction he later returned to his old charge and survived until 1695, dying at the age of eighty-five (*Fasti,* vol. 3, p.282).

Chapter 13 — Cameron leaves for Holland

1. Cf. Herkless, *Richard Cameron,* p.77.

2. *Letters of John Graham of Claverhouse,* Bannatyne Club, 1826, pp.24-5.

3. According to an official report of this encounter Robert Hamilton, who was in command of the horse, reproached the government party in words of coarse insult (*Lauderdale Papers,* ed. O. Airy (Camden Society), 1884, iii, p.163).

4. R. M'Ward, *Earnest Contendings,* 1723, p.156.

Chapter 14 — Rutherglen and Drumclog

1. For Douglas, see *Fasti,* vol. 2, p.225; also *No King but Christ,* chapter 9, note 8 (see also chapter 19, note 9, below).

2. This version of the declaration is reproduced from the contemporary *London Gazette* (9-12 June 1679) and may be taken as authentic. Various alternative versions later appeared, representing attempts to give the declaration greater force and fluency. One of these is quoted by Wodrow (*History,* III, pp.66-7).

Chapter 15 — Bothwell Bridge and its aftermath

1. Wodrow notes: 'Those occasional meetings, in this persecuted state of the church, did not assume any determining power' (*History,* III, p.155). This is,

however, contrary to a contemporary account by John Dickson, in letters of 17 August and 25 September to Robert M'Ward (*Wodrow MSS,* fol. lix, ff.118, 121). In these, Dickson records that some time after Bothwell a group of ministers had met at Edinburgh and had taken upon themselves 'to send to all places in the nation to convocate ministers here against the 7th of August to cognosce upon what are the proper duties of the time'. On the due date (or, according to other accounts, 8 August) some fifty to sixty ministers had convened and, after meeting for several days, had adjourned on 14 August after deciding that all ministers throughout the country should group themselves into synods and 'act synodically'. This had been done, the synods proceeding to enact judicially that 'none preach in their several bounds but such as are commissionate by them'. They had then commissioned 'all their members through the whole kingdom to sit a General Assembly'. It was this meeting which convened in Edinburgh on 16 September and resolved that the liberty offered by the Third Indulgence could be accepted without compromise of principle. Dickson rightly divined that these attempts to revive ecclesiastical structures were aimed expressly at those who, in the eyes of the older ministers, were sowing discord and division among the people. He noted: 'When acutely examined this looks more directly towards the detriment than the edification of the church; seeing the edge of church censures in their project does now point directly towards the curbing of the faithful in the church, more than towards the censuring of scandals.' M'Ward of course shared this view, and it was the determinative power assumed by the so-called 'General Assembly' which explains the vehemence in his later letter to Cameron.

2. The term 'Cameronian' was coined around 1678 or 1679 by their opponents to describe those who shared Cameron's views on the supremacy and the Indulgence. After 1688 it was applied to those elements of the United Societies which did not join the Revolution Settlement (cf. *Six Saints of the Covenant,* vol. I, p.251). It was always regarded by those to whom it was applied as a 'by-name' or nickname and they never described themselves in this way (for further discussion of this point see Grant, *No King But Christ,* chapter 9, note 7).

3. Hog (not to be confused with the better-known Thomas Hog of Kiltearn) was the son of yet another Thomas Hog, former minister of Larbert near Stirling. After an initial career in the law he was licensed to preach by some of the nonconforming ministers on 7 March 1678 (W. Steven, *History of the Scottish Church in Rotterdam,* 1833, pp.140-44). The date of his licensing suggests that he could well have been licensed along with Cameron, who was said at the Edinburgh meeting in August of the same year to have been licensed 'but five months since'. Hog's notoriety as an incendiary preacher for a time matched that of Cameron himself, and he came to the attention of the Edinburgh ministers for advocating non-payment of taxes due to the government. The contemporary evidence strongly suggests that his departure for Holland around March 1679 was related to his continuing difficulties with the older ministers. That he received ordination there is avouched by Robert Law (*Memorialls,* p.153) who brackets his name in this context with that of Cameron. While it cannot be proved for certain that Hog was ordained along with Cameron, he was, on his own testimony, present at Cameron's ordination (*Six Saints of the Covenant,* vol. i, p.236). Hog's subsequent career was more subdued. Despite his close association with Cameron in Holland he did not join with him in field-preaching on their return to Scotland but decided in 1681 to make his way back to Holland, where he was successively minister at Delft,

Campvere and Rotterdam. He declined numerous calls to return to Scotland and died in Holland in 1723 at the age of sixty-eight (*Fasti,* vol. 7, p.551).

Rightly or wrongly, Hog was seen by a number as one who did not fulfil his early promise. Robert Hamilton clearly regarded him as a defector (*Faithful Contendings Displayed,* 1780, pp.198-9) and he alleged that Hog joined with others in Holland in trying to block James Renwick's ordination (*Ibid.,* p 214; see also Grant, *No King but Christ,* chapter 7, note 5).

4. There exists a rather puzzling letter from John Hog, collegiate minister of the Scottish Church in Rotterdam, to John Brown, dated 30 May 1679, in which Hog recounts that he and three fellow-ministers had met at the Rotterdam church the previous day, 'which was the day designed for ordaining three young men by imposition of hands after sermon publicly in and before the congregation'; that the work intended had not been done because the young men had objected to one of the ministers, who had then dissuaded the others from proceeding; and soliciting Brown and M'Ward to join him and Koelman in carrying out the ordination as soon as possible. Hog adds: 'There shall none I promise you know of your being here; there shall be none present but Mr Russell and Mr Gordon [i.e. two elders of the Rotterdam church] or any other elder you desire. I hope neither yourself nor Mr M'Ward will refuse; your answer I expect with the first.' Nothing further is known of this, and there is no record of Brown's reply. If Cameron and Thomas Hog (who was John Hog's nephew) were two of the young men referred to, the implication is that M'Ward and Brown wanted more time to test their credentials, since other evidence suggests that their ordination did not take place until late July or early August. Whether John Hog eventually participated in the ordinations is not clear; his status as collegiate minister of the Rotterdam church (with Robert Fleming) may well point to this possibility.

Chapter 16 — Return to Scotland

1. J. King Hewison suggests that Cameron married after his return from Holland (*The Covenanters,* 1908, vol. ii, p.327). This appears to be deduced from Patrick Walker's statement that 'Another old Christian sufferer told me that he married him a little after he came home' (*Six Saints of the Covenant,* vol. II, p.110). The 'him' here, however, clearly does not refer to Cameron himself, but rather indicates that he officiated at the marriage.

2. Cameron's letter to M'Ward was sent under cover of a letter of the same date to Andrew Russell, a prominent local merchant and elder of the Rotterdam church, with whom Cameron had lodged during his stay in Holland. In his letter to Russell, dated from Edinburgh on 30 October, Cameron expressed his thanks for the hospitality extended to him and asked after the welfare of other friends. He wrote, 'I came but this week to this town, else I had sooner by a line signified my sense of the singular kindness you and your wife showed to me in a strange land. I cannot requite it, but think myself bound to wish you and yours well. Oh what need is there of living nigh God in this so sad a time! I'm now straitened and intend to write afterward at more length. My respects to your mother-in-law and Mr Gordon. I am, Sir, yours much obliged to serve you in the Lord, R. C.' He added a postscript: 'You'll do me the favour as to present my service to Madam Hosshopie and to deliver the enclosed to our friend [i.e. M'Ward]. Be pleased to tell my other intimates as you have occasion that I intend shortly to write to them.'

Chapter 17 — Field-preaching resumed

1. Dalzell was one of the local commissioners appointed by the government to enforce the laws against conventicles (Wodrow, *History*, II, p.366, III, p.182). He appears to have undertaken the task with enthusiasm; the *Cloud of Witnesses* records him as a noted persecutor (1871 ed., pp.540, 561).

2. The record of Cameron's movements at this time comes from the evidence of Robert Smith of Dunscore, who was one of those questioned at the time of the Rye House plot (*A True Account and Declaration of the Horrid Conspiracy Against the Late King*, 1685, pp.120-21). While, as Professor Herkless says, Smith's evidence was that of an informer, there seems no need to doubt his record of Cameron's field-preaching, on which he had no cause to fabricate any evidence, and his references to people and places can be verified from other sources. More questionable is the rest of Smith's account, in which he alleges, among other things, that Cameron and his brother had gone to Holland to buy arms, which they were holding in readiness for use when required, and that Michael Cameron had plotted with David Hackston of Rathillet to assassinate the Duke of York as he sat at dinner.

3. According to Smith's account, those with whom Cameron found sanctuary at this time were the Carmichaels of St John's Kirk, near Biggar, and the lady of Gilkerscleugh House (Anna Hamilton) at Crawfordjohn. Both were noted sympathizers with the persecuted preachers and they endured their own hardships as a result.

4. The Duke of York, writing to the Duke of Lauderdale from Edinburgh on 29 November 1679, noted: 'The weather is very favourable, for I have not seen a finer season at this time of year than it is now here' (*Lauderdale Papers*, vol. III, pp.185-6). To the same effect was a letter from a Roman Catholic priest to his correspondent: 'As for the weather it has been a summer rather than a spring, much less a Scottish winter' (*Blairs Archives*, Charles Whytford to Lewis Innes, 27 February 1680).

5. Because of his family connections, Andrew Cameron was seen by the United Societies, formed after Cargill's death, as a prospective adherent to their cause. They were doomed to be disappointed. He supported Argyle's expedition in 1685, which the societies disowned, and he attempted, unsuccessfully, to induce James Renwick to give it his support (*Renwick's Letters*, Carslaw ed., 1893, pp.125, 128).

In May 1688, just before the day of final deliverance, the societies wrote to Andrew Cameron in Utrecht to ask him to consider returning to Scotland to be their minister (J. Howie, *Faithful Contendings Displayed*, 1780, pp.332-5). They did not hesitate to remind him of his connections: 'Sir, we expect more of you, in whom we claim more than a common interest and plead a nearer relation and respect, both on account of your faithful and famous brother, a renowned minister and martyr of Jesus Christ, who owned and sealed with his blood these truths we contend and suffer for; and who had great hopes of you, that the Lord would engage and spirit you to own the same; and upon your own account, for the savoury report we have, of the Lord's grace conferred upon you, fitting you for his service in the work of the gospel; and for that we know you were once with us, and we hope that when you shall make a nearer enquiry into our way, you shall not be far from us now.'

Andrew Cameron, however, was never over-impressed by reminders of his brother. He wrote the societies a somewhat dismissive reply (not published by Howie) in which, while making professions of sympathy, he took pains to distance himself from their position. 'As to your alleging', he wrote, 'that I was sometime one with you (that is in judgement) you know that I never had a hand in any of your proclamations, neither so much as knew of them till they were published and so made generally known.' The societies, with a candour which was perhaps more honest than prudent, had expressed to him their dismay that in supporting Argyle he had associated himself with those who had been his brother's 'murderers' (no doubt referring particularly to Sir John Cochrane). Cameron professed not to have been offended at this, though it could scarcely have warmed his heart to the societies' invitation.

At the revolution of 1688 Andrew Cameron returned to Scotland and was minister successively at Carsphairn and Kirkcudbright (*Fasti,* vol.ii, pp.401, 417). In the latter capacity he continued to display every evidence of his dislike of dissenters. He was a member of the Presbytery of Kirkcudbright which deposed John Macmillan of Balmaghie for contumacy in 1703 (Reid, *A Cameronian Apostle,* 1896, p.67) and he was the acknowledged leader of the presbytery's campaign against Macmillan. He was equally opposed to attempts to disturb the peace of the church from within, and in 1715 he was appointed to a Committee of Assembly charged with preserving purity of doctrine, in the context of James Webster's case against Professor Simson (*Acts of the General Assembly,* 16 May 1715; see also Walker, *Six Saints of the Covenant,* vol. i., p. 13). Andrew Cameron died at Kirkcudbright in 1721 in the thirty-second year of his ministry.

6. M'Ward, *Earnest Contendings,* pp.331-68. The letter does not bear the name of an addressee and in the printed copy is said to have been directed to 'Mr Donald Cargill or Mr Richard Cameron'. The directness of the style, however, makes it highly unlikely that it was directed to Cargill, who was equally senior in the ministry to M'Ward, and who in any event had not returned to Scotland by this time. Patrick Walker has confirmed (*Six Saints of the Covenant,* vol.1, p.226) that the letter was addressed to Cameron.

Chapter 18 — Powerful preacher and faithful friend

1. *Six Saints of the Covenant,* vol.1, pp.227-8. Henry Erskine was the father of the noted Ebenezer Erskine and his brother Ralph.
2. *Six Saints of the Covenant,* vol. II, pp.111-13. 'Horsecleugh House has long since disappeared' (J. Warrock, *The History of Old Cumnock,* 1899, p.193).
3. *Letters of Samuel Rutherford* (ed. A.A. Bonar), 1891, pp.132-3.
4. It was probably Cameron in particular that Lady Earlston had in mind when she later wrote, 'It was ministers who were valiant for Christ that were sent in my way, such as did not flatter me in my sin, but faithfully and freely did hold out, in the gospel, what was sin and duty, and sealed the same with their blood' (*Lady Earlston's Soliloquies,* Wodrow Society, Select Biographies I, pp.498-9).
5. This letter and Cameron's two subsequent letters to Alexander Gordon were published in John M'Millan's *Collection of Letters,* 1764, pp.244-9. Given what they reveal of Cameron's character, it is surprising that Professor Herkless should dismiss them as of no importance (*Richard Cameron,* p.115).

Chapter 19 — The bond is drawn up

1. The repeated co-ordinate clauses, and the use of 'as also' are typical of Cameron's composition; the same traits are to be seen in the Sanquhar Declaration.

2. Buchanan, *De Jure Regni Apud Scotos,* quoted in Shields, *A Hind Let Loose,* p.347.
3. *Jus Populi Vindicatum,* 1669, p.117.
4. *Ibid.,* pp.140ff.
5. Rutherford, *Lex Rex,* 1644, p.462.
6. Brown, *Apologetical Relation,* 1665, pp.149-50.
7. *Jus Populi Vindicatum,* 1669, pp.139, 141-2.
8. The bond was subscribed as follows: 'Thomas Douglas Minister of the Gospel, Ri. Cameron Minister of the Gospel, Robert Dick, Alexander Gordon of Creuch, Will. Stewart, David Farrie, James Stewart, Robert Stewart, John Patterson, John Potter, James Grierson, John Hamilton, James Edward, John Moody, J. Vallance, Thomas Campbell, John Crichtoun, John Gemmill, John Maccolm [often known as John Malcolm], Patrick Gemmill, John Wilson, Samuel Macmichael, Joseph Thomson, Michael Cameron, John Fouller, James Macmichael' (*A True and Impartial Account of the Examinations and Confessions of Several Execrable Conspirators,* 1681, p.12).

According to this source (p.11), John Potter stated at his trial that the bond 'was signed in a moor near to Galloway in summer last'. This contrasts with a statement in a letter from William Livingstone (*Andrew Russell Archive,* 9 December 1680), also reporting Potter's trial, that the bond was subscribed 'in March last'. The two statements can probably be reconciled on the supposition that the bond was originally subscribed in March, as seems consistent with other evidence, and that Potter and possibly other subscribers added their signatures later.
9. Writing from London on 5 August 1682, Douglas notes: 'The matter of the difference was concerning Mr Fleming; a friend did at Rotterdam withdraw from his ministry upon the account of the indulged men; another friend was dissatisfied with his practice at that place; their debate was so hot about it that I suppose the grief of it put both into their grave.' Douglas is referring, respectively, to Robert Ker of Kersland and Robert M'Ward, the former of whom died on 14 November 1680 and the latter on 26 May 1681. Kersland's cause was espoused, on his arrival in Holland, by Robert Hamilton, who similarly set himself against M'Ward because of his refusal to debar Fleming from fellowship. The dispute was soon to involve Douglas himself. He records that when based at Utrecht on taking refuge in Holland after Bothwell he received an invitation from M'Ward, in Fleming's absence, to assist at communion services at the Scottish Church in Rotterdam. Though well aware of the controversy, he had yielded to pressure from M'Ward, who had protested that 'He would rather choose to be in his grave than that I should refuse.' On his return to Utrecht Douglas was taken to task by some of his fellow-exiles for what they saw as an act of compromise. The dispute proved extremely acrimonious and split the exiles into two camps. Its effects were to catch up with Douglas after his return to Scotland (see chapter 25) and effectively ended his usefulness as a preacher until the revolution of 1688 (see also Grant, *No King but Christ,* chapter 9, note 8).

Chapter 20 — The movement gains impetus
1. *Cloud of Witnesses,* 1871 ed., pp. 60-61.
2. M'Ward, *Earnest Contendings,* p.357 note.
3. *Lauderdale Papers,* ed. O Airy (Camden Society), 1884, p.198.

4. *Blairs Archives,* Charles Whytford to Louis Innes, 30 March and 13 April 1680.
5. M'Millan's *Collection of Letters,* 1764, pp.246-7.

Chapter 22 — Cameron preaches at Crawfordjohn

1. *Airlie Muniments,* Dalyell to Airlie, 29 May 1680.
2. John Howie reckoned that, with the possible exception of John Livingstone's famous sermon at Kirk o'Shotts in 1630, no sermon was 'more remarkably blessed with success from the Lord in Scotland since the primitive times' (*A Collection of Lectures and Sermons,* 1779, p.386 note).
3. Walker, *Six Saints of the Covenant,* vol. II, p.112.

Chapter 23 — The Queensferry Paper

1. The paper refers at one point to the Privy Council's 'last letters to the king and Duke of Lauderdale' in which the Reformed religion was stigmatized as a 'slavery'. The fact that the letters in question were written as early as 17 February suggests that Cargill had been working on the paper since soon after his return from Holland.
2. The circumstances in which the paper was found are somewhat obscure. According to popular belief, as expressed, for example, in the *Cloud of Witnesses,* it was found on Hall, but government sources speak of it being found on Cargill. However, this cannot literally be true, as Cargill did not fall into government hands. The most likely explanation is that in his haste to escape Cargill was forced to abandon his horse, leaving the paper in his saddle-bag, where it was subsequently discovered with other books and papers. The *London Gazette* of 5-8 July speaks of the paper having been found in a 'port-mantle' (i.e. a travelling or saddle-bag used when riding). An extract from a contemporary diary quoted by Dr Hay Fleming gives a similar account and adds that Cargill made his escape on a horse belonging to Governor Middleton, who had come to arrest them (*Six Saints of the Covenant,* vol. II, p.206).
3. The version of the paper published by Wodrow (*History,* III, pp.207-11) is much longer and more developed than the one published at the time by the government. It would appear to have been expanded and developed to express the principles of its authors in a more coherent form. It is by no means certain that all the additional material included in Wodrow's version was the work of the original authors (see Grant, *No King But Christ,* chapter 10, note 2).
4. Calvin, *Institutes,* IV. 20.8.
5. The Queensferry Paper was to be invoked by later separatists in support of their views, chief among them James Russell and Patrick Grant. Russell had been one of those involved in the killing of Archbishop Sharp, and has left his own account of the affair (Appendix to Kirkton's *History of the Church of Scotland,* pp.397-482). Both Russell and Grant were founder members of the United Societies in 1681 and were apparently instrumental in drawing up the Lanark Declaration (see chapter 24, note 2). Soon afterwards, however, they separated themselves from the societies and set themselves in opposition to them and to James Renwick. Grant, who far outlived Russell, proved to be a thorn in the side of the societies for upwards of forty years. He was the author of numerous pamphlets including *The Nonconformist's Vindication* (1700), *Rectius Declinandum* (1709), *A Bond of Union* (1714), *A Letter to a Friend* (1716) and, most notoriously, *A Manifesto, or The Standard of the Church of Scotland* (1723). In all of these he propounded his theory

of the right of private persons to assume magisterial powers in order to overthrow tyrannical governments, a right which he claimed was inherent in the Queensferry Paper and the Sanquhar and Lanark Declarations, but which had in his view been compromised by the societies in their *Informatory Vindication.* The societies, while belittling Grant and his influence, nevertheless felt obliged to answer his *Manifesto* with an elaborate *Confutation* (1724).

Chapter 24 — The Sanquhar Declaration

1. As with the Queensferry Paper, the version of the Sanquhar Declaration given here is taken from the copy published by the government. The versions later published by the United Societies show slight variations, mainly in syntax and grammar. In no case, however, are there major differences. While the government version may be taken as an authentic copy of what was posted up at Sanquhar, it does omit a line of the original (the words from 'Britain' to 'crown of' in the second paragraph). That this was merely a transcription error is proved by the fact that the missing words are quoted in the contemporary *London Gazette* (5-7 July 1680) which gave a summarized version of the Declaration.

2. The United Societies were the general gathering of the 'Society people' who continued the testimony of Cameron and Cargill after the latter's death. They held their first General Meeting in December 1681 and arranged for the ordination of James Renwick in Holland. Their proceedings were published by John Howie in 1780 under the title *Faithful Contendings Displayed.*

3. The Lanark Declaration was the first product of the United Societies formed after the death of Donald Cargill (*Faithful Contendings Displayed,* 1780, pp 9-15). There seems little doubt that at this early stage the societies were dominated by some extremist elements whose views were reflected in the Declaration and which, under James Renwick's direction, they later repudiated in their *Informatory Vindication* (1687, pp.55-6). The passage which so offended Renwick reads: 'Must the people, by an implicit submission and deplorable stupidity, destroy themselves, and betray their posterity, and become objects of reproach to the present generation, and pity and contempt to the future? Have they not in such an extremity, good ground to make use of that natural and radical power they have, to shake off that yoke, which neither we nor our forefathers were able to bear? Which accordingly the Lord honoured us (in a general and unprelimited meeting of the estates and shires of Scotland) to do; a convention of unprelimited members, a convention of men who had only the glory of God and the good of the commonwealth before their eyes; the like whereof the present reigning tyrant could never, since his homecoming, pretend to. At which convention, he was most legally, and by general consent cast off, by the declaration afterward published at Sanquhar, by especial warrant from the said convention.' Apart from its attempt to invest the Sanquhar Declaration with authoritative status, this passage is interesting in identifying the declaration as the product of a preceding 'convention'. No record of such an event survives, and its nature can now only be guessed at. Given, however, the highly-coloured tone of the Lanark Declaration, it is doubtful if the 'convention' was anything more than a general meeting of Cameron's followers. It is significant that Cameron himself never made any extravagant claims for it.

4. So far were the moderate Presbyterians from identifying with Cameron's Vindication that they regarded it as an attempt by the episcopalian party to discredit

Presbyterian principles in general. In that belief a number of refutations were penned, all of them seeking to distance mainstream Presbyterianism from the arguments in the Vindication. While there is no reason to doubt that the Vindication was penned by Cameron, there is some evidence to suggest that the episcopalian party, and in particular Bishop Paterson of Edinburgh, may mischievously have promoted it for their own ends to embarrass the moderate Presbyterians. For some obscure reason the Vindication was usually referred to in contemporary writings under the nickname of *Hackston's Ghost.*

Chapter 25 — A price on his head

1. *A True and Exact Copy of A Treasonable and Bloody Paper, called the Fanaticks New-Covenant ... Together with their Execrable Declaration...* Edinburgh and London, 1680.

2. *Minutes of High Court of Justiciary,* 28 June 1680. There is no evidence that any reprisals were exacted from the Town Council of Sanquhar on account of the declaration. In that respect they fared better than their counterparts in Lanark, who were heavily fined for permitting the publication of the subsequent declaration there (*Register of the Privy Council,* 3rd series, vol. VII, pp.329-30).

3. 'If your Excellency's letter had come a little sooner to my hands it would have saved us a great deal of toil' (*Airlie Muniments,* Airlie to Dalyell, 2 July 1680).

4. There is some evidence to suggest that Cameron visited the north of England, though not necessarily at this stage in his career. Robert Gray, a Northumberland man who was executed in the Grassmarket on 19 May 1682, referred in his last testimony to 'the faithful warning these two worthies [i.e. Cameron and Cargill] gave in Northumberland'. Cargill is known, from other evidence, to have had friends in Northumberland with whom he and Cameron could have lodged on this occasion.

5. *Airlie Muniments,* Ross to Airlie, 5 July 1680.

6. 'As for Mr Richard Cameron, I never heard anything from him, in the Lord's truth, but I am both ready and willing to confirm it' (Cargill to Lady Earlston, younger, in M'Millan's *Collection of Letters,* 1764, p.241).

7. Wodrow doubts whether Thomas Douglas was at Sanquhar (*History* III, p.217). The list of names in the proclamation is, however, very specific, and was compiled from the testimony of eyewitnesses (*Register of the Privy Council,* 3rd Series, vol. VI. pp.481-5). Douglas was certainly well enough known to be recognized and identified by the local population.

8. Hackston's account took the form of an open letter to a person unnamed, who had sent Robert M'Ward a report strongly critical of Hamilton and his management of affairs at Bothwell. It remains unpublished, and what appears to be the only surviving copy — itself unreadable in places — is preserved among the *Laing MSS.* William Wilson made use of Hackston's account, among others, when writing his own *True and Impartial Relation of Bothwell Bridge* (1751, also appended to some early editions of John Howie's *Scots Worthies*).

Howie notes elsewhere that Hackston's account was written to correct 'a false information' sent to M'Ward by 'one of chief note' (*Faithful Contendings Displayed,* pp.199-200). He does not identify the 'one of chief note' concerned, but from a comparison of Hackston's account with that by Wilson it is possible to identify him as John Dick, who was among Welsh's supporters at Bothwell and who acted as clerk to the council of war which drew up the supplication to Monmouth. Dick was later arrested for his part at Bothwell and was condemned to death. He escaped from prison but was subsequently recaptured, and was executed in the Grassmarket of Edinburgh on 5 March 1684. There is a touching account of his last hours by John Erskine of Carnock (*Journal,* 1893, pp.42-4). Dick earned a somewhat perfunctory reference in the *Cloud of Witnesses* (1871 ed., p.400), which provoked an angry comment from Robert Wodrow (*History,* IV, p.59). His own *Testimony* appeared, in a pamphlet of fifty-eight pages, shortly after his death. Dick's letter to M'Ward, which provoked Hackston's reply, appears to be no longer extant.

9. The shipmaster, James Cassels, protested that he had not recognized Hackston and was liberated on taking the oath of allegiance (*Register of the Privy Council,* 3rd Series, vol. VI, p.525).

10. *Airlie Muniments,* Airlie to Dalyell, 5 July 1680.

11. Patrick Walker asserts: 'There is a fool story handed down, that that handful was divided among themselves, which is false; they were of one heart and soul' (*Six Saints of the Covenant,* vol. 1, p.231). However, while there was no open breach, it is beyond doubt that Hackston's arrival did precipitate tensions and strains which did not altogether disappear with the removal of Douglas. In a letter written after his capture, Hackston wrote, 'It [i.e. the defeat] was not altogether unexpected to me, for, not to reflect on any that sealed the truth and cause as we stated it with their blood, I cannot deny it but it was over [i.e. against] conscience and light I joined with some of our party; for some of them had not their garments clean of the late defection, and there was too much of pride amongst us. Neither dare I allow that taking of satisfaction for practices, which are the homologating of the public sins, which we did of one about half an hour before our break, which checked me exceedingly in the time. I think real sorrow should be like the prodigal, to think themselves not worthy to be employed in that work. Real evidences of reconciliation to God should be seen before an admission to such an employment. Oh that all would take warning by my reproof, not to venture to follow any man over conscience. There were choice godly men among us, but one Achan will make Israel to fall before the enemy. I fear the want of faith amongst us, first and last, all alongst our late business made us to fall. I know many mouths will be opened against me because of what I did before this business, but I dare not but speak it, that this is a stumbling-block to drive them to more sin; and alas that I did not more to purge us of every sin, especially known sin among us' (*Cloud of Witnesses,* 1871 ed., p.45; the above is taken from a contemporary copy which shows some variations from the printed version).

There is little doubt that Hackston is speaking here mainly of Douglas, and that by 'the late defection' he means the controversy in which Douglas was involved in Holland (see chapter 19, note 9) and in which Hackston had sided with Robert Hamilton against him. It is clear too that the ejection of Douglas did not rid Cameron's following of all the elements of which Hackston disapproved. However, it is to Hackston's credit that he did not allow these frictions to influence his high regard for Cameron, or to diminish his feelings towards him. 'Some of them have come to me', he wrote afterwards of his captors, 'and regretted that such a man as I should have been led away with Cameron. I answered, he was a faithful minister of Jesus Christ.'

Chapter 26 — New Monkland and Cumnock
1. Cameron's prediction came true — James II and VII, the last of the Stuart kings, never took the Coronation Oath in Scotland.

Chapter 27 — Cameron's last sermon
1. The evidence for Cameron's preaching at Crawfordjohn comes from Patrick Walker, who quotes the testimonies of hearers (*Six Saints of the Covenant,* vol. II, p.113). Given the impression it made, it is somewhat surprising that no written record of the sermon survives, the published sermon on this text having — as John Howie proves — been preached at Shawhead on 30 May (*A Collection of Lectures and Sermons,* 1779, p. 380 note; see also chapter 22). The record of the Shawhead sermon includes a pause for prayer, as Walker records of the Crawfordjohn sermon, and Howie appears to deduce from this that Walker's record is incorrect. However, there is no compelling reason to accept this view; Cameron could well have preached from the same text on the two occasions, with similar effects on himself and his audience.

Chapter 28 — The last days
1. *Airlie Muniments.* These contain numerous contemporary despatches which throw interesting light on the military manoeuvres and intelligence-gathering involved in the search for Cameron.
2. There is evidence that Dalyell had become increasingly impatient with Airlie's methods in tracking down Cameron. He wrote to him on one occasion: 'I wonder to have had no account of the success of your last party, and much more to hear that a few skulking rogues still stay together within ten or twelve miles of you; you shall immediately march with both troops towards Mauchline for the dispersing of these villains...' Much of Dalyell's correspondence is in a similarly robust strain.
3. Wodrow, *History,* III. p.219.
4. Robert Wodrow, who characterizes Cannon as 'very bloody', says of him: 'He got money at Edinburgh and undertook to lead the soldiers to Mr Richard Cameron; and when the Duke of York came down this winter [i.e. 1680-81] he made his boast that he had directed Earlshall to him, but for anything I can find, without any ground; for the rencounter was unforeseen' (*History* III, p.224). The documentary evidence, however, points strongly to Cannon's involvement, at least at the start of the final search for Cameron. An unsigned document in the *Airlie Muniments* reporting Cameron's presence at Roberton (given as 'Sunday the 18th day of July' but in fact 11 July) notes: 'This is a part of Mardrogat's intelligence.' Intriguingly, the document goes on to say that 'the week before' Cameron had 'made public intimation for excommunication of His Majesty and to all persons whatsoever to come and hear it done'. Cameron did not live to carry out this action himself, but it was later performed by Donald Cargill at Torwood (see *No King But Christ,* chapter 11). The reference is interesting, however, as showing that the excommunication was already being contemplated by both Cameron and Cargill, and was not, as some have claimed, an individual aberration on Cargill's part.
5. An unsigned copy of Airlie's orders to Bruce is preserved in the *Airlie Muniments.* In full, it reads: 'You are to march with your party with all convenient speed in pursuit of the rebels, who are said to have been at Roberton upon Sunday

last, near Crawfordjohn, and in the march to secure all the passes which lead into Annandale and other places upon the south and east hand, and to get what intelligence you can of Cameron and his accomplices, whom you are to pursue to the uttermost; and to give me notice from time to time in case ye hear of their motion. Given under my hand at Newtown of Galloway, the 19th of July 1680.' The government party was in the nature of a task force, comprising elements from three troops of horse (Airlie's, Claverhouse's and Hume's) and three companies of dragoons (Strachan's, Stuart's and Inglis's). One of the dragoon commanders, John Creichton, many years later related to Dean Swift his own highly-coloured account of the action at Airdsmoss (*Memoirs of Captain Creichton,* 1731). Hackston, in his account, put the strength of the government force at 120 (not 112, as in the published version). Government sources put their number at only eighty (*London Gazette,* 29 July - 2 August 1680) but, on the other hand, Bruce estimated Cameron's force at 140 as against its true strength of only sixty-three.

6. John Livingston, Airlie's ensign, wrote to him on 21 July: 'As for Earlshall [i.e. Andrew Bruce] I have heard nothing from him as yet, neither can I hear anything of the rebels.' Airlie himself, now at Strathaven, wrote to Dalyell: 'I have not heard anything from Earlshall nor none of his party since I sent them off at Newtown of Galloway, but how soon I hear from him your Excellency shall be acquainted.' It would seem, however, that by this time, or shortly thereafter, Dalyell had made his own rendezvous with Bruce. This may have taken place at Lanark, where Dalyell was now known to have been stationed (*Memoirs of Captain Creichton,* p. 86). In his later dispatch after Airdsmoss, Bruce implies strongly that he had recently been with Dalyell.

7. *Lauderdale Papers.* ed. O. Airy (Camden Society), 1884, iii, pp.149-51.

8. William Row, who gives the account involving Miller, records that Cochrane passed the information direct to Dalyell, who sent Bruce (or rather redirected him) on the track of Cameron (*Life of Robert Blair,* Wodrow Society, p.569). Patrick Walker, on the other hand, makes no reference to Miller but says that Cochrane sent a message to Bruce telling him where Cameron could be found (*Six Saints of the Covenant,* vol. i. p.232; ii. p.115). Whichever version is true, the evidence involving Cochrane seems conclusive.

9. The *Airlie Muniments* contain a record of the interrogations of William Manuel of Shotts, who was wounded at Airdsmoss and died on entering Edinburgh. Manuel is said to have disclosed that Cameron lodged mainly at Middle Welwood, 'where he preached and lectured, besides other occasions in the fields'; that Cameron rode on 'a white grey horse, pinch-mouthed'; and that the party's password was 'God is our refuge'. James Wharry, of Lesmahagow, another of Cameron's party, testified when captured that 'Cameron commanded in chief, that his brother was there with him and John Paterson exercised them sometimes, and that their number was sixty or thereby.'

10. Robert Law, *Memorialls,* p.55.

11. The only surviving account of Airdsmoss on Cameron's side is the somewhat sketchy one given by David Hackston (*Cloud of Witnesses,* 1871 ed., pp.45-7). A fuller account, though obviously biased as regards casualties, was given in a dispatch by Bruce of Earlshall to General Dalyell, the substance of which was reported in the *London Gazette* of 29 July - 2 August. In his despatch (which was not generally known to be extant until it was acquired by the National Library of

Scotland in 1991) Bruce wrote, 'I have had the good fortune since I parted from you in my march towards Cumlock about three miles other side the Moorkirk to discover the rebels by our fore party, whereupon I sent a second party with order to engage them, but before they could reach them they had posted themselves in a morass, having to the number of an hundred foot well appointed and about forty horse on the wings of their foot well ordered. So soon as I came near and found the ground to be inaccessible for horse I drew the horse and dragoons to the side of the morass and then sent a party of dragoons on foot to vex their horses on the flanks. No sooner did they perceive my design than they sent a party of foot to receive ours, and in the meantime they advanced their body and made very smart fire, which was well returned by our dragoons and carabines so as their horse began to reel. Our horsemen and dragoons being forced to quit their horses both we and they being afoot [went] pell-mell through other. The dispute continued a quarter of an hour very hot; the rebels, refusing either to fly or take quarter, fought like madmen, in which contest we have lost Mr Kerr of Hume's troop, Mr Parker, Ja. Lisle, Archibald Eliott of Claverhouse's troop wounded to death, two or three of Airlie's troop, three or four dragoons wounded and killed, five or six horses killed. There are odds of 20 killed to the rebels whereof the great Cameron is one, in whose pockets are found a great many papers directed to him which I have not yet had time to peruse. Hackston of Rathillet is now our prisoner and four more, one whereof we left on the place being mortally wounded.'

Bruce's despatch claims to have been written 'at 11 o'clock at night' and it bears the marks of hasty composition. Though admitting that the engagement was for a time 'very hot' and that Cameron's party 'fought like madmen', Bruce may well have understated the true nature of the action. An account sent from Edinburgh on 24 July, apparently by a government agent, speaks of 'great disadvantage' having been suffered by the government troops, and of 'a sharp dispute for half an hour' (*An Account of the Total Defeat of the Rebels in Scotland,* 1680). There is also an account sent by a Roman Catholic priest in Edinburgh to a correspondent in Paris, which goes so far as to say that for some time the 'day was doubtful' (*Blairs Archives, Correspondence of Charles Whytford,* 1680).

12. Bruce records: 'I gave those who killed him a mark to know him, by his want of two joints of his mid finger and a nail upon it, which they found, for security whereof they cut off both his hands and brought [them] along.' The fact that Bruce was able to give his men these personal distinguishing marks of Cameron may have derived from personal acquaintance in their early days in Fife or, more probably, from information gleaned from informers.

Chapter 29 — M'Ward's words come true

1. According to John Creichton (*Memoirs,* 1731, p.83) Parker was a volunteer from Lancashire who had gone to Airdsmoss 'to see the sport'. Parker was to pay dearly for his day's entertainment. Severely wounded at the beginning of the action, he was left for dead by Earlshall and, on his own testimony later 'was forced to lie on the ground with the dead men all that night'. Though rescued by Cochrane, Parker never fully recovered from his wounds and died the following year.

2. Both Bruce and David Ramsay applied to the Privy Council for rewards, Ramsay describing himself as 'a gentleman but of a mean fortune' and with 'no other thing to live upon but his pay, which is very small'. Their applications were referred to

the Treasury for favourable consideration (*Register of the Privy Council,* 3rd Series, vol. VI, pp.524-5).

3. A contemporary letter, of which only a fragment remains, from the Roman Catholic priest Charles Whytford to his friend Louis Innes in Paris confirms this account by Walker, with the additional information that among those meeting the party was the Lord Provost in his coach, and that the hangman washed Cameron's head before exhibiting it (*Blairs Archives*). The latter circumstance would seem to corroborate Walker's account of the outrage perpetrated by the soldiers.

4. 'The fair house of Sir John Cochrane at Ochiltree is by an accident burnt to ashes in two hours and nothing but his papers saved' (*Calendar of State Papers, Domestic Series,* 15 October 1681).

5. *Letters to the Earl of Aberdeen,* Spalding Club, 1851, p.127.

6. Some doubt has been cast on Patrick Walker's horrific account of Hackston's execution (*Six Saints of the Covenant,* vol. 1, p.233) because of his inclusion of some particularly gross barbarities not mentioned in the sentence. It should be remembered, however, that the infliction of such barbarities was ordinary in cases of hanging, drawing and quartering, which was what Hackston — contrary to all Scottish practice — was subjected to. The fact that Hackston refused to forgive the executioner, prior to the sentence being carried out, may also account to some degree for the severe treatment he received. It is interesting that a contemporary letter from the Roman Catholic priest Charles Whytford (*Blairs Archives,* 13 August 1680) confirms Walker's account in every circumstantial detail.

Index